The Medieval Mystical
Tradition in England

THE MEDIEVAL MYSTICAL TRADITION IN ENGLAND

Papers read at

Dartington Hall, July 1984

Edited by Marion Glasscoe

D. S. Brewer

Published with the aid of grants
from The British Academy and
the Isobel Thornley Bequest, University of London

ISBN 0 85991 160 8

First published 1984 by
D. S. Brewer, 240 Hills Road, Cambridge,
an imprint of Boydell and Brewer,
P.O. Box 9, Woodbridge, Suffolk IP12 3DF

Typesetting by Paragon Photoset, Aylesbury
Printed and bound by Short Run Press Ltd., Exeter

CONTENTS

FOREWORD

While the nature of contemplative experience is essentially unacademic, the records of the medieval English mystics have attracted a wide spectrum of academic interest. Historians, textual scholars, theologians, literary critics, psychologists and those involved in the practice of psychiatric medicine all engage with the subject; yet it is one which does not lend itself fruitfully to any one academic discipline in isolation. The aim of the Exeter Symposia is to bring together scholars from a wide variety of disciplines who are actively engaged in the field in order to promote a context for flexible, but disciplined, study and understanding of the realities witnessed to by the medieval mystical texts. Despite the broad framework – the medieval mystical tradition as it relates to England – the papers have on each occasion formed significant groupings and generated coherent patterns.

The meetings are deliberately restricted to a small group which includes both well-established scholars and those just entering the field, thus promoting healthy, relaxed and open inter-disciplinary exchanges on a subject which seems to be in a seminal stage of its development. From the occasion of the first Exeter Symposium at the University in 1980 it was clear that such a meeting attracts a vigorous and world-wide response; scholars have come not only from mainland Europe and the United States, but from as far apart as Finland and Japan. We owe a debt of gratitude to the editors of the *Fourteenth-Century English Mystics Newsletter* (now retitled *Mystics Quarterly*) for generous help over publicity. To compensate for the necessary restriction in numbers we have tried to publish the proceedings promptly in order to share them immediately with a wider audience. This has only been possible through the courteous cooperation of the contributors in submitting their copy well in advance and foregoing the opportunity to correct in proof. While every attempt has been made to observe a uniform editorial procedure, any inconsistencies in this respect must be my responsibility.

I would like to express especial gratitude for the financial help of both the British Academy, who have most generously aided the present volume and also that published in 1982, and the University of London trustees of the Isobel Thornley Bequest. Such assistance in these times of financial stringency has been crucial. Finally I acknowledge with gratitude the active support of Boydell and Brewer Ltd in absorbing us into an already extended schedule.

Marion Glasscoe   University of Exeter 1984

THE SPECULUM IMAGE IN MEDIEVAL MYSTICAL WRITERS

RITAMARY BRADLEY

IN CHRISTIANITY THE inner self is simply a stepping stone to an awareness of God. Man is the image of God, and his inner self is a kind of mirror in which God not only sees Himself, but reveals Himself to the 'mirror' in which He is reflected. Thus, through the dark, transparent mystery of our own inner being we can, as it were, see God 'through a glass.' All this is pure metaphor. It is a way of saying that our being somehow communicates directly with the Being of God, Who is, 'in us.' If we enter into ourselves, find our true self, and then pass 'beyond the inner I,' we sail forth into the immense darkness in which we confront the 'I AM' of the Almighty.[1]

In these words a mystic of our time, Thomas Merton, uses the mirror metaphor, with Scriptural overtones, to speak of the contemplative experience open to those still in the wayfaring state. So pervasive has this metaphor been in writings about the mystical life that I am led once again to examine it, this time with a view to seeing how the major fourteenth-century English mystics employ it. For, though an impressive number of mystics fall back on this metaphor in the difficult task of finding language to express the encounter with the divine, few use the analogy in the same sense.

The mirror metaphor is more ancient than the Platonists, and as new as our own contemporaries. Understandably, literature about this metaphor is far from sparse. Nonetheless, Margot Schmidt, in a major survey article in 1980,[2] affirms that there is not yet a systematic study of the mirror analogy, especially of its uses in mysticism. This is still true. The most comprehensive work to which Schmidt refers, that of Herbert Grabes, has been recently updated and issued in an English translation[3]; but even this valuable work focuses on the strictly literary uses of the metaphor, and, though rich in information about mirror titles of devotional and mystical works it does not deal in depth with religious experience. In fact, Grabes cannot be quite right when he says that '. . . English literature . . . made no use of the convention of mystical transformation via contemplation of the mirror of God, as argued by Porphyry, pseudo-Dionysius the Areopagite, Zosimo of Panopolis and Raban Maur'.[4] This is not true, if we include, as we should, mystical texts within English literature.

Only one passing reference to the mirror metaphor occurs in Wolfgang Riehle's otherwise thorough study of metaphors used by the medieval mystics.[5] In that one passage he mentions Eckhart's mirror metaphor of the birth of God in the soul and recalls in this context what Walter Hilton says: 'For þi soule is bot a mirrour in þe whilk þu schalt see God gostly.'[6] But Riehle limits his remarks to saying that the image serves to distinguish the divine substance from the substance of the soul and thus preserves the writers from the suspicion of heresy.

Nonetheless, in the work already done, there is a gathering of facts and a beginning of analysis on which we can build. Schmidt, for example, deals to some extent with the mirror as a metaphor for religious experience, though she limits her examples to what is found in the continental mystics. Grabes in his general classification of mirror metaphors cites examples which are later reflected in medieval mystical writings.

First, God is the paramount mirror, a concept found in Alcibades I and in the Odes of Solomon: the soul sees the invisible in the visible and is cleansed by contemplation in the divine mirror.[7] The *Pricke of Conscience* and Wyclif supply medieval examples of this class. Second, Christ is a mirror, a metaphor going back to the first century and expressed by Clement of Rome. This concept develops into the exemplary mirror, or pattern of right living, as alluded to in the Rule of St Benedict; and also into the mirror of creation, which in Bonaventure is the Word of God.[8] From here on, Grabes' multiple classifications are, as one reviewer noted, not distinct classes but rather are like promiscuous families.[9]

But his classifications yield some help for discerning the basic analogy drawn from the mirror metaphor: the mirror shows us what we are and what we should be. For example, the exemplar mirror, which overlaps several of Grabes' categories, has this meaning: Mary is an exemplar mirror, as indicated by Ephrem[10] and affirmed in the Council of Ephesus; angels and all mortals distinguished for their virtues are mirrors, either in a positive way, by showing us what to imitate, or in a negative way, by pointing out what we should avoid, as in the reference to a 'mirror of wretchedness' in the *Orcherd of Syon*.[11] Holy Writ is a prime source of such exemplars, offering us a sight of what we are and what we should be. This tradition of the twofold view in the mirror goes back, in ecclesiastical writings, at least to John Chrysostom, who draws the analogy out of what happens at the hairdressers, where the mirror shows us our initial sorry condition and allows us, sometimes after consulting our friends, to project the ideal or corrected image which we ought to see reflected.[12]

These analogies refer to the function of a mirror, whereby we see ourselves. But it is also common for the eye to be called a mirror, in which something is reflected, whether it be the eye of the senses, of the mind, or of the spirit. With overtones from the medieval theory of sense perception, the eye is passive and receives a faithful image, if it is healthy and clear. Only God can open the eye of the spirit, and sometimes even of the reason, to enable us to see spiritual realities. The image received in the heart or mind differs from that received by the sense of sight,[13] giving a basis for dealing with illusion and deception in images.

Of prime importance for interpreting the mirror images in the mystical tradition is a study by Norbert Hugedé.[14] He identifies the echoes of Hellenic literature and Hebrew Scriptures in the key mirror texts in the Epistles to the Corinthians, texts which are often read in the light of each other. They are 1 Corinthians 13:12 and 2 Corinthians 3:18, which say:

> Now we are seeing a dim reflection in a mirror; but then we shall be seeing face to face; Now I know in part; but then I shall know even as I am known;

> And we with our unveiled faces reflecting like mirrors the brightness of the Lord, all grow brighter and brighter as we are turned into the image that we reflect; this is the work of the Lord who is Spirit.

Hugedé demonstrates that these passages, overall, though influenced by Greek antecedents at the level of expression, are permeated with Scriptural themes. Especially is this true in the way Paul opposes knowledge here on earth, which is to know God's revealed will, with knowledge in the parousia, which will be face to face. But the immediate context of the first passage reveals Greek influence, in that mirror knowledge is likened to the imperfect, but perfectible, knowledge of a child still under a tutor. Therefore the enigma is not so much a darkness as an imperfect vision stemming from the condition of being a child. But also, as an enigma, it is a symbolic or indirect representation of reality.

From Paul on, it is necessary to note the difference between the Neo-Platonic meaning of the mirror and the Christian senses. In Neo-Platonism only the 'pure of heart' could see perfectly in the divine mirror—but this purity of heart meant, of course, escape from matter and the life of the senses. Hence, there was a hierarchy of mirrors, built on their relative remoteness from immersion in matter. Because of his Neo-Platonic bent Clement of Alexandria commands attention for what he transmits about mysticism through the mirror image. Despite Neo-Platonic leanings, Clement interprets mirror knowledge in general to stand for the 'partial apprehension of true reality', according to a recent reassessment of his writings by Raoul Mortley.[15] Clement develops basic concepts conformable with Christian mysticism. Echoing Paul, he presents imperfect mirror knowledge in the context of stages of instruction. He goes even further, by attaching the mirror image, thus understood, to the metaphor of Christ, the Mother, who first feeds at the breast, then gives himself as milk, and finally proffers solid food to the mature. This consuming of solid food corresponds to the union of face-to-face vision:

'Wherefore also I have given you milk to drink', he says; meaning, I have instilled into you the knowledge which, from instruction, nourishes up to life eternal. For those who are full-grown are said to drink, babes to suck. . . . In saying, therefore, 'I have given you milk to drink,' has he not indicated the knowledge of the truth, the perfect gladness of the Word, who is the milk? And what follows next, 'not meat, for you were not able,' may indicate the clear revelation in the future world, like food, face to face.[16]

The mirror knowledge which Clement speaks of is not only inward but is also outward looking, to the neighbour, and to Christ in the flesh:

'For now we see as through a glass,' knowing ourselves in it by reflection, and simultaneously contemplating, as we can, the efficient cause, from that, which, in us, is divine. For it is said, 'Having seen thy brother, thou hast seen thy God': methinks that now the Saviour God is declared to us. But after the laying aside of the flesh, 'face to face'. . . .[17]

In the context of the whole of Clement's writings, Mortley paraphrases this elliptical passage thus:

The sequence of his thought is as follows: we may know ourselves by contemplating ourselves in a mirror; by self-contemplation we are in fact contemplating the efficient cause in ourselves (among us?) that is, God. We are able to do this because of the fleshly presence of Christ as our 'brother', i.e. one of us. By contemplating ourselves, or one of our number in particular, we in fact are contemplating God.[18]

This is the sense also of another passage from Clement:

But if . . . they follow in the Master's footsteps, this now joins them to those who are to be enrolled in heaven. For it is thus that one truly follows the Saviour, by aiming at sinlessness and His perfection, and adorning and composing the soul before it as a mirror, and arranging everything in all respects similarly.[19]

Thus Jesus, visible to us, becomes the mirror in which we discern what we should become—in the journey from the condition of sin on earth to the state of transformation into Christ's likeness in heaven. As Mortley has shown, and these passages confirm, Clement sidesteps Neo-Platonism by making the divine element in us equivalent to Christ: 'We have here a christological interpretation of the idea of self-knowledge through a mirror. . . '.[20] This form of the analogy derives in part from the exegesis of Wisdom 7:26, which presents Christ as Wisdom and the mirror of God.

Thus there are in Clement important Christian mystical elements sometimes overlooked. With Augustine the problem is not the same but similar: it is a question of separating out the philosophic passages from those on the mystical life. It is surprising that more has not been done on this question. Probably best-known of the philosophic mirror images in Augustine are those in the *De Trinitate*, in which the human soul is a mirror of God—a mirror in which human reason can discern in the mind some natural analogy for the Trinity.[21] Specifically, the mind has three activities rooted in one substance, and in the mind, as in God, simultaneously things past, present, and future exist. We are bidden to reflect on these likenesses in order '. . . that we might see in some way or other by this image which we are, Him by whom we are made, as by a glass'.[22] Yet even in this rational approach to God by analogy, whereby we can see, unless we are blind, a likeness between our soul and the Trinity, we are cautioned to take note of the 'great unlikeness', too.[23]

There are other passages in Augustine with more direct bearing on the mystical life. A glass, and an enigma, signifies for Augustine any image whatsoever, adapted to the understanding of God, who can only be known darkly. To see darkly in a glass, however, is most appropriately spoken of with reference to the soul, since it is 'not vainly called his image'.[24] Nor is the soul a static image of God, but as in 2 Corinthians 3:18, it grows into Godlikeness. We are transformed by the Spirit from glory to glory, by what we see in a glass: 'And we with unveiled faces [unlike Moses coming down from the mountain] . . . are turned into the image which we reflect'. 'With face unveiled' means freed from the law, which is the shadow of things to come when we shall see face to face.[25] From glory to glory—the stages of transformation into his image—means, primarily, from the glory of creation to the glory of justification';[26] but also from a defaced image to a beautiful one;[27] from faith to vision;[28] and from the glory of being children of God to being like him when we see him as he is.[29]

Mirror vision becomes brighter in proportion as we make progress.[30] In fact, can anticipate the face-to-face vision reversed for heaven. 'We now, in order that we may be led to face-to-face vision of the one whom we see now in a glass darkly.[31] A heart made pure is necessary for seeing even 'in part' (with an allusion to 1 Corinthians 13:12)—and hence a speaker cannot be sure that the hearer sees God, for impurities of heart would hamper that communication.[32] To see in this life is always to see through a glass and is therefore imperfect knowledge.[33] Neither purity of heart nor knowledge, in fact, can anticipate the face-to-face vision reversed for heaven: 'We now, however great may be our human understanding, know but in part, and 'see through a glass darkly'.[34] Even love is not powerful enough to pierce the heavens: 'For in this life who sees except as "in an enigma and through a glass?" Neither is love itself of might sufficient to rend the darkness of the flesh, and penetrate into that eternal calm from which even things which pass away derive the light in which they shine'.[35] Such face-to-face vision was not granted in this life even to the writers of the New Testament, who said, that while they preached secrets which were revealed, they themselves only saw in a glass, darkly.[36]

Yet the one whom we shall see is truly Christ himself, the same Christ who was crucified, but is now transfigured. He is the reward of our toils.[37] He is also the mirror in whom we see the Father. This is what Paul means when he speaks of seeing through a glass: 'because the Father shall be seen through the instrumentality of the Son'.[38] The face-to-face vision of the last day, reserved for the just, will include the form in which Christ is equal to the Father, together with the kingdom, which is all creation as subject to God, including 'that wherein the Son of God was made the Son of man', that is, united to human nature.[39] The darkness which obscures the vision in the mirror is 'our own mortality', a darkness which will give way to light: '. . . when Christ who is our life shall appear, then shall ye also appear with Him in glory' (Colossians 3:3, 4). But until that time we see through a glass—in similitudes—and only then face to face.[40] There is no hierarchy of mirrors in Augustine. Rather, God's righteousness is one, and this righteousness is reflected in all who follow the truth: as in many mirrors there are seen many reflections of one face.[41]

Lastly, Augustine also correlates the mirror image with the motherhood of the Church, as she is now in labour and will later give birth:

> And this is life eternal . . . that they might know thee . . . and Jesus Christ. . . . Of this vision and knowledge the apostle says, 'Now we see through a glass, in a riddle, then face to face. . . .'. At present the Church is in travail with the longing for this fruit of all her labors, but then she shall bring to birth in its actual contemplation; now she travails in birth with groaning, then shall she bring forth in joy; now she travails in birth through her prayers, then shall she bring forth in her praises.[42]

In addition to the use of the mirror image to contrast imperfect knowledge of the divinity with face-to-face vision, Augustine also interprets God's face in other ways. For example, 'God's face is the power by which he is made known to them that are worthy'.[43] Again, 'His presence in the Church' has been called his face.[44] And his face is the 'manifestation itself of the Wisdom of God.'[45] Generally, it is the 'spiritual eye', itself a mirror, which is able to look upon God's face in these senses.

These are a few of the most significant ways, then, in which the mirror analogy reached the English mystics, when the texts in Corinthians were the primary basis for the metaphors. In summary, we can see that the underlying notion of these texts is not so much a contrast between the visible and the invisible, but an emphasis rather on moving into spiritual maturity. At every stage this emphasis allows for an insight into what one now sees in the mirror and what one projects as the ideal or perfected image. Only passing mention will be made, for this reason, of the mirror references in Dionysius, the Pseudo-Areopagite, because his mirrors—though they are exemplars—relate to fixed gradations which reflect the divine perfections.[46]

The purpose served by this selective survey of some of the major mystical themes in the tradition of the *speculum* metaphors is to help identify this mirror image in the English mystics when the analogy is incomplete and indirect; and also to explicate the image—direct or implicit—in the light of some Biblical commentary on which it may depend in part for its meaning.

The medieval mystics, I will now show, use the mirror metaphors to teach the whole mystical life, as a growth and an unfolding, and to contrast what one is and what one should be or will become. One misses this purpose, in part, by following Grabes' and Schmidt's models of simply classifying the mirror metaphors—as, for example, the mirror of Scripture, God as mirror, sinners as mirrors, and exemplar mirrors.

First, as an example of the mirror metaphor in its relation to the whole mystical life, I will cite from the *Cloud*-author's version of Richard of St Victor's *Benjamin Minor*. The soul, being a mirror, must be kept clean, if one is to know oneself and God. When grace enlightens reason in this mirror, one can see more clearly, becoming able to perceive one's un-worthiness along with God's goodness. Next, the knowledge based on reason gives way to beholding, as the light of God's face reforms the divine image which has been obscured by the darkness of sin on the soul-mirror. This signals the birth of contemplation, and then one shares in 'the fair food of angels', which is the sustenance of spiritual maturity.[47]

Next, I will draw up a selection of illustrations for the growth stages of the mystical life, as these are explained by the experience of looking into a mirror. There are many differences, of course, among these medieval English mystics when they speak of the mystical life. But the mirror metaphor is a common link they have with tradition, as I have briefly traced it. The variants of their uses of the mirror metaphor serve to bring out their originality and differences.

Mirrors and Beginners

First, metaphorical mirrors tell beginners and those progressing what changes should be made in their lives—what blots on their conscience must be cleansed. The Scriptures are the mirrors which help the literate in this task; the teachings of those who can read assist the unlearned. For example, the *Cloud*-author says:

> Goddes worde, ouþer wretyn or spokyn, is licnid to a mirour. Goostly, þe iȝe of þi soule is þi reson; þi concience is þi visage goostly, & riȝt as þou seest þat if a foule spot be in þi bodily visage, þe iȝe of þe same visage may not see þat spotte, ne wite wher it is, wiþoutyn a myrour or a teching of anoþer þan itself: riȝt so it is goostly. Wiþouten redyng or heryng of Goddes worde, it is impossible to mans vnderstondyng þat a soule þat is bleendid in custom of synne shuld see þe foule spot in his concyence.

> & so folowyng, when a man seeþ in a bodily or goostly myrour . . . þan at erst, & none er, he renniþ to þe welle to wasche hym.[48]

Similarly, one of the medieval texts deriving from Augustine's *Speculum Peccatoris* uses Scripture as a mirror throughout, like a motif. Summing up the warnings to sinners to reform, the writer says: 'Be-hold in this myrour and see what þou hast been, what þou art, and what thou shalt bee'.[49] To destroy vice and plant virtues the sinner should have recourse to the Scriptures for inward beholding of the last things as reflected therein. Richard Rolle, while not explictly calling the Scriptures a mirror, as many do, assigns to the reading of the sacred text the twofold insights gained in mirror knowledge: we see what we ought to avoid and what we ought to do, because in the sacred books we recognize our defects.[50]

For those who cannot read, mirrors are in the form of visible examples, both positive and negative. Margery Kempe is instructed to be a mirror among others, who should take example from her.[51] The *Orcherd of Syon* refers to Gregory as a mirror of holy living, which gave us light.[52] And negatively, the same text speaks of those who were a mirror of wretched-ness.[53] The *Cloud*-author cites Mary, in contrast to Martha, as a mirror or example for all contemplatives.[54]

A Talking of the Love of God cautions the 'blynde wrecche' who is only virtuous in his own eyes to awaken to the fact that he is looking in the devil's mirror and shaping himself to the devil's likeness:

> þus he lokeþ at him-self. wiþ a fals eȝe, seoþ þat þat is nouȝt. and demeþ al wrong. Hit is þe deueles Mirour. þat he in lokeþ, and þe fendes argumens. þat him þinkeþ resouns, þat he bobbeþ him wiþ. and ledeþ as him lykeþ.[55]

The devil intervenes in mirror knowledge in another way in *Ayenbite of Inwyt*: the spirits of men and angels are spiritual mirrors, and one mirror can receive the form seen in another. Hence, the devil can reflect his thoughts on the soul-mirror of a man, waking or sleeping, and some of these thoughts, originating with the fiend, are hard to distinguish from godly thoughts.[56]

Mirrors for Progressives

For those progressing, and even entering into union, mirror metaphors are used to convey spiritual guidance. For example, in the *Book of Privy Counseling*, the naked thought and blind feeling of one's own being is a darkness and a mirror. If this dark mirror is not befouled by extraneous thoughts and feelings, one will be 'secretly fed' by the touching of grace— though 'blindly and in part, as it may be in this life'.[57] Here the mirror image is joined, as in earlier writings, with that of feeding—Christ as our spiritual food—measured according to one's maturity.

Again, counselling those who are progressing, Walter Hilton, in the *Scale of Perfection*, Book Two, as Riehle has noted, commends meditating on the nature of the soul, which is a mirror in which one can see God spiritually. But for the effective seeking of God in this way, the soul-mirror must be kept clean and above the earth.[58] In Book One Hilton uses the parallel of the clarity of the mirror, and the food appropriate to one's stage of spiritual maturity. In the third stage of contemplation, even, we see 'not clearly, but in darkness', though enjoying a 'taste' of heavenly vision. Intertwining the mirror and food images more explicitly, he says: 'The second stage of contemplation is milk for children, while the third stage is solid food for men of tested intelligence, who can discern good from evil'. To this he adds the mirror text from 2 Corinthians 3:18, which says that while we reflect the brightness of the Lord in mirrors, we are turned into the image which we reflect. 'With face unveiled' is interpreted to signify that with the opening of the spiritual eye the face of the soul is unveiled. Then: 'We behold as in a mirror a heavenly joy: we are fully formed and joined to the image of our Lord; we are transformed from the clarity of faith to the clarity of understanding or from the clarity of desire to the clarity of blessed love'. Yet even this state is a darkness, for 'My night is my light'.[59]

The same conflating of images occurs in Book Two, where it is said: 'To the pure soul who has his palate purified from the filth of flesh-governed love, Holy Scripture is life-giving food and delectable sustenance. . . . This is one way of seeing Jesus, as I have said before, but clothed in the images of words and works . . . in a mirror and through an image, as the Apostle says.'[60] Hilton has just said that he does not refer to seeing Jesus 'as he is in Himself, in the fulness of His blessed godhead, but Jesus as He chooses to show Himself to a pure soul, held within the body, according to the degree of purity it has'.[61]

In Rolle's *Meditations on the Passion* the speaker gives thanks for Christ's suffering caused by the spitting on his face—a face which is then called 'þat swete myrrour and bodily blis of heuene, upon which aungels & seintis haue deinte to loke'. The image in the mirror is that of Jesus in the passion, in heaven, and in the soul, who desires to become like the image of Jesus, for the text continues: 'swete Ihesu, restore þe liknes of þi face in my soule þat foule synness han faded'.[62] Similarly, in the lyric 'My trewest tresowre sa trayturly taken', the poet after contemplating Jesus 'naked and nayled' and 'hydusly hyngand', prays that: 'þe mynde of þis myrour þou lat me noght mysse;/Bot wynd vp my wylle to won wyth þe ay', thereby asking for grace to think on the passion and to keep the will fastened on heaven.[63]

The mirror metaphors dealing with spiritual progress focus then on the soul, but not the body, as a darkness, on the soul as the defaced image in which the likeness of Christ is to be restored; and particularly on the face of Jesus as a mirror in which one contemplates all the mysteries of his life, passion, and glorified state.

Mirrors of Mystical Union

The mirror image also supplies language for describing the highest reaches of the contemplative life. Richard Rolle aptly illustrates this use in

Emendatio Vitae: the 'contemplation of the saints'—those who are seized by the sweetness of divine love—is mirror vision:

> . . . the mental vision is snatched up above, and contemplates heavenly things through a mysterious and spiritual vision, not through a clear and penetrating sight, because when we see through faith we see 'through a glass in obscurity' (1 Cor. 13:12). For if the intellectual eye rests in spiritual light to contemplate, it does not see that light as it is in itself. Nevertheless it feels itself to have been there, when it keeps the savor and fervor within itself in limited light. Whence it says in the Psalm, . . . 'As is its darkness, so is its light' (138:11). For although the shadows of sins have vanished from the holy soul, obscurities have receded, and the spirit is purged and illumined in purity, nevertheless, while it is forced to remain here in mortal flesh, that ineffable glory is not perfectly seen.[64]

This remarkable passage synthesizes variations of the mirror analogy from tradition, especially from Augustine: the mirror knowledge of faith in contrast to face-to-face sight in heaven; the eye as a mirror, which sees not the light but sees by the light; mirror knowledge as felt presence: the paradox that the light in the mirror is really a darkness; the blurring of the mirror image by sin and its cleansing by virtue; and mortality as the ultimate darkness which prevents face-to-face vision even in those who are advanced in holiness.

Further expanding on the Corinthian text, Rolle adds that 'saints and contemplative men contemplate the glory of God with His face revealed'. Yet it is not the Face itself, for 'we do not see the invisible light'. 'And Christ takes His hiding place and from there speaks to us in a column of cloud, but what is felt is exceedingly delectable'.[65] These lines correspond to Augustine's commentary, wherein the shadows on the mirrors are the Old Law, with the same implied reference to Moses, who veiled his own face to shield the people from the glory of God—still blinding, though only reflected.

This passage has been prepared for throughout the preceding chapters, with references to the unveiled Face and taste and food: 'O Shining Love, come into me and seize me within Yourself, so that I may be present before the Face of my Creator. For you are seasoning savor. . .'.[66] Almost at the end of the final chapter, with the food image again included, a passage recalls that the Face—no longer in the mirror—will be seen as one like ourselves:

> And because it is delicately fed inwardly with delights, it is no wonder if, sighing, it should say, 'Who will grant me, my brother, that I may discover you and kiss you?' —that is, may I deserve to discover you freed from flesh, and seeing You face to face, may I be joined to you totally, forever. . . .[67]

This then, is the contemplative man, who is 'fastened by . . . great desire into that invisible light. . .'.[68] Thus the mirror text in 1 Corinthians 13:12

influences the whole of the concluding chapter of *Emendatio Vitae*, in which the highest experiences of contemplation are described.

It is not the Corinthian text but the mirror image of Wisdom 7:26 which is echoed in the *Orcherd of Syon*, but there, too, Jesus Christ—the image of divine goodness—is the face in the mirror. Contemplation of that mirror shows the soul its unworthiness but also stirs its desire to be one with the Wisdom which mirrors God:

> In þe beholdynge, or in þe myrrour of þe dyuyn goodnes, þis soule knew her owne unworþines. . . . A soule . . . lifteþ up his entent and affeccyoun by an vnward feruent desier to biholde & loke ynward . . . to se hersilf in þe holy myrrour of God. . . .[69]

And again, in *The Treatise of Perfection of the Sons of God*, the author, after having cautioned that only God can teach the contemplative life, identifies Jesus Christ in his divinity as the mirror without spot:

> By þis litel stone we vnderstande oure lorde iesu cryste, whyche by his dyuynyte is the whitnesse of euerlastande lyght, and the schynere of the ioye of god, also the myrroure withoute spotte, in the whiche alle thynge hase lyfe.[70]

Linking the analogy of 1 Corinthians 13:12 the author says that our state of mortality is the shadow on the mirror of our understanding, so that we know God only imperfectly:

> . . . owre state, whiche is ȝit mortalle and rude, cawses and schaddowes oure vndeyrstondynge, þat god ne ȝit hevenlye thynges as sayntys we may (not) knowe. For it is manyfestly knowen that we may not se the sonne in his substaunce, that is to say in his perfyte beynge, also longe as we goo in a schadowe, wherefore that our knowlyche is be a myrroure in a schadowe the apostle beres witnesse.[71]

In line with a familiar theme in tradition, the writer then associates this imperfect mirror knowledge with the kind of food that is proportioned to our growth in grace: 'Alle m(e)t(e) the whiche ys gyffen vs in this mornetyde schadowe is not ellys bot a preuynge of the m(e)t(e) that is to comme in the mydday of the ioye of god . . . vnto hym it pertenyes to feede vs'.[72]

Lastly, *The Pricke of Conscience* explicitly calls on the authority of Augustine for the interpreting of the mirror metaphor: when the redeemed see God 'face to face' nothing that he has done will be hidden from them. In the mirror of God—Jesus Christ—they will see his humanity and divinity; they will see God in that mirror of his brightness, God become human. They will also see themselves in that same mirror. Then the text makes explicit what is rarely specified elsewhere: in heaven in the mirror there will also appear all creation and all humanity:

> Right swa men salle se God als he es,
> In þe myroure of his bryghtnes,

Als properly als possible may be,
Tylle any creature him to se.
þai salle se þam-self so bryght,
And alle men to-gyder, at a syght,
And alle other thyng þat salle knawe,
And se over-alle, both hegh and lawe.[73]

There are, then, many passages in Middle English mysticism, both in original texts and in translations, which employ the mirror analogy. (Books with the title of mirror or glass usually are books of instruction, and only some of them explain the meaning of the title). These English mystics use the analogy, as would be expected, to signify the imperfection of our knowledge of God and of our self here on earth; but beyond that, in harmony with what Hugedé finds to be the original significance of the Corinthian mirror texts, these writers relate the imperfect mirror knowledge—not just to the darkness caused by our earthly condition or even by sin—but to the steps in growing and perfecting of the experience of God. In particular, they link growing clarity of vision to milk and food, for it belongs to Christ who is Divine Wisdom to feed us—sometimes under the analogy of the mother giving food to her child.

Julian in Relation to the Mirror Analogy

It will not go unobserved that in this survey of how the English mystics used the mirror analogy in relation to growth stages in the mystical life, I have not drawn any examples from Julian of Norwich. Of course, this is because she makes no direct and explicit mirror references in her *Showings* Nonetheless, there is language in Julian's work which seems to presume as context the mirror tradition which she inherited and in particular the sense of 1 Corinthians 13:12: 'We see now in part, dimly, then face to face'. In fact, the way the sense of this text controls much of Julian's thought throws light on how she regarded her showings and the contemplative experiences open to her even-Christians.

First, in line with tradition, Julian, like Augustine, finds within our humanity a mirror of the Trinity:

And thus was my vnderstandyng led of god to se in hym and to wytt, to vnderstonde and to know that oure soule is a made trynyte lyke to the vnmade trynyte, knowyn and lovyd fro with out begynning, and in þe makying onyd to the maker. . . .[74]

But for Julian, it is not just the rational mind, as in Augustine, which images the Trinity; rather we can see God in all our natural capacities to do, know, and love.[75] Nor does she speak of the defacing of the image of the Trinity as a result of the Fall, but rather a blindness and darkness:

. . . for our goostly eye is so blynde, and we so boren down with weyght of our
deedely flessch and darknes of synne that we may nott see oure lorde god *clerly* in
his blessydfull chere.[76]

But even in this life God may open the spiritual eye, as happened to Julian in
the sixteenth revelation: 'And then oure lorde opynnd my gostely eye and
shewde me my soule in þe myddys of my harte'.[77] She sees Christ dwelling in
her soul. More precisely, she sees him at work (not just in her memory or
mind) but in her heart—the same human heart that has been filled with love
for her even-Christians[78] who populate the city in which the Lord reigns. It is
the same heart that in periods of dryness and temptation has summoned up
the memory of the passion for comfort, and at other times has felt the very
joy of heaven in part.[79]

Colledge and Walsh in the critical edition identify four passages which
seem to allude to Biblical mirror texts. These editors find an echo of 1
Corinthians 13:12—we see now darkly but then face to face—in four
passages:

. . . the vse of oure reson is now so blynde, so lowe and so symple that we can nott
know the hygh marvelous wysdom . . . at the last end thou shallt se verely in
fulhede of joye;[80]
[he loves us now] as he shalle do when we be there before hys blessyd face;[81]
And ther shall we se god face to face, homely and fulsomly;[82]
. . . we haue knowyng here, as it were in an A B C . . . we shulde haue fulhed in
hevyn.[83]

They also identify two passages with allusions to 2 Corinthians 3:18—reflecting like mirrors the brightness of the Lord, we are turned into his
likeness. These are: 'The channgyng of hys blessyd chere channgyd myne'—
a rather distant allusion;[84] and a closer one: for the soul that beholds Jesus
dwelling in the soul, 'it makyth it lyke to hym that is beholde'.[85]

The most striking parallels to the sense of 1 Corinthians 13:12, however, are several passages in the *Showings* where Julian notes that what she
sees of the godhead or even of the passion, is only 'in part'. For example, in
the second revelation, in a bodily sight, while she is looking on the face of the
crucifix, she sees only a '*parte* of his passion'. She sees 'bodely and . . .
darkely' because we are now 'so blynde' that we cannot see, unless God
shows us more, in which case 'he shal be thy light'.[86]

'In parte' brings out, in particular, that even in the highest beholding of
God which she experiences, her showing is only indirect and by faith. For
she says of every showing, and especially of the exalted twelfth revelation,
that she had 'in perty' 'touchyng, syght, and feelyng in three propertees of
God . . . lyfe, loue and lyght'.[87] (Here, by the way, I am differing from the
editors of the critical edition, who hold that here it 'is evident that Julian
means "in this matter" and not "partially." '[88]) In another place she says
similarly, 'I had *in perty* touchyng, and it is growndyd in kynd,' which is to

say that her experience was rooted in her human nature, bonded to Christ. The reservation—that she experienced God's presence only partially—follows after she explains what the 'full knowying of God' consists in: for 'full knowyng' it is required that 'our sensualtye be brought vp in to þe substance, with all þe profytes of our trybulacion that oure lorde shall make vs to gett by mercy and grace'.[89] She stresses that for the soul to see 'in fulhed' is to see 'in his owne lycknes'—that is, in the humanity of Christ.[90] Likewise when she sees how Mary mirrors God, it is only in part: 'Also god shewed *in part* the wisdom and the truth of her sowle. . .'.[91] This partial vision extends, too, to the human faces of sinners, who have become saintly and been acknowledged already by the Church as images of Christ: 'And therefore oure curtesse lorde shewyth for them here *in party*, lyke as it is ther *in fulhed*; for there the tokyn of synne is turnyd to worshyppe'.[92]

The vision 'in part' in this life grows under the guidance of grace, linked as it is to our partial knowledge of the substantial self. In the forty-sixth chapter: We may 'increse and wax' in the knowledge of self by the 'fortheryng and spedyng of mercy and grace'[93], but in our life here, 'in oure sensualyte' we do not know 'what oure selfe is but in our feyth. And whan we know and see verely and clerly what our selfe is, than shalle we verely and *clerly* see and know oure lorde god in *fulhed of joye*'.[94] Similarly, in the fifty-first chapter, the servant (as man) neither 'seeth *clerly* his lovyng lorde' nor 'seeth truly what hym selfe is'; when these two are seen we will find rest and peace—'here *in party* and the *fulsomnesse* in the blysse in hevyn'.[95]

'In part' in the final showing, marks off the special mystical gifts from the ordinary ways in which God is present to us. There are three expressions of the divine countenance:

> And thus in the tyme of oure payne and oure woo he shewyth to vs chere of his passion and his crosse. . . . And in the tyme of oure synnyng he shewyth to vs chere of reuth and pytte. . . . And theyse two be þe comyn cherys whych he shewyth to vs in this lyfe, therwyth medlyng þe thyrde, and that is his blessyd chere lyke *in perty* as it shal be in hevyn; and that is by gracyous toucchyng a swete lyghtenyng of goostly lyfe. . . .[96]

Following almost immediately on this passage, Julian again distinguishes between the clear light in which we shall see God in heaven and the partial knowing of him on earth:

> The hyghest blesse that is to haue god in cleerte of endless lyght, hym verely seyng, hym swetly felyng, hym all peasable havyng in *fullhede of joye*; and thus was þe blessydfulle chere of our lorde god shewde *in perty*.[97]

Further on—in chapter 85—she speaks of the mysteries, now hidden, which will be then seen clearly. 'And . . . whan . . . we be alle brought vppe, than shalle we *clerely* see in god the prevytees whych now be *hyd* to vs'[98]—namely, how the endless purpose of his love has been achieved.

All of this growth to spiritual maturity is to be brought about under the tutelage of mother Jesus: as one 'waxith in age and in stature', one will find that 'she channgyth her werkes, but nott her loue'.[99] Julian explicitly links the motherhood of Jesus—'our goostly forth bryngyng'—with the partial knowing of the godhead: 'Ande in our *gostly forth bryngyng* he vsyth more tendernesse in kepyng . . . he lyghteth oure harte and gevyth vs *in party* knowyng and louyng in his blessydfulle godhede, with gracyous mynde in his swete manhode. . .'.[100] In faith and by reason we know something of all that has been made. But to see more, we are to look to holy Church, which is mother Christ's breast, and to his dwelling in our soul, and await the clear vision to come: '. . . and ther shulde we fynde alle, now in feyth and in vnderstandying, and after verely in hym selfe *clerely* in blysse'.[101]

Thus, without explicitly using a mirror metaphor, Julian integrates into her account the insight of 1 Corinthians 13:12 in another way—by repeating the phrase 'in part' to distinguish vision here from vision hereafter. She does, indeed, note that the human being images the unmade Trinity, but not precisely in Augustinian terms. Her vision is never of the divinity apart from Christ. What she experiences is rooted in Christ, and she never leaves behind his life and victory on earth, while always including the Trinity to whom we are united through our grounding in Christ. She includes, too— and this is not frequent among her English contemporaries and pre- decessors—all members of the Church, Christ's body and crown. She has ample antecedents in tradition however, when she incorporates that motif of the mirror tradition which links increasing clarity of vision with growth towards spiritual maturity, through the nourishing we receive from Christ, the mother. Julian is at pains to stress that any experience of God as bliss and joy in this life—no matter how ecstatic—is only 'in parte'. The fullness of face-to-face vision will include the unveiling of the mysteries of his love, obscure now in the midst of sin and suffering. However, a direct mirror image does not serve Julian's purpose, because what she wishes to convey is not a spiritual sight alone, but is related to all the senses in a context of joy.

Conclusion

From this selective overview of the use of the *speculum* image by the English mystics, a few points become clear. First, it is evident that an artificial typology of mirrors and what they signify cannot adequately show how that image functions for the mystics. Second, despite some literary and philosophical ramifications, the mirror image in the English mystics stays quite close to a single theme: the maturing process within the mystical life. Hence it conveys a general sense of moving from what we see in the mirror to what we shall become. This sense frequently links with the appropriate kinds of food on which the maturing soul is nourished, and sometimes on being fed, according to childhood's changing need, by mother Christ or mother Church.

In all cases the influence of Platonism is minimal or non-existent. The image in the mirror, in one way or another, is Jesus Christ. Occasionally, the image is Jesus Christ united with all the redeemed, and in this vision we see what humanity is to become. And, somewhat surprisingly, in Julian, where the direct allusions to the mirror analogy are obscure and almost negligible, the intent of the Biblical mirror passages is emphatic and clear. In heaven indeed we shall know the fullness of joy; but meantime, on earth, all is by faith, and only in part.

NOTES

1. Thomas Merton, 'The Inner Experience: Notes on Contemplation (1)', ed. Patrick Hart, *Cistercian Studies*, 18 (1983), 3–15. Note also that William Johnston in *The Mirror Mind*, New York, 1981, says of his title: 'Buddhism loves to speak of the mind as a mirror— sometimes an empty mirror, sometimes a mirror that reflects the universe. And Christian mystics also speak of the ground of the soul as a mirror that reflects the glory of God and the beauty of the human person' (p. ix). And elsewhere: 'Just as the pure and polished mirror is completely transparent, receiving everything into itself without distortion and reflecting all objects as if they were appearing in it for the first time, so the enlightened mind is completely receptive and filled with wonder, seeing everything as if for the first time' (p. 36).
2. Margot Schmidt, 'Miroir', *Dictionnaire de Spiritualite*, Paris, 1980, 10, 2, 1290–1303.
3. Herbert Grabes, *The Mutable Glass: Mirror-imagery in titles and texts of the Middle Ages and English Renaissance*, trans. Gordon Collier, Cambridge, 1982.
4. *Ibid.*, p. 134.
5. Wolfgang Riehle, *The Middle English Mystics*, London, 1981, p. 154.
6. *Ibid.*
7. Grabes, *op. cit.*, p. 139; pp. 331–332.
    Despite these early texts, Andrew Louth, *The Origins of the Christian Mystical Tradition from Plato to Denys*, New York, 1981, pp. 79–80, believes that Athanasius is the first to develop explicitly the metaphor that the soul, when pure, is a mirror which can reflect the image of God: 'He speaks of the soul "being a mirror in which it can see the image of the Father" (*Contra Gentes* 8). And later in the same work he says: "So when the soul has put off every stain of sin with which it is tinged, and keeps pure only what is in the image, then when this shines forth it can truly contemplate as in a mirror the Word, the image of the Father, and in him meditate on the Father, of whom the Saviour is the image" (*C.G.* 34)'. This metaphor depends on the Greek idea of vision, in which light from the eye mingles with rays from the thing seen on the surface of the mirror. Hence, the mirror image actually exists, on the surface of the mirror. The metaphor suggests that there is a real similarity between the soul and God, though the similarity discloses a much deeper dissimilarity at the level of substance. Divinization then means that as the soul becomes purified it becomes more truly God's image.
8. Grabes, *op. cit.*, p. 332.
9. Alastair Fowler, 'Through the Looking Glass', *Times Literary Supplement* (August 19, 1983), p. 872.
10. Grabes, *op. cit.*, p. 79; Schmidt, *op. cit.*, p. 1298.
11. Grabes, *op. cit.*, pp. 81–2.
12. *Ibid.*, pp. 140–141.
13. *Ibid.*, p. 335; Fowler, *op. cit.*, p. 872.

14. Norbert Hugedé *La Metaphore du Miroir dans les Epîtres de Saint Paul aux Corinthiens*, Paris, 1957.
15. Raoul Mortley, 'The Mirror and 1 Cor. 13:12 in the Epistemology of Clement of Alexandria', *Vigiliae Christianae*, 30 (1976), 109–120.
16. *The Instructor*, Bk. I, in Ante-Nicene Fathers, American Edition, ed. A Cleveland Cote and A Menzies, Grand Rapids, Michigan, 1951–1965, II, p. 218.
17. *The Stromata*, Bk. I, in Ante-Nicene Fathers, *op. cit.*, II, p. 322.
18. Mortley, *op. cit.*, p. 117.
19. *Who is the Rich Man That Shall Be Saved?*, in Ante-Nicene Fathers, *op. cit.*, II, ch. 21, p. 597.
20. Mortley, *op. cit.*, p. 117.
21. For example, *De Trinitate*, Bk. 9, ch. 12.
22. *On the Trinity*, Bk. 15, ch. 8, in Nicene and Post-Nicene Fathers, First Series, ed. P. Schaff, Michigan, 1956—, 3, p. 206.
23. *Ibid.*, Bk 15, ch. 11, p. 210; Bk 15, ch. 16, p. 215; Bk 15, ch. 20, p. 221.
24. *Ibid.*, Bk 15, ch. 9, p. 207.
25. *Ibid.*, Bk 15, ch. 11, p. 210.
26. *Ibid.*, Bk 15, ch. 8, p. 207.
27. *Ibid.* Also: Bk 14, ch. 17, p. 196: 'For the likeness of God will then be perfected in this image when the sight of God will be perfected'.
28. *Ibid.*, Bk 14, ch. 2, p. 184.
29. *Ibid.*, Bk 15, ch. 8, p. 207.
30. *On the Psalms*, Psalm CXIX, in Nicene and Post-Nicene Fathers, First Series, 8, 33, p. 565 and *On the Gospel of St John*, Tractate cxxiv, Nicene and Post-Nicene Fathers, First Series, 7, p. 451.
31. *On the Psalms*, Psalm XXXVII, *op. cit.*, 7, p. 96.
32. *On Faith and the Creed*, ch. 9, in Nicene and Post-Nicene Fathers, *op. cit.*, 3, p. 331.
33. *On the Gospel of St John*, Tractate 102, ch. 16, *op. cit.*, p. 390; '. . . when the spiritual man begins to discern all things . . . he perceives, even though in his life it still be through a glass and in part, not by any bodily sense . . . but by the clearest understanding of the mind, that God is . . . spiritual'.
34. *On the Psalms*, Psalm XLIX, *op. cit.*, 5, p. 170: Commenting on 1 Corinthians 13:12: 'Howsoever a man may cultivate his heart and apply himself to apprehend mysteries, so long as we see through the corruption of the flesh, we see but in part'.
35. *On the Catechising of the Uninstructed*, ch. 2, in Nicene and Post-Nicene Fathers, First Series, 3, 4, p. 284.
36. *On the Psalms*, Psalm XLIV, *op. cit.*, 4, p. 141.
37. *Ibid.*, Psalm XCI, *op. cit.*, 20, p. 452: 'He appeared in that shape in which those who saw Him crucified Him.. . .When shall we, as the Apostle saith, see Him "face to face"? which God promised us as the high reward of all our toils'. '. . . all our reward is seeing'. '. . . our Lord Jesus Christ is that very sight'.
38. *On The Gospel of St John*, Tractate 102, *op. cit.*, p. 390.
39. *On the Trinity*, Bk I, ch. 13, *op. cit.*, p. 33: 'And that sight is face to face, the very sight that is promised as the highest reward to the just, and which will then take place when He shall have delivered up the Kingdom to God, even the Father; and in this "kingdom" He means the sight of His own form also to be understood, the whole creature being made subject to God, including that wherein the Son of God was made the Son of man'.
40. *Ibid.*, Bk I, ch. 8, p. 26.
41. *On the Psalms*, Psalm XII, *op. cit.*, 2, p. 44: 'The truth is one, whereby holy souls are enlightened; but forasmuch as there are many souls, there may be said to be many truths: as in mirrors there are seen many reflections from one face.' Also *On the Psalms*, Psalm XI, *op. cit.*, 11, p. 44: '. . . there is one only righteousness of God whereof . . . all participate. Like as when one face looks upon many mirrors, what is one only, is by those many mirrors reflected manifoldly'.
42. *On the Gospel of St John*, Tractate 101, *op. cit.*, p. 388.
43. *On the Psalms*, Psalm XI, *op. cit.*, 11, p. 44.
44. *Ibid.*, Psalm LXVIII, *op. cit.*, 2, p. 286.

45. *On the Trinity*, Bk 2, ch. 17, *op. cit.*, p. 51.

46. Dionysius, the Pseudo-Areopagite, *De Coelesti Hierarchia*, Cap. III: 'Scopus igitur hierarchiae est, quanta fieri potest, assimilatio conjunctioque: quem cum habeat omnis sacrae et scientiae et operationis ducem, ad divinissimum ejus decorem constanter intuendo, eumdem quad potest exprimit, nec non divinos sui consortes sacra quadam perficit simulacra, speculaque clarissima et immaculata quae primitivae lucis summaque deitatis radium excipiant: cujus indito splendore sacro plena, denuo eumdem ex divinis legibus, in ea quae sequuntur, sine invidia transfundant' (Patrologiae Graeca, 3, 166). *De Divinis Nominbus.* cap. IV: '. . . certe angelus est imago Dei, et arcani luminis declaratio, speculum purum, clarissimum . . . totam in se recipiens (si dictu fas est) pulchritudinem boniformis deiformitatis, liquidoque (quoad fieri potest) in semetipso resplendere faciens secretissimi illius silentii bonitatem. . . . (Patrologiae Graeca, 3, 723).

47. '. . . he þat desireþ to se God, hym behoue to clense his soule, þe whiche is as a mirour in þe whiche alle þing is cleerly seen when it is clene. And when þe mirour is foule, þen maist þou see noþing cleerly þerin. And riȝt so it is of þi soule. When it is foule, neiþer þou knowest þiself, ne God. . . . by þe liȝt of his grace þat he seendeþ in þi reson, þou maist boþe seen þin vnworþines, & his greet goodnes. . . . þan byginniþ þer a maner of cleerte of þe liȝt for to schyne in þi soule . . . þi goostly siȝt, þe whiche is þe iȝe of þi soule . . . is openid to beholde God & godly þinges, heuen & heuvenly þinges, and alle maner of goostly þinges. . . . De liȝt of Godes face is þe shinying of his grace, þat reformeþ in us his ymage þat haþ ben disfigurid wiþ þe derknes of synne.' *The Cloud of Unknowing and Related Treatises*, ed. Phyllis Hodgson, Salzburg, 1982, pp. 143–4.

48. *The Cloud of Unknowing*, *op. cit.*, pp. 39–40.

49. *The Myror of Synneres*, abridged from *Speculum pecatoris*, Patrologiae Latina, VI, 283, in C. Horstman, *Yorkshire Writers, Richard Rolle of Hampole and his Followers*, New York, 1896, I, p. 437.

50. *The Fire of Love*, ch. 9, in *The Fire of Love and the Mending of Life by Richard Rolle*, trans. M. L. del Mastro, New York, 1981, p. 74. See *The Fire of Love and the Mending of Life or The Rule of Perfect Living*, ed. Ralph Harvey, Early English Text Society, O.S, 106, London 1896, 121.

51. 'I haue ordeyned þe to be a merowr amongys hem . . . þat þei ȝulde takyn exampil by þe'. *The Book of Margery Kempe*, ed. William Butler-Bowden, New York, 1944 (London, 1954), p. 186/13.

52. 'Gregory [ȝeue liȝt] wiþ his kunnyng . . . and also wiþ þe myrrour of holy lyuynge'. *The Orcherd of Syon*, I, eds. Phyllis Hodgson and Gabriel Liegey, Early English Text Society, O.S, 258, London, 1966, p. 264.

53. *Ibid.*, p. 277: 'þese wrecchis ben to hem a myrrour of wrechidnes'. For other exemplar mirrors, see p. 319: 'myrrouris of wrecchidnesse þere þe schulden be myrrouris of vertu'; p. 271: 'wiþ þe myrrour of good lyuynge'; pp. 287–88: 'þou schuldist be a myrrour of honeste, & þou art a myrrour of dishoneste'.

54. *The Epistle of Discretion*, ed. Phyllis Hodgson, *op. cit.*, p. 116: '. . . and chese þee þe best, wiþ Mary þi mirour, þat neuir wil defaile'.

55. *A Talking of the Love of God*, ed. C. Horstman, II, *op. cit.*, p. 350.

56. *Dan Michel's Ayenbite of Inwyt or Remorse of Conscience*, ed. Richard Morris, Early English Text Society, New York, 1965, I, p. 158.

57. *The Book of Privy Counselling*, ed. Phyllis Hodgson, *op. cit.*, pp. 75–6: 'Dis nakid entent . . . schal be nouȝt elles . . . bot nakid þouȝt & a blynde feling of þin owne beyng. . . . Dat meek derknes be þi mirour & þi mynde hole. . . . wiþ þe touching of grace be priuely fed in þi felyng only wiþ hym as he is; bot blyndly & in partie, as it may be here in þis liif. . .'.

58. *The Stairway of Perfection*, trans. M. L. del Mastro, Garden City, New York, 1979, p. 273.

59. *Ibid.*, pp. 72–3.

60. *Ibid.*, p. 330.

61. *Ibid.*, p. 326.

62. Horstman, *op. cit.*, I, 95.

63. *Ibid.*, p. 72. This poem was once attributed to Richard Rolle. It is discussed briefly in

Rosemary Woolf, *The English Religious Lyrics in the Middle Ages*, Oxford, 1981, p. 163.

64. *The Mending of Life*, trans. M. L. del Mastro, *op. cit.*, p. 87. See Ralph Harvey, *op. cit.*, pp. 128–29, especially: 'Myendly sight truly is takyn vp heuenly to behald þe schadoly syght ʒit and meroly, not clere and opyn; qwhils we go be faith, þe mero as wer & schado we see'.
65. M. L. del Mastro, *op. cit.*, p. 88; Ralph Harvey, *op. cit.*, p. 129.
66. M. L. de Mastro, *op. cit.*, p. 84.
67. *Ibid.*, p. 90.
68. *Ibid.*, p. 89.
69. *The Orcherd of Syon*, *op. cit.*, p. 47. Another passage (p. 130) says 'þis soule . . . say in þe swete mirrour of þe godheed creaturis goynge in dyuerse maneris'. A passage explaining the Eucharist, but not directly related to the mystical life says (p. 245): 'Riʒt as a myrrour þat is dyuydid, in euery diuysioun is seen þe ymage of a man, and ʒit þe ymage is not diuydid, riʒt so þis hoost [is] diuydid'.
70. *The Chastising of God's Children and The Treatise of Perfection of the Sons of God*, ed. Joyce Bazire and Eric Colledge, Oxford, 1957, p. 234.
71. *Ibid.*, p. 252.
72. *Ibid.*, p. 253.
73. *The Pricke of Conscience*, ed. Richard Morris, New York, 1973, p. 221.
74. *A Book of Showings to the Anchoress Julian of Norwich*, ed. Edmund Colledge and James Walsh, Toronto, 1978, 2, ch. 55, p. 568. All references are to this edition and to the long text. Emphases are mine.
75. Brant Pelphrey, *Love Was His Meaning. The Theology and Mysticism of Julian of Norwich*, Salzburg, 1982, p. 147.
76. *Showings*, *op. cit.*, ch. 72, pp. 662–63.
77. *Ibid.*, ch. 68, p. 639. According to Pelphrey's explication of this vision Julian has insight into the substantial relationship of humanity to God, i.e. the Trinity in its substance. Jesus is understood mystically as human nature as it was made, the source of all humanity, the chief example of it, as well as humanity fulfilled by God (Brant Pelphrey, *op. cit.*, p. 163).
78. *Showings*, ch. 8, p. 319.
79. *Ibid.*, ch. 41, p. 467.
80. *Ibid.*, ch. 32, p. 423.
81. *Ibid.*, ch. 37, p. 444.
82. *Ibid.*, ch. 43, p. 481.
83. *Ibid.*, ch. 80, p. 708.
84. *Ibid.*, ch. 21, p. 379.
85. *Ibid.*, ch. 68, p. 644.
86. *Ibid.*, ch. 10, p. 325.
87. *Ibid.*, ch. 83, pp. 722–23.
88. *Ibid.*, p. 722, note.
89. *Ibid.*, ch. 56, p. 573.
90. *Ibid.*, ch. 72, p. 661.
91. *Ibid.*, ch. 4, p. 297.
92. *Ibid.*, ch. 38, p. 447.
93. *Ibid.*, ch. 46, pp. 490–91.
94. *Ibid.*, ch. 46, p. 90.
95. *Ibid.*, ch. 51, p. 522.
96. *Ibid.*, ch. 71, pp. 657–8.
97. *Ibid.*, ch. 72, pp. 659–60.
98. *Ibid.*, ch. 85, p. 729.
99. *Ibid.*, ch. 60, p. 599.
100. *Ibid.*, ch. 61, pp. 601–2.
101. *Ibid.*, ch. 62, p. 613.

'SINGULER LUFE': RICHARD ROLLE AND THE GRAMMAR OF SPIRITUAL ASCENT

ROSAMUND ALLEN

1

Luf es a byrnand ȝernyng in God, with a wonderfull delyte and sykernes.[1]

LIKE MOST MEDIEVAL MYSTICS, Richard Rolle draws on the imagery of the Song of Songs to express his yearning for union with God. Reinforcing the Biblical love song by analogy with contemporary secular song, he describes his love as heat (*fervor*, *calor*; *byrnyng*) and sweetness (*dulcor*), in which he longs to run to God, to seize God to him, be drawn into the divine embrace. But the metaphor Rolle uses to echo the highest degree of his apperception of God comes not from the senses of touch, taste, or sight, which other mystics appeal to for a sense equivalent to the experience of ecstasy, but from hearing. Rolle does not often deploy the metaphor of hearing in terms of the commonplace allusion to the divine bridegroom whispering in the secret chamber from the Song of Songs, (1:12), for Rolle conceives of the celestial harmony he enjoys in terms of the communal activity of the medieval feast, with satisfaction supplied to all the spiritual senses in the image of heavenly conviviality. As in a medieval great hall, heaven is a place of warmth, security, light, food and mirth, where each individual has his seat (*setel*) reserved for him:

Intil þi lyght me lede, and in þi lufe me fede.[2]

What Hilton describes as gleams of light from the caves of the City of Jerusalem, Rolle presents in the blended sense image:

Capimur autem ad contemplacionem sonantibus epulis,[3]
'we are carried away into contemplation by melodious banquets',

feasting anticipated from the sounds of joyful merriment proceeding from the castle.

But this favourite feast image is a paradox: the solitary longs for a union with God that is also communal. The solitary life is a purgation by seclusion from intimate friendship, in preparation for the harmony of a communion of joy, perhaps a reflex of Rolle's intense but retiring nature. The paradox is two-fold. First, it was not until his own emotional maturity that Rolle himself solved the problem of communicating with his fellow men on earth;

as I shall suggest, he does not resolve the tone of address in his prose writings until the late epistles. Second, the metaphor of communal joy in God does not provide an available image for the silence,[4] or darkness, that lack of all sense awareness which in more standard mystic terminology precedes the divine union. Because he is silent about this 'sleep' of the senses, Rolle has been demoted by some commentators, to the second grade of mystics who reach only *illuminatio* and not full union with God.

In his lack of reference to 'darkness', Rolle is very different from Hilton and the *Cloud*-author. In the closing chapters of part II of *The Scale of Perfection*, Hilton describes the preliminary stages of full contemplation, with a tantalising glimpse in chapter 46 of the highest stages of all, culminating in an extreme instance of the figure *occultatio*:

> These biholdynges . . . maken a soule wise & brennyng in desire to þe face of iesu . . . & I do but touche hem alitel . . . ffor a soule þat is clene, sterid bi grace to vse of þis werkynge may see more in an houre of swilke gostly mater *þan miȝt be writen in a grete book*. . . .[5]

Hilton's account of the preliminary stages of higher contemplation, following 'reformyng in faiþ'[6] and the 'openynge of þe gostly eiȝe' which 'luf techiþ . . . is . . . liȝty mirknes & riche nouȝt'[7] leaves us at the moment where this 'mirknes' will lead souls so graced to 'felen þe knowynge of hem self'.[8] In passages of great beauty, Hilton describes the state of 'gostly rest' which then ensues, using the tactile imagery which is his common metaphor for the 'touchynge'[9] of grace, but again evading full analysis of ecstasy itself. The 'riche nouȝt' brings 'mikel gostly ese' and 'fulle softnes'.[10] Then,

> Whan þu art broȝt into þis gostly rest þan schalt þu *more esily tent to god* & nouȝt elles do bot lufen him and þan schal he with bemes of gostly liȝt fulfil alle þe miȝtes of þi soule.[11]

This is to take us to the 'gate' of contemplation, but not to attempt any further description of this ineffable experience than the reference to the allegory of light shining from the distant city,[12] promising 'þe whilk vndirstondyng þat I calle þe siȝt of God'.[13]

Hilton's nearest approach to an account of ecstasy occurs at the end of *Scale* II.41:

> He comiþ pryueily sumtyme whan þu art last war of him bot þu schalt wel knowen him or he go. ffor wu[n]dirfully he stiriþ & miȝtily he turneþ þin herte into beholdynge of his godnes & doþ þin herte make delitably as wax ageyn þe fire into softenes of his lufe & *þis is þe voice þat he souniþ*. Bot þan he goþ er þu wite it.[14]

In Hilton's terminology, the state immediately antecedent to ecstasy, after the restful darkness, is the firing of the soul with love, which provides the impetus to contemplation, as the soul is turned into 'fire of lufe' where every secret prayer is like 'a spercle spryngande out of a fire bronde þat chaufiþ alle þe miȝtes of þe soule & turneþ hem in to lufe.'[15]

But Hilton is emphatic that such ardour, like the restful darkness, is not full contemplation, nor 'þe wirkyng of lufe bi it self', but is 'a party of contemplacioun' so that a soul experiencing 'þis fredam & þis gracious felyng in praier with gostly sauour & heunely delite' does have 'þe grace of contemplacioun in maner as it is'.[16] In alluding to the intensity of full ecstasy in *Scale* II.46 Hilton tends to employ imagery from the senses of sight and hearing,[17] while still describing the effect on the soul, as Rolle had, in terms of burning love; the account is very lightly sketched, the metaphor essentially nuptial.[18]

Hilton's state of 'rest' preceding the union of the soul with God is similar to the reference which the author of *The Cloud of Unknowing* makes to the pause which comes after the intense spiritual discipline, metaphorically presented in terms of violent physical activity:

> & þerfore trauayle fast awhile, & bete apon þis hiȝe cloude of vnknowyng, *and rest* *siþen.*[19]

For both Hilton and the *Cloud*-author, the metaphors of sense imagery and physical activity precede a quiet, a 'mirknes' or 'cloude' beyond which is silence, punctuated by secret murmuring perhaps,[20] but better expressed by a 'failyng', since God 'an vnmaad goostly þing' cannot be known by the understanding, and the most apt expressions for *raptus*, ecstasy, and its intuitions, are therefore negative:

> And herfore it was þat Seynte Denis seyde: 'þe moste goodly knowyng of God is þat, þe whiche is knowyn bi vnknowyng.[21]

Moreover, not only in the apophatic mystic way of *The Cloud of Unknowing* do we find that 'the rest is silence'. Even Julian of Norwich, while attempting to transpose into the medium of words what she experienced in her sixteen showings, has to admit that the 'words' of the visions were merely metaphors for her communion with God:

> The nomber of the words passyth my wyttes and my vnderstandyng and alle my myghtes, for they were in þe hyghest, as to my syght, for ther in is comprehendyd [–] I can nott telle what. . . . And therfore theyse wordes be nott declaryd here; but evyry man, aftyr the grace that god gevyth hym in vnder standyng and lovyng, receyve them in our lordes menyng.[22]

What Hilton left as secret murmurings, Julian translates, in the case of 'bodyly syght', into words we can comprehend; the second 'part' of her visions had already been translated as 'worde formyd in my vnderstondyng', but the 'goostely syght' Julian has to admit cannot be shown 'as openly ne as fully as I would'.[23] Even the 'worde formyd in my vnderstondyng' has to be converted from that personal communication into words which can be generally understood. But the *Cloud*-author prefers metaphor, and silence:

þan wil he sumtyme parauenture . . . schewe þee sum of his priuite, þe *which man may not, ne kan not, speke.* þan schalt þou fele þin affeccion enflaumid wiþ þe fiire of his loue, fer more þen I kan telle þee, or may, or wile, at þis tyme.[24]

The author is alluding to the effect on the soul of the aspirant of the 'peersyng' of the 'cloude' from God's side. Like Hilton, he uses the image of setting flame to the soul, and like Hilton means more than merely physical response. The similarity between such 'enflauming' and Julian's 'words' is made very clear in the passage from Cassian quoted by Hodgson; the imagery here is from light and water:

> The mind, enlightened by the infusion of that heavenly light, describes in no human and confined language, but pours forth richly as from a copious fountain in an accumulation of thoughts, and *ineffably utters to God* expressing in the shortest possible space of time such great things that the mind when it returns to its usual condition cannot easily utter or relate them.[25]

The 'word' is clearly a metaphor, as the paradox 'ineffably utters' shows; it will not bear translation into the language of men.

As Riehle has recently remarked, the English mystics rarely attempt description of God in anthropomorphic terms;[26] except for Julian, they are reluctant to convey more of their experience of ecstasy than an oblique reference to its effect. Affective mysticism naturally assumes a dialogue between the soul, reaching out in love to the Creator, and God, who responds. But the dialogue which is actually conducted in the writings of Hilton and the *Cloud*-author is that between the mystic and his pupil, the writer and his reader. Essentially, this is Julian's mode as well: what Christ said to her was for her 'even Christians', and her dialogue with Christ is translated into a talking with her audience; her ecstasy, filtered through the medium of her own personality by further meditation, is made ready for instruction to others. The instructress stands alongside us and views God from a point of view which she draws us to. There is little distance between us and her, but she warns us to leave a 'courteous' distance between ourselves and God.[27]

In Rolle's earlier, Latin, works, we note a more subjective mode, with Rolle's personal address to God actually recorded, and this mode is retained in some of his English lyrics; but even in his most apparently personal reminiscences, Rolle is probably writing for the edification of others, as an instructor who has himself been divinely instructed; he shows us his experience and the means he uses to recapture the divine *afflatus* by means of song, as an example to follow.[28] Rolle is quite unlike Margery Kempe, who records some experiences which seem superficially similar to Rolle's, but as autobiography. Rolle's metaphor for the divine 'touch', 'murmur' or 'beam of light', the song,[29] is perceived by him in physical terms as a song or 'symphony' which he both hears and himself voices spiritually. The harmony is played on the instrument of his own soul. How was this communication beyond words, between himself and God, to be rendered in transferring the experience to the understanding of others? Rolle seems to have chosen the two most obvious methods: circumstantial record, and verbal echo patterned so as to suggest the eternally ordered harmony of which this is a mere strain.

But did Rolle 'translate' his experience to himself? Did he think of spiritual experience in terms of actual, rather than metaphorical sense experience? Hilton carefully distinguishes the 'mony gostly felynges' of those who experience 'grete deuocions and feruours in here praiers' from the consolatory sweetness accorded to the soul as it sets out on its spiritual journey; but, as carefully, he makes distinction between psycho-physical response and the 'feelings' produced by the act of contemplation itself. Those who experience 'felynges of counfortable hete & grete swetnes' nevertheless 'come neuer fully in þis restful mirknes þat I speke of with feruent desire.'[30] Hilton poses for us the degree of their contemplative vision:

> þan askes þu wheþer þese soules be reformed in felynge or nouȝt. It semiþ ȝis. in as mikel as þei haue swilke grete gostly felynges. þat oþer men . . . fele not of; . . . I may say as me þenkiþ þat þese gostly felynges wheþer þei standen in conpunccioun or in deuocioun. or in gostly ymaginacioun. are nouȝt þe felynges whilk a soule schal han & felen in þe grace of contemplacioun.[31]

Whatever the explanation of Rolle's manifestations of *dulcor*, *calor* and *canor*, and it sounds as if Hilton were a little puzzled that they short-circuit the 'mirk', the question which puzzled Rolle's contemporaries was whether he had known the dark, the desolation; whether he were reformed in feeling.

2

. . . þe lofe of þi hert be ay vpwarde . . .

. . . þi thoght . . . now be ay upwarde, als fire, sekand þe heghest place in heven, right til þi spows, þare he syttes in hys blys.[32]

Both Hilton and the *Cloud*-author are content to describe the method by which the chosen soul attains ecstasy; both decline to categorise the modes of mystic apperception of divine truth:

> For of þat werke þat falliþ to only God dar I not take apon me to speke wiþ my blabryng fleschely tonge; & schortly to say, al-þof I durst, I wolde not.[33]

But Richard of Saint Victor does attempt to classify and evaluate mystic experience in his works. He treats of the 'grades' of love in two works, one being *De Quattuor Gradibus Violentae Charitatis*, which must have been known to Rolle. In *Benjamin Maior*, Richard assesses the objects and then the 'modes' of contemplation. Like his predecessor, Hugh of Saint Victor, he considers the psychological bases of contemplation, distinguishing six kinds in the first four books of *Benjamin Maior*, two in each category, of imagination, reason and 'beyond reason'. In the fifth book, Richard considers the nature of the last two types: beyond the reason but not contrary to it, and beyond reason and, on the mind's return from ecstasy, apparently contrary to all that reason can explain. In both of these last two categories it is usual 'to see by ecstasy', although all kinds of contemplation may be experienced with or without ecstasy.[34] It would thus be not impossible for Rolle to have experienced the highest mode of contemplation without knowing ecstasy. Referring to the top of the mountain, where Moses saw the Ark on the Mount, Richard explains 'so by the Holy of Holies we understand the innermost part of the human mind'.[35] He is clear that ascent, or penetration into the Holy of Holies, are both merely metaphors:

> Quid igitur est montis verticem, vel interius tabernaculum subire quam summum et intimum mentis sinum ascendere, apprehendere, et tenere?[36]

This is the acme of contemplative progress: the second tabernacle, known by very few, reached by ecstasy, where we contemplate the invisible things not of human nature, where the rational sense operates, but of the divine world.[37] What these are, we are of course not told. Richard is merely describing how contemplation takes place. To signal the separation between reason and the experience of *excessus mentis* he uses the metaphors of veil and cloud, indicating the influence of pseudo-Dionysius on his work. Richard was a notable theologian[38] and may well be working from his own perceptions of *excessus mentis*[39] as he clarifies his concept of ecstasy in his works. In the appended fifth book of *Benjamin Maior*, Richard analyses the three *modi* or manners[40] by which progress is made in contemplation. Here he envisages a hierarchy of methods of attainment: by divine inspiration alone (typified by Moses), by personal application and effort combined with grace (the type is Bezaleel), and by the direction given by others (Aaron).[41] But all three see the ark. Richard makes greater allowance for the application of reason than the *Cloud*-author,[42] who draws on him; Rolle's understanding of contemplation as an experience to be had 'at will' may derive something from Aaron who could 'see the Ark' as often as he wished, though Rolle also emphasises the importance of *affectus* in meditative preparation. This apparently volitional contemplation may perhaps have led to some misunderstanding of the degree of Rolle's mystical experience: he surely progressed beyond *illuminatio*,[43] but may never have experienced ecstasy with 'Moses'.[44]

Richard of Saint-Victor considers the effect of contemplation on the mind, in terms of a triple progression: an enlarging of the mind, a raising of the mind, and an abstraction of mind.[45] When the mind is enlarged, the soul's gaze is expanded and sharpened, when it is raised, intelligence transcends human effort, but has not passed over into ecstasy and withdrawn from its 'accustomed ways of knowing',[46] but in ecstasy there is alienation of the mind and withdrawal of normal sense perception. These three 'modes' are experienced by 'those who deserve to be raised to the height of that grace'.[47] He has thus adopted the commonplace image of 'ascent' to God to indicate the stages of the soul's advance. In categorising the third mode, ecstasy, Richard expends the full force of his considerable eloquence, using metaphors: abundant sweetness, infused gladness, the soul being carried away out of herself, and, yearning to fall into rapture, being urged to 'Sing to the Lord, sing Praises to his name' (Psalm 31:11 [Vulgate]).[48] In her joy, the soul dances and gesticulates and is raised up and passes over (*transire*) in ecstasy to contemplation of heavenly things.[49]

It may well have been under inspiration from Richard of Saint Victor rather than Augustine that Rolle first sought the analogy of music for his mystic experience.[50] Certainly Rolle had read the Victorine Richard,[51] and his famous division of love into the degrees of insuperable, inseparable and singular is taken from Richard's *De Quattuor Gradibus Violentae Charitatis*.[52] Here once again, Richard grades the effects of divine love on the soul. It is possibly his final work.[53] In this work, as a reciprocation of the three degrees of apperception of the divine, we have four degrees of response, four types of uncontrollable love, a metaphor from carnal affection first explained in human, sexual terms, then given a spiritual signification. The psychological states of mystic love are graded in ascending degrees of *affectus* for God. This is not a classification of the actual stages on the mystic way, but an analysis of the effects on the soul of its graduated progress to—and beyond—ecstasy. Love is *insuperabilis* 'when it will not yield to any other feeling'; *inseparabilis* when it never leaves the memory; *singularis* 'when it will have no companion'; in the fourth degree, *insatiabilis* 'when it cannot be satisfied.'[54] As in secular love poetry, the states are described metaphorically in terms of burning, wounding and piercing, binding, taste and thirsting, sickness and strife; for the spiritual interpretation, Richard mainly uses imagery of taste, drink, melting and dissolution, all metaphors put to full use in his turn by Rolle. In mystical terms, the first degree seems to cover introversion, the second describes the effect on the soul of being 'raised', and the third the effect of ecstasy. But it is the fourth degree which is most interesting: the return of the soul from her ecstasy, to reveal the experience to others, in so far as the 'remains' of the divine feast can be gathered at all. At this stage the soul takes pleasure in its own infirmity and any persecution it has to endure; it has in some way become immortal.[55] In this state the soul descends below itself and goes out on God's behalf to others:

In primo itaque gradu Deus intrat ad animum, et animus redit ad seipsum. In secundo gradu ascendit supra seipsum et elevatur ad Deum. In tertio gradu animus elevatus ad Deum totus transit in ipsum. In quarto animus exit propter Deum, et descendit sub semetipsum.[56]

This final degree, *insatiabilis*, is not named by Rolle. As is well known, he refers four times to the degrees of love, three times naming them as *insuperabel*, *inseperabel* and *syngulere*.[57] Although he never mentions the degree *insatiabilis*, Rolle insists that he has reached the highest grade of love:

Alii autem, qui illud donum nesciunt, nec illud ideo ab aliis percipi putant; et sane paucissimi sunt qui illud habuerunt, quoniam quidem inter mortales nulla vita alcior, nec ita alta, est; quia hec altissima est qua ad Christum graditur.[58]

The *donum* is his own gift of song, usually placed in his triad of *dulcor*, *calor*, *canor* as if it marked the highest grade. In chapter one of *Contra Amatores Mundi*, Rolle refers to the need for all '*de gradu in gradum* proficere' but adds 'felix est qui eciam habet minimum gradum'.[59]

The influence of Richard of Saint Victor is noticeable throughout *Contra Amatores Mundi* (although no grades of love are designated), especially in the metaphors of dissolving in and being uplifted by the divine love, and it seems likely that already for some time by this middle period of his writing, Role had been familiar with the works of Richard, and in a fairly complete form, not in selections in a *florilegium* without the full context. Why then did he omit the fourth grade, *insatiabilis*? Margaret Jennings suggests that he excised it because it did not correspond to his own experience.[60] This brings us back to Hilton and his speculations about exuberant mysticism such as Rolle's. Did Rolle never experience *unio*, full contemplation? Had he not only never experienced the state of return from ecstasy but never known *excessus mentis* itself, which he would have encountered as a term in Richard of Saint Victor's lyrical descriptions? This we cannot know since Rolle himself, like Hilton, does not analyse ecstasy. It is surprising that he did not mention the 'silence' one would have expected to precede ecstasy, and much of his writing does suggest a consciousness that his vision of God is very imperfect, but this is a mystical commonplace even with those who mention ecstatic knowledge. Possibly Rolle did mistake the physical manifestations of the early mystic way for the full contemplative awareness. Hilton, as we have seen, allowed him the benefit of the doubt; modern critics tend not to.[61]

That Rolle should have failed to identify all the categories of his experience is not proof that he did not experience the final stages of contemplation. The degrees which we must look for in Rolle are not categorised stages in the mystic way: his lack of full scholastic training denied him the expertise in ordering phenomenological experience,[62] an almost impossible task anyway when the experience itself is ineffable.

Rolle's temperament seems to have led him away from the abstractly (even if symbolically) numbered analyses of the theologians, towards the evocative use of rhythm, balance, iteration, and the cumulative surge of the list, as a reflex of the mystic experience itself.[63] Rolle seems to have been vague about terms as well as degrees; his account of the preliminary devotional exercises of reading, meditation and prayer is self-contradictory on their definition and order.[64] His definition of *raptus* in *Incendium Amoris*, chapter 37, as either the raising of the mind in love or a detachment from the senses is theologically orthodox,[65] but elsewhere he seems to conflate the term with ecstasy.[66] He states in *Incendium* that 'rapt' can describe those who are bound in love to God, and hence rapture of the senses is a foretaste of heavenly sweetness;[67] there is some kind of muddle here.

Many of Rolle's terms are echoes of his reading. He employs the term *exire* apparently for the passing out of the spirit in ecstasy, but might have taken it from Richard of Saint-Victor; his use of the terms 'rest', 'darkness', 'cloud' and 'flight' are taken from the Psalms where they were traditionally accorded mystical exegesis, although not in his own Psalm Commentary.[68] This is no more than the habit of Biblical *imitatio* noted by a recent critic as a characteristic of Rolle's compositional method throughout his career:[69] Rolle could even have learned the technique from reading in Anselm, Bernard and their successors, if no further. Even when Rolle says:

Sed tamen quamvis in contemplacionem *per excessum mentis evolent*, nondum propter carnem quam inhabitant illud incircumspectum lumen videre possunt,[70]

this is no more than what the Victorine Richard calls meditation, despite the use of the word *excessus*, which is properly *ravysching* in medieval English, what we now tend to call ecstasy.[71] When Rolle defines two meanings for *raptus* he seems to understand only the non-mystical one.[72]

At least at the time when Rolle wrote *Contra Amatores Mundi*, which its editor considers a fairly mature work,[73] Rolle had not experienced for himself the state of *raptus*.[74] Although Hope Allen equates Rolle's reference to the 'opening of the heavenly door' with *raptus*,[75] it is unlikely that Rolle would have written the strangely unfocussed account of the state of *unio* which results from *raptus*, although not apparently exclusively by that means, if this were so, for in *Contra Amatores Mundi*, ch. 5 the pronouns of reference shift uneasily between first and third. Thus he says 'contemplative men are most holy—as all affirm—and *they* long for that vision of eternal brilliance', but '*I* sigh with desire . . . *I* look forward to heavenly joy'.[76] He cannot quite identify himself with those of the highest degree, and employs a rhetorical *diminutio* by distancing them into the third person. In the same part of the chapter he longs 'not that another glory be given me, but that this be given in a different way, namely, that I may see my

God . . . clearly. I wish that the joy of love . . . be truly brought to perfection in the kingdom of my God'.[77] Although, as we have seen, the first person functions here as a directing device, urging the reader to experience similar longings, the distance of the narrator from his subject seems to be only partly rhetorical, and seems to show a lack of that unitive experience which Hilton calls 'seeing God's face'.

Whatever the degree of Rolle's mysticism, the steps we may chart in his progress are not to be found in his record of his actual experience; they are found in the way he writes: in his acquisition of the techniques of modulating tone, simplifying diction and making syntax more elastic, which we note in his mature works.

3

Calore coactus, curro in cantum.[78]

Now I write a sang of lufe, þat þou sal delyte in when þow ert lufand Jhesu Criste.[79]

For some time, critics have been steadily redeeming Rolle from the earlier indictment that his Latin prose is 'a kind of scandal' written in rhetoric of the most strained and fantastic variety' and 'the most alliterative Latin ever attempted'.[80] Rolle's use of alliteration is now acknowledged to be a device common in early medieval Latin, even in the extremes practised by Rolle,[81] and the rhythmic patterning of his Latin and English prose, especially in the use of repetition, antithesis, *isocolon* and *similiter cadens*, are found to echo the usage of the Fathers of the Church, many medieval scholastics, and parts of the Vulgate itself.[82] From regarding him as individualistic[83] and eccentric, and, in his English writings, an innovator, criticism tends now to find him more derivative, both in content and in style. His exuberant love of metaphor, especially in piling up and even blending imagery derived from Psalms, Canticles, Job and other books of the Bible he seems especially to have loved, is now a critical commonplace,[84] and it is nearly thirty years since it was first claimed that he owed a marked debt to the English devotional tradition.[85]

A recent study of Rolle's theological position has, however, endorsed the impression of every reader of his work that there is a softening and rounding of view in the final works,[86] compared to the frequent acerbity and defensiveness of his Latin writings, even within the middle period.[87] The comparative urbanity of tone in his later prose, in both languages, has also been noted, and accounted for in various ways: he was writing for those who were ignorant of Latin and 'beginners' in mysticism;[88] he was writing in English, where he had less expertise and no formal training;[89] he was writing works of instruction rather than descriptive autobiography.[90]

In both Latin and English works, the most prominent feature of Rolle's style in his later writing is his reliance on the verb forms, as has frequently been noted.[91] The explanation for this marked preference may lie partly in Rolle's observance of *cursus* and of rhetorical patterning: the verbal inflexions of Latin, especially the third person singular and plural, the present and past participles, and gerunds, for example, provide readily identifiable examples of *similiter cadens*:

> Uelut seraphym succensus ardet, et amat, canit et iubilat, laudet et estuat.[92]

> Vulneratur qui vulnerat, quia amatur qui amat.[93]

> Liquet igitur quia omnino odiendus et contempnendus est amor istius mundi, atque amplectendus et amandus amor dei.[94]

But in fact Rolle seems more frequently to employ the sibilants of the nominative and genitive singular, and dative and ablative plural, often in combination with verbal inflextions, for this effect:

> De possessionibus tuis constituis tibi heredem, et tu criminibus involutus pergis ad gehennam![95]

In the last example he has drawn on an array of *-s* inflexions to reinforce the effect. The succeeding sentence of the first example above is: 'Et tanto fit acceptabilior quanto in amore est feruencior', which shows *similiter desinens* (tanto . . . quanto) as well as *similiter cadens* on *-ior*. Although, therefore, Rolle does not only rely on verbal inflexions for these figures of speech, the verbals do afford opportunity for more sustained instances:

> Amatum pro seipso amans et se totum in amato figens, nichil extra ipsum querens, de ipso contentus, flagrans, estuans, uehemens, illum in se ligans . . . omnem modum excedens, ad solum amatum se extendens, cuncta alia contempnens et obliuiscens, in amato iubilans, ipsum cogitans, ipsum incessanter reminiscens, ascendens in desiderio, ruens in dilecto, pergens in amplexibus, absortus in osculis, totus liquefactus in igne amoris.[96]

Verbal patterning in the English works also may account in part for Rolle's prominent use of the present participle and of verbal nouns there too: because final 'e' is falling silent during his lifetime, especially in Yorkshire, the unambiguous inflexional endings in dentals (-[e]d, -and) and velar (-ing)[97] which are not in the process of erosion, will secure the aural effect he desires; they also give a dynamic quality to the prose, reinforcing Rolle's own dictum 'I wil þat þow never be ydel',[98] 'Luf wil noght be ydel':[99] the prose surges with the force of the impelling repetitions:

> -and   *Mykel lufe he schewes,* þat never es irk to lufe, bot ay standand, sittand, gangand or wirkand, es ay his lufe thynkand, and oftsyth þarof es dremande.[100]

> -yng   And þat (schrift of mouth) salle be hasty withouten delaying, naked withouten excusing, hale withouten partyng, als for to tell a syn till a prest and another til another. . . .[101]

-ed (as ppl.) . . . swa perfytely festend, sett and stabeld in Jhesu Cryste, þat þi thoght comes never of hym, neuer departyd fra hym. . . .[102]

(as pret.) for some pulled, some schoven þe, drowen þe, despised þe, skorned þe, tugged þe, and toren þe.[103]

Frequent use of the present participle and verbal noun is not a native idiom in English. Within fifty years of Rolle's death the Introduction to the Wycliffite Bible acknowledges this by recommending methods of avoiding this common device in the Latin Vulgate:

In translating into English, manie resolucions moun make þe sentence open, as an ablatif case absolute may be resoluid into þese þre wordis, wiþ couenable verbe, þe *while, for, if,* as grammariens seyn; as þus þe *maistir redinge, I stonde* mai be resoluid þus *while þe maistir rediþ, I stonde.* . . . And sumtyme it wolde acorde wel wiþ þe sentence to be resoluid into *whanne* eiþer into *aftirward.* . . . And sumtyme it mai wel be resoluid into a verbe of þe same tens as oþere ben in þe same resoun, and into þis word *et,* þat is *and* in English. . . . Also a participle of a present tens eiþer pretert, of actif vois eiþer passif, mai be resoluid into a verbe of þe same tens and a coniunccioun copulatif, as þus *dicens,* þat is *seiynge,* mai be resoluid þus *and seiþ* eiþer þat *seiþ.*[104]

Rolle must have been as aware of the difference in native colloquial idiom as the Wycliffite Bible commentator. It is too simple an explanation to account for Rolle's heavy reliance on verbal forms in English prose as an echo of his Latin writings,[105] or to explain his preference for participial constructions as an imitation of passages in the Bible. For one thing, the use of verbal nouns has been noted recently as a common feature in German mystical writings of the Middle Ages,[106] and it forms part of the listing techniques of Wulfstan in Old English, and the prose of MS. Bodley 34 in Middle English. The verbal noun and present participle, probably in Julian's dialect identical in inflexion, form a frequent and effective means of showing the vigour and completeness of her universe:

And then shall we alle come in to oure lorde, oure selfe clerely knowyng and god fulsomely hauyng, and we endlesly be alle hyd in god, verely seyeng and fulsomly felyng, and hym gostely heryng, and hym delectably smellying and hym swetly swelwyng.[107]

In medieval Latin, the present participle was used in constructions where classical Latin would have required subordination with a *cum* clause or an ablative absolute, and was used mainly in relation to the subject and rarely in predicative functions.[108] In other words, it had an increasingly descriptive function, and yet retained the dynamic force of the verb without restricting meaning to any precise location in time or the kind of causal relationship which the Wycliffite theoriser wished to restore in his 'open' English renderings.[109] Modern English of course resolved the matter by evolving the durative aspect of the verb. But in medieval grammatical theory, the participle and verbal noun were considered to be part verb, part noun. Rolle often uses present participles substantivally: *arguentes*, *insipiens*, *Omnipotens*, *Vivificans* etc., and, conversely, will vary the items in a long list by using, now a verbal noun, now an abstract noun, and now an infinitive used as a noun:

> þe synnes of þe mowthe er thir: to swere oftsyth . . . to neuen his name withouten reuerence, agaynsaiyng and strife agayne sothfastnes, grotchyng agayns God for any angwys . . . to say Goddes servys undevowtly and withouten reverence, bakbityng, flateryng, lesyng, missaiyng, wariyng, defamyng, flytyng, manasyng, sawyng of discorde, treson, fals wytnes, ill cownsell, hethyng, unboxumnes with worde; to turne gude dedes to ill. . . .[110]

The powerful hortatory effect of the repetitions is arrested just before the incantations induce somnolence and the reader instead of being impressed by the force of repetition grows bored. Rolle can handle his audience reaction by subtle adjustment of the verbs and nouns.

Now the speculative grammarians of the thirteenth century had given careful consideration to the very nature of nouns and verbs. Among the most prominent of these '*modistae*' is Martin of Dacia, who died about 1300. His *De Modi Significandi*,[111] written about 1270, which relies on an interplay between grammar and logic, treats most fully of nouns and verbs, chiefly because Aristotle distinguished these two parts of speech in his *Topica*. The *modistae* retained the terminology of Donatus and Priscian, but followed Peter Helias, in his glosses on Priscian, in associating grammar with philosophy and using terminology derived from contemporary philosophical theories, notably Realism.[112] They maintained that it should be possible to devise a single, universal grammar, its basis lying outside language itself but within reality.[113] For Siger de Courtrai, the essentials of grammar are 'permanence, becoming, and arrangement', the 'nominals expressing permanence, verbals becoming, and the indeclinables arrangement'.[114] The *modistae* were concerned to 'set up the contrast between the *nomen* and the verb'.[115] It was Nominalism which refuted the *modistae* and their theories in the fourteenth century. Rolle may well have encountered some of the contemporary fourteenth-century controversy between Nominalists and *modistae* while at Oxford. If he really did attend the Sorbonne in the 1320s he would certainly have met it there.[116]

Rolle's degree of education will presumably also always remain a controversial point. If he went to University at fourteen or fifteen years of age, then by eighteen when he left,[117] he would certainly have studied Donatus, probably since seven, and the new, more advanced grammar of Alexander de Villa-Dei, the *Doctrinale* at about fourteen. By the time he was ready to become a questioner, Richard should have studied logic and rhetoric and begun the natural sciences and astronomy.[118] His more advanced studies of grammar and logic at University could well have introduced him to the notion expressed by the *modista*, Martin of Erfurt, the last but one of them all, who taught briefly in Paris in the early fourteenth century, that

> So that we may know from which property of the thing this mode of signifying is derived, it should be noted that in things we find certain properties or common modes of being, i.e. the mode of an entity and the mode of being. The mode of an entity is the mode of condition and permanence inherent in the thing from which it has essence. The mode of being is the mode of change and succession inherent in the thing, from which it has becoming.[119]

Thomas defines *Nomen*, the noun, in terms of its mode of entity 'derived from the property of condition and permanence which is found first and above all in substance'.[120] The adjective, including interrogatives, indefinites, relatives, demonstratives and comparative and superlative degrees of adjectives, are described as 'modus adiacentis' (modes of adhering).[121] Of the verb, Thomas writes: 'The verb is therefore the part of speech that signifies by means of the mode of being separate from the substance'.[122]

Now whatever Rolle's degree of learning and philosophical opinions, it is clear that much of this type of grammatical reasoning would be inherently inapplicable to someone struggling to express a union, not modes of separation, with the one being of real permanence. For Rolle the only *Nomen* which could truly be said to have permanence and substance was *the Nomen*, Iesu, the object and the voice of his yearning, and being separate from him was a 'mode' to be transcended.

When Thomas of Erfurt does try to deal in his terminology of the verb as a mode of flux and separation, with the problem of the being of God, observing, 'the being of God is not in flux and succession, and yet we say 'God is' and 'Intelligence is', he is forced to chop logic:

> It must be said that, although the being of God and of Intelligences may not be successive in terms of the succession of time, they are however successive in terms of the succession of eternity; and although eternity may, according to Boethius, be a total simultaneity and a perfect possession, yet because we understand from the standpoint of lesser beings, therefore in this instance we imagine succession and the duration of eternity in terms of different spaces of time.[123]

To Rolle, God is the one real 'thing': 'Nam tam admirabilis *res* Deus est, et tam delectabilis ad uidendum'.[124] Clearly, for one whose message is consistently not to delight *in rebus transitoriis*,[125] to abandon 'ille amor qui magis delectatur in creatura quam in Creatore',[126] and to consider that those do best who 'will na erthly thyng',[127] any theory which holds nouns to represent permanence and finds it hard to account for one whose own title is verbal: 'I am who am', would be nonsense. And yet his Latin style, abounding in metaphor, seems to be making use of the very substance he is denying. He celebrates the Creator by means of his creatures, providing a profusion of metaphors for the divine lover, and using the earthly as an image of the heavenly in *The Bee*, and in the dove, honeycomb and meadow images in *The Meditations*. In describing God as 'cithara mea' in the *Incendium* and Christ as an entirely rubricated book in *The Meditations* he is even describing God in terms of his creatures' creations, although admittedly the simile is rare in Rolle, and this section of the *Meditations* may be a non-authorial addition.[128]

This use of metaphor produces the paradox in the relationship between Rolle's subject-matter and style, whereby he uses the erotic secular love song, which he runs away from when he hears it, as a medium, in style and imagery, for his heavenly 'song', both lyric and prose poem, to God, Christ and the Virgin.[129] In *Contra Amatores Mundi* this produces a work whose very polarity is expressed in its title—*De Amore Dei, Contra Amatores Mundi*—and in the deliberate syntactical and verbal contrasts which form its entire message. The world is to be rejected as such, but its fruits must be used as holocausts to praise the Creator in appropriately ornate language.[130]

It was Rolle's ornateness which some earlier critics found tasteless. Yet in Rolle's early and middle style the decoration is an expression of the notion that God cannot be adequately praised except in the most elaborately contrived language. All the resources of Rolle's *eloquium* are accordingly drawn on, the rhymes, internal rhymes, use of *cursus*, alliteration, *isocolon*, repetition, antitheses: everything must echo the richness of the Creator and the fecundity of the harmonious love he has inspired in Rolle. We can appreciate that such prose has its own kind of beauty. This is not art for art's sake, and is far from being any form of self-advertisement. If anything, its aim may have been the reverse: to draw attention away from Rolle the man towards his gift of song, especially in *Melos Amoris*, the most ornate of all his works, and surely an attempted echo of the divinely infused song itself.

And yet this style, with its rich profusion of nouns, especially in metaphor, which inherently suggests some point of identity between the Divine and the created, between the world of sense and the world of spirit, ultimately leads away from the very objective it is designed to lead us to. The cataphatic mystic way ultimately cannot say enough. Hence Rolle has to have recourse to the negative. In *Contra Amatores Mundi* we see one of the consequences of his sustained attempts at definition by contraries; as its editor recently observed 'in a sense everything is defined by its opposite; it is what its opposite is not'.[131] God's love is what worldly love is not. But this again is to bring before our attention the very qualities which are to be rejected.

An alternative to using a profusion of nouns in metaphor might have been the sustained use of adjective. Rolle in fact tends not to use cumulative heaping of epithets in the way he uses listing with nouns. He prefers the genitival noun construction, of the type 'celi amor' to 'amor caelestis'. When Rolle uses adjectives, they tend either to be traditional, usually Biblical epithets for one of God's attributes, or, and most frequently, pejorative terms harshly vituperative of the lovers of this world and its possessions:

O quam dulcis, delectabilis et desiderabilis est dileccio Dei.[132]

Deus meus, o Iesu iudex iustissime. . . .

O Dilecte dulcescens, descendere dignare, dulicissima Deitas . . . O Bonitas beata . . . fidem fregerunt fidelissimo Factori.[133]

O miser homo, et plane infelix . . . cum omnia terrena vana sunt, fallibilia insolida. . . .[134]

. . . of þe foule servys of syn, and of þe ugly felyschip of þe deuels.[135]

The substantival use of the adjective is one of Rolle's distinctive features. When he uses adjectives they are usually emotive or evaluative, and this is the case even in his one sustained exercise in the use of the adjective, the *Meditations on the Passion*: emotion is aroused not by describing how Christ looks, but how he feels. Naturally, Rolle is not concerned with the appearance of things, even in the case of the suffering Christ. Here he is using the traditional affective style such as that of the thirteenth-century *Wooing Group*, where the epithets are also emotive, but, in þe *Wohunge of Ure Lauerd*, tend to connote the desirability of Christ as an object of devotion; the adjectives, centring on *swete*, relate to the subjective response aroused in the meditator:

þu art lufsum on leor. þu art al schene . . . for þi leor is swa unimete lufsum & lusti on to loken.[136]

A nu of þa honden & of þa fet swa luueli. streames te blod swa rewli.[137]
Ne mai i naman ʒiue mi luue to swettere biʒete.[138]

Derre druri ne ʒef neauer na lefmon to oder.[139]

This is different from the effect produced by Rolle in focussing on Christ's human weakness, pain, and degradation, by means of extended use of the adjective, but still more of the participles and verbal noun:

þi bodi is so seek, so febyl and so wery, what with gret fastynge before þat þou were take, and al nyʒt wooke withowten ony reste, with betynge, with bofetynge so fer ovurtake, þat al stowpynge þou gost, and grym is þi chere.[140]

The passage most closely akin to Rolle's *Meditations* among the *Wooing Group* is þe *Lofsong of ure Lefdi*:

Ich bide þe & biseche þe . . . bi þe herde hurtes & þe unwurðe wowes ðet he for us sunfule willeliche þolede. bi his deað.fule grure. & bi his blodie swote . . . bi his scornunge. & bi his spotlunge. & buffetunge. & his hel[i]unge. bi þe þorne[ne] crununge . . . bi his owune rode. on his softe schuldres. so herde druggunge. bi þe dulte neiles. bi þe sore wunden: bi þe holi rode. bi his side openunge. . . .[141]

The effect in the *Lofsong* is no longer decorative; this is not a static crucifix; in both Rolle and the thirteenth century poem what we are invited to experience is the progression of events in Christ's passion. By using verbal nouns, the writers put us in the scene, and in their use of adjectives relating to the object of meditation, they bring Christ and the Virgin to life. When he celebrates the human aspects of God, Rolle displays that aspect of the divine with which alone we can really identify: the element of change. Here, at least, the divine does exhibit the state of flux predicated by the speculative grammarians: God becomes man, is acted upon, cruelly, by man. No longer is he to be viewed as a static image, unimaginable in the permanence and totality of his heavenly being.

Although the dynamic use of verbs characterises Rolle's style from the beginning, it is in his later work that we find this feature most expressively used as a reflex of the aspiring, reaching, yearning desire of the mystic to touch God. Rarely does Rolle allow anything simply to 'be'. His worshipper typically 'runs' to God[142] and implores God to 'grant me grace . . . stidfastly to stond,[143] while God causes his lovers 'ryse into þe solace of hym'.[144]

So, in the use of the participle, the verbal noun and the verb of action, for which he is so noted, Rolle expresses the movement of the soul to God, the ascent *into* God which is a 'transformacio affectus in rem amatum':[145] 'Transformatiuam eciam uim habet amor, quia amantem transformat in amatum et transfert in ipsum'.[146]

The speculative grammarian Thomas of Erfurt's pronouncement on the present participle was that it partakes of both noun and verb, or of permanence and becoming. Even if Rolle knew nothing of the speculative grammarians, by intuition if not imitation, he hit upon a verbal mode which ideally expressed his apprehension of the busily active state of God's lovers:

þi lufe es ay lastand, fra þat we may it fele.
þarein make me byrnand, þat na thyng gar it kele. . . .[147]

When will þow com to comforth me, and bryng me owt of care,
And gyf me þe, þat I may se, havand evermare?[148]

The verbal nouns in Rolle, and the reliance on verbs of action to connote movement of the soul rather than 'states of mind', contribute to his message that the one, singular, love above all negative earthly loves is constantly to be aspired to, as the one real thing among all the multiple vanities of the world is unceasingly reached for. It is as active a mode of life, despite the eremetical seclusion, as the verb form which so characterises it; it is as much a 'work' as the *Cloud*-author's similarly dynamic imagery indicates.

4

(Anima) descendit sub semetipsum.[149]

Til þe I write specialy . . .[150]

Briefly, in conclusion, we return to the puzzling of the fourteenth-century mystics: had Rolle been reformed in feeling? Had he reached the dark, returned from the upward and outward surge of rapture, and returned 'below' himself, as Richard of Saint-Victor characterises the final state of *insatiabilis?*

The question of Rolle's alleged claim to a 'continual' state of ecstasy— and its improbability—has been refuted by recent critics.[151] The prayers of the *Carmen Prosaicum* culled from the *Melos*, and those in the *Incendium*, are adequate proof that Rolle's *jubilus* was not uninterrupted, and that he did not mean to claim uninterrupted joy and intimacy with God: he understood the periods of desolation described by all mystics:

> Langor uero in anima perseuerat, donec dederis quod tanto ardore desideraui.[152]

> Ergo ne, Deus meus, cui deuocionem offero absque ficcione, recordaberis mei in miseracione? quia miser sum, misericordia indigeo.[153]

And though there is no mention of the 'dark', in *The Form of Living* Rolle announces:

> And þan þou comes intil swilk rest and pees in sawle, and quiete withowten thoghtes of vanitese.[154]

Rolle's mention of peace and rest in his later writings (there are several instances) may be a sign of his late attainment to that state subsequently described by Hilton and the *Cloud*-author. It may simply reflect a new poise in his personality. What is noteable in Rolle's later prose, however, does correspond to the degree of love designated *insatiabilis* by Richard of Saint-Victor, in which the soul 'goes forth on God's behalf' teaching others: it is a change of tone.

Rolle's earlier works, which seem to have been the scriptural commentaries, are appropriate to the discipline of *redynge*, which Rolle conflates with what the Victorines called *meditatio*. In these works, Rolle helps beginners with the purgative stage of the mystic way, explaining the scriptures. It is a shared process, in which he is both utilising and expounding the scriptures. He accordingly changes his mode of address from 'they' to 'we' to correspond to his topic:

> *Qui dilexit nos*, non nostro merito, sed gratis, quia uoluit . . . Mundamur a peccatis si, quod credimus, opere et uirtute imitamur.[155]

In commenting on the Psalms, Rolle uses 'I' as a reflex of the Psalmist's own lyric utterance; it is overliteral reading which reckons all such interpretative comments to be verging on the autobiographical; as Alford points out, it may well be equally naive to read all first person singular references in the Latin treatises as simple autobiography: Rolle's 'own identity merged with the reflection, until he was himself Job, and David, and Paul'.[156] The 'audience' of the commentaries could well have been both secular and regular religious, and the exegesis might have formed part of Rolle's own process through *purgatio* before he saw the gate of heaven opened,[157] subsequently recorded for others' benefit.

The works of the middle period are less easy to account for in terms of an audience.[158] Their unsystematic method would seem to rule out those with scholastic training, and the use of Latin would, in England anyway, rule out nuns and female recluses and lay brothers; the defensive tone Rolle adopts with reference to his solitary state and movement from one abode to another seems to exclude enclosed religious, except the very tolerant. Often, in these works, Rolle's stance almost seems to be that of one primarily addressing God, with a few remarks tossed over his shoulder to the world at large, which he has firmly turned his back on. The tone is adulatory and hortatory by turns, according to whether he is addressing God or men, and the style fluctuates accordingly.[159] In *Contra Amatores Mundi*, Rolle addresses : a reader,[160] young men in general,[161] young girls,[162] God,[163] and his own love;[164] in the *Melos*, his address is to men,[165], women,[166] a reader ('*tu* lauda qui legis'),[167] the rich (pl. 'mementote'),[168] God,[169] his own 'melos'[170] and interspersed vocative addresses are distanced into the third person within a paragraph, as also is the case with first person narrative. The habit of writing *postillae* on texts has been carried over into Rolle's more extended writing, not merely in the compositional technique but in the tone as well.[171]

This lack of focus may reflect a lack of a specific audience. Rolle is not writing autobiography in *Incendium* and *Melos* so much as using himself as the Psalmists did, as an exemplum, an instance of prayers addressed to God in particular circumstances. Even in the signed *Cantus Amoris* to the Virgin, Rolle uses himself as a mouthpiece, a practice he mentions explicitly in *Ego Dormio* and *The Form of Living* when he supplies lyric prayers to be used by his disciples.

In the last works it seems as if the plea voiced in *Incendium* (ch. 39) for a sympathetic friend has been answered; in the epistles, addressed to a single recipient, there is inevitably a clarification both of addressee and speaker. The use of þu or *tu* instead of the fluctuating *tu/vos/ei* and the even vaguer *quicumque es* ('whoever you are', *Contra Amatores Mundi*, ch. 6), produces that intimacy of tone, invitation, not empty exhortation, which is lacking in the earlier works. At the beginning of ch. 10 of *The Form of Living*, Rolle allows his recluse a series of questions (he finds them hard), exactly in the manner of the author of *Ancrene Wisse*, and of the *Cloud*-author and Hilton after him. The balanced prose, rhyme, and some verbal decorations are still present, together with lyrical 'orationes', because these echo the measured cadence of his divine 'gift'. But now an individual reader is identified, not, exclusively, 'Margaret' or 'a nun of Yedingham' but 'you, my solitary reader'. In communicating with an actual or supposed solitary, Rolle has found exactly the medium which corresponds to his own 'singular' love. His love was singular in the first instance because unusual in its actual impact on his personal life: eccentric if not bizarrely singular at first; it is singular in his own sense because it 'hase na pere'[172] and leaves him alone in the presence of his maker; but in the final analysis it is singular because it allows Rolle the dynamic, one to one address to a single reader which informs and characterises Rolle's most mature prose. He has indeed returned from the mystic heights to advise and direct ('lere, rede') others on God's behalf.

NOTES

1. 'The Form of Living', ch. 10, in *English Writings of Richard Rolle*, ed. H. E. Allen, Oxford, 1931, pp. 108–109. (in the following abbreviated *E.W.*).
2. 'Cantus Amoris' in 'Ego Dormio', *E.W.*, p. 70.
3. *Melos Amoris*, ed., E. J. F. Arnould, Oxford, 1957, ch. 7, p. 20, 1.21, cited in W. Riehle, *The Middle English Mystics*, tr.B.Standring, London, 1981, p. 120. Rolle's preference for the feast metaphor may owe something to his experience in the Dalton's manor at Pickering, where, on his first evening, he was very uncommunicative at the dinner given in his honour. *Office*, Lectio Tertia, in Hope Emily Allen, *Writings Ascribed to Richard Rolle Hermit of Hampole and Materials for his Biography*, New York, 1927, p. 57 [*W.A.*]. The analogy with the feast is noted by Riehle on pp. 109 and 120.
4. For this purpose, mystical writers use the verse in Apocalypse 8:1, 'Factum est silentium in caelo quasi media hora', which immediately precedes the blowing of the four trumpets. But Rolle exhorts: 'Musa et musica nolite tacere, confluite in canticum Cunctipotenti', *Melos, op. cit.*, p. 142.
5. *The Scale of Perfection*, in British Library MS. Harley 6579, f. 140[r], abbreviations silently expanded, italics mine.
6. *Ibid.*, f. 71[v]: 'þis reformyng, in faiþ is liȝtly begeten bot it may not so liȝtly ben holden'.
7. *Ibid.*, f. 123[r].
8. *Ibid.*, f. 95[r].
9. *Ibid.*, f. 130[r]: 'Bot þan comiþ þe liȝt of grace' and 'makiþ it [þe soule of a man] scharp & sotil redy & able to gostly werk'.
10. *Ibid.*, f. 97[v]. Riehle, *op. cit.*, p. 61, equates Hilton's use of *ese* with the Latin mystical term *vacatio*.
11. British Library MS. Harley 6579, f. 98[r].
12. *Scale* II, 25. (The ladder of Perfection, trans. Leo Sherley Price, Penguin, Harmondsworth, 1957, p. 169.)
13. British Library MS. 6579, f. 73[v]. At the beginning of this section (*Scale* II, 11) Hilton has admitted that ecstasy may produce total abeyance of the senses, as Richard of St Victor describes in the exegesis of the death of Rachel (=Reason) in *Benjamin Minor*, ch. 86. Hilton's familiarity with *Benjamin Minor* is noted by Clare Kirchberger, *Richard of Saint-Victor, Selected Writings*, London, 1957, pp. 70f, and notes. As noted by Riehle, *op. cit.*, p. 95, there is a reference to *raptus* itself in Scale I, 8: 'Bi *rauischinge* of lufe þe soule is oned for þe time and conformed to þe ymage of þe Trinite'.
14. British Library MS. 6579, f. 130[r].
15. British Library MS. Harley 6579, f. 130[v].
16. *Ibid.*, f. 131[r].
17. *Ibid.*, ff. 139[v]–140[r].
18. In *Scale* II, 40 Hilton has referred to the secret chamber (pryuey chamber), a common image also used by Rolle in *Emendatio Vitae* ch. 11, but Hilton only alludes to the secret counsels the soul hears there. In *Scale* II, 40 he has previously declared his incapacity to describe the experience of *unio*. The concluding chapter, II, 46, mentions 'lufly daliaunces of priuey speche' but does not develop further this image from Song of Songs 2:10. The

'secret chamber' image, Hosea 2:14 as Riehle, *op. cit.*, pp. 100f notes, is also used by Rolle in *Incendium Amoris*, ch. 37.

19. *The Cloud of Unknowing*, ed. Phyllis Hodgson, Early English Text Society, O.S, 218, London, 1944, p. 61. (Abbreviated *The Cloud*, all quotations from *The Cloud* are from this edition, italics mine.)

20. *Scale* II, 40, 46. (L. S. Price, *op. cit.*, pp. 223–229, 250–253).

21. *The Cloud*, p. 125. The *Cloud*-author explicitly refutes the possibility of being able to approach God beyond the 'cloude of vnknowyng' even if 'hiȝe rauischid in contemplacion' (p. 47). As Riehle *op. cit.*, notes p. 93, in the *Book of Privy Counselling* the author follows Richard of St Victor in interpreting *excessus* as loss of reason: 'alle þou þat in excesse of loue ben rauisc[h]id abouen mynde', *The Cloud of Unknowing and the Book of Privy Counselling*, ed. Hodgson, Early English Text Society, O.S, 218, p. 150.

22. Julian of Norwich, *A Book of Showings to the Anchoress Julian of Norwich*, ed. Edmund Colledge and James Walsh, Toronto, 1978, Vol. 2, p. 403, (in the following this edition is abbreviated *Showings*), repunctuated, since I believe Julian's words suggest *aposiopesis*. Colledge and Walsh, note to line 15,imply that this remark is unrevised from the Short Text, and that in the Long Text the explanation is given in ch. 59, (p. 590, ll. 13–14), an expansion, after fifteen years' meditation, on the significance of the words *I it am*. The meditation has surely provided a translation into human terminology (fatherhood, motherhood and unity) of a communication lying far beyond the reach of words. See Riehle, *op. cit.*, pp. 104, 126–7.

23. *Showings*, p. 323. Colledge and Walsh here cite Mechtild of Hackeborn, whose work translated as *The Book of Gostlye Grace* describes how 'sodaynlye god inspyrede here ande schewede here the inwarde felynge and clere vnderstondynge of thees wordes', ed. T. Halligan, unpubl. diss., Fordham, 1963, p. 77, (cited in note to line 30).

24. *The Cloud*, p. 62, the similarity to Hilton's imagery in *Scale* II, 25 in the 'beme of goostly liȝt' is noted by Hodgson, p. 193.

25. *Ibid.*, from Cassian, *Collationes*. ix. 25, cited from Cuthbert Butler, *Benedictine Monachism*, London, 1919, p. 79, in note to p. 62, ll. 17–19, (italics mine).

26. Riehle, *op. cit.*, p. 76.

27. E.g. *Showings*, p. 695: 'but be we ware þat we take not so rechelously this homelyhed for to leue curtesye . . .', noted by Riehle, *op. cit.*, p. 99.

28. This point is made most effectively by Rolle himself in ch. 5 of *Contra Amatores Mundi*, ed. P. Theiner, University of California Press, 1968, p. 93: 'Non enim propter me loquor, sed propter gloriam et laudem dei, et lectorem utilitatem'.

29. See Vincent Gillespie, 'Mystic's Foot: Rolle and Affectivity', in *The Medieval Mystical Tradition in England*, ed. M. Glasscoe, Exeter, 1982, p. 210: 'Rolle uses the term *canor* to describe a central part of his own mystical experience in terms of harmony, melody, and joyful singing'.

30. British Library MS. Harley 6579, f. 100^r. Here in *Scale* II, 29 Hilton does not mention sounds, which are covered in *Of Angels' Song*, where comfort and sweetness which are felt to sound like a song in the heart are similarly said to come from God but to be, not angels' song, but a song of the soul (ed. from British Library Add.MS. 27592 by Toshiyuki Takamiya, in *Studies in English Literature*, 1977).

31. British Library MS. Harley 6579, ff. 100^r–100^v. Similar observations in *Scale* I, 10, 26, and II, 30.

32. 'The Form of Living', chs. 7 and 4, *E.W.*, pp. 104 and 94–95.

33. *The Cloud*, p. 62. Cf. Hilton's disclaimer, *Scale* II, 40.

34. Richard of Saint Victor, *Benjamin Maior* IV, 22, Migne, Patrologiae Latina, [P.L.] 196, col. 164: 'Quamvis autem familiare sit, et quasi proprium videatur duobus novissimis contemplationum generibus per mentis excessum videre, econtra autem quatuor primis quasi domesticum est et pene velut singulare, sine ulla animi alienatione in contemplationem assurgere, possunt tamen omnia atque solent modo utroque contingere'.

35. *Richard of Saint-Victor, Selected Writings*, Tr. Clare Kirchberger, London, 1957; *Benjamin Maior* IV, 23, P.L. 196, col. 167.

36. P.L. 196, col. 167. This looks like an identification of identical goals for both transcendent and immanent mystic contemplation.

37. *Benjamin Maior* IV, 23, P.L. 196, col. 167.
38. Kirchberger, *op. cit.*, introd., pp. 24f.
39. This is Richard's usual term for ecstasy, taken from the Vulgate (mis) translation of Psalm 67:28: 'Ibi Beniamin adulescentulus, in mentis excess'.
40. Kirchberger, *op. cit.*, explains the term as referring to 'states of mind of the contemplative' or 'ways of contemplation'.
41. *Benjamin Maior*, V, 1, P.L. 196, col. 167: 'Modis autem tribus in gratiam contemplationis proficimus, aliquando ex sola gratia, aliquando ex adjuncta industria, aliquando ex aliena doctrina'.
42. Noted by Riehle, *op. cit.*, p. 93.
43. Contrast Hodgson, echoing Conrad Pepler, in *'The Orcherd of Syon and the English Mystical Tradition'*, Sir Israel Gollancz Memorial Lecture, British Academy, 1964, p. 243, n. 1: 'Rolle is thought not to have progressed beyond that (stage) of Illumination'.
44. Rolle uses the term *extasis* in *Emendatio Vitae*, 'quasi in extasim rapitur', MS.Bodl. 16, f. 75^r, (cited by Riehle, *op. cit.*, p. 92), but he may be adopting the term from e.g. Hugh of St Victor: 'In extasim, id est mentis excessum' (Riehle, *loc. cit.*). Rolle seems to equate it with *raptus*, as Riehle notes.
45. *Benjamin Maior* V, 2, P.L. 196, col. 170.
46. *Ibid.*, tr. Kirchberger, *op. cit.*, p. 183.
47. *Idem.*
48. *Benjamin Maior* V, 18, P.L. 196, col. 191: 'Satagamus coram ipso, cum intima devotione psallere'.
49. Tr. Kirchberger, *op. cit.*, p. 211; P.L. 196, col. 191–2: 'Ad ejusmodi itaque psalmodiam, spiritalemque harmoniam anima contemplativa spiritalibus theoriis assueta incipit tripudiare, et prae gaudii nimietate suo quodam modo gestire, et ad spiritales quosdam et sui generis saltus dare, et se a terra, terrenisque omnibus suspendere, et ad coelestium contemplationem tota mentis alienatione transire'.
50. See Vincent Gillespie, *op. cit.*, esp. 211f., for discussion of the role of psalms in contemplation, and the medieval attitude to music.
51. See Allen, *WA*, pp. 79, 202; J. P. H. Clark, 'Richard Rolle: A Theological Re-Assessment, *Downside Review*, 101 (April, 1983), 108–139, note 102, p. 138. Rolle apparently echoes *Benjamin Maior* IV, 16, P.L. 196, col. 155, the explication of *Cant*. 5:1: 'Comedite, amici, et bibite . . . carissimi' in *Contra Amatores Mundi, ed. cit.*, ch. 2, p. 72. Hilton also echoes the passage in *Scale* I, 44.
52. P.L. 196, cols., 1213f. Also *Epitre à Sévérin sur la Charité: Richard de Saint-Victor, Les Quatre Degrés de la Violente Charité*, ed. Ives G. Dumeige, Paris, 1955.
53. Kirchberger, *op. cit.*, p. 45.
54. Kirchberger, *op. cit.*, pp. 220–1; P.L. 196, col. 1212: 'Quartus itaque violentae charitatis gradus est, quando aestuantis animi desiderio jam omnino nihil satisfacere potest'.
55. Kirchberger, *op. cit.*, pp. 220–1.
56. P.L. 196, col. 1217.
57. 'The Form of Living', ch. 8, *E.W.*, p. 104; all critics agree that the *Form* is likely to be Rolle's final work, produced within months of his death, yet it shows no amplification of the triple scheme outlined in 'The Commandment' ll. 33–4, *E.W.*, p. 74; Ego Dormio, p. 61ff, ll. 85–8, 118–20, 132–6 cites the degrees without naming them; they are named in *Emendatio Vitae*, tr. R. Misyn, *The Mending of Life*, ch. 11, ed. Ralph Harvey, Early English Text Society, O.S, 106, pp. 122–6, Oxford Bodl. MS. 16, ff. 11^v–12^v. The terms *insuperabilis* and *singularis* are used in *Melos*, ch. 50, *Contra Amatores*, ch. 7; *Comment. on Cant.* (MS. TCD 153) has *singularis*, but the latter term is apparently used by Rolle in the sense 'solitary, secluded from the world' in some of these cases, rather than 'unique'; cf. Richard of St Victor, *Benjamin Maior* I, 15; P.L. 196, col. 153: 'Quoniam vero singularis amor solitudinem amat, solitarium locum requirit. . .'. In *Contra Amatores Mundi*, Rolle dismisses grades of love: 'Cum ergo de gradibus divini amoris plurimi loqui nituntur, profecto cognoscant singuli, quia si quis gradum istum pre-notatum conscenderit, alciorem invenire nequit', *op. cit.*, ch. 7, p. 108.
58. *Contra Amatores Mundi*, ch. 2, *op. cit.*, p. 72.

59. *Contra Amatores Mundi, op. cit.*, p. 68.
60. 'Richard Rolle and the Three Degrees of Love', *Downside Review* 93 (1975), p. 198. Allen, *W.A.*, p. 202, suggests that Rolle modified the scheme under the influence of Gregory, observing also that *Melos* has four (and different) degrees (ch. 47, *op. cit.*, pp. 145f). Clark, *op. cit.*, note 102, p. 138, refutes suggestions by M. G. Sargent, 'Contemporary Criticism of Richard Rolle' in *Kartäusermystik und-Mystiker*, I, ed. J. Hogg, Analecta Cartusiana, 55, 1981, p. 174, that Rolle's use of three terms derives from David of Augsburg, *De Profectu Religiosorum* 2, 25, or Rudolf of Biberach, *De Septem Itineribus Aeternitatis*, 4 itin. d. 5, a 1; the latter does not use *singularis*, and has six degrees.
61. E.g. Evelyn Underhill, in Introd. to *The Fire of Love or the Melody of Love*, ed. F. M. Comper, London, 1914, p. xxi, calls Rolle an 'outgoing mystic'; Allen, *W.A.*, p. 5 terms him 'the simplest possible type of mystic'.
62. Carl Horstman praised Rolle's versatility but called his taste into question and referred to his 'restless mind' and rambling compositional method (*Yorkshire Writers*, 1896, rpt. 1981, Vol. II, pp. xxxv–vi). Clark, *op. cit.*, finds 'greater theological rigour' in Hilton.
63. See Gillespie, *op. cit.*, p. 215, for a discussion of the function of music in the early stages of mystic ascent; also Antonie Olmes, *Sprach und Stil der englischen Mystik des Mittelalters unter besonderer Berücksichtigung des Richard Rolle von Hampole*, Göttingen, 1933, p. 99, points to the familiar observation by, e.g. E. Underhill (*Mysticism*, London, 1911, p. 94f. that rhythm and balance best capture the mystic experience by their suggestion of order and completeness. A similar point is made by Lois Smedick, 'Parallelism and Pointing in Rolle's Rhythmical Style', *Medieval Studies*, 41 (1979), 404–67.
64. See Clark, *op. cit.*, p. 127.
65. *Ibid.*, p. 115.
66. See Riehle, *op. cit.*, p. 92: *Emendatio Vitae*, Oxford Bodl. MS. 16, f. 35^r: 'quasi in extasim rapitur'.
67. 'Dicuntur itaque rapti sunt Saluatoris sui desideriis integre et perfecte sunt mancipati . . . Unde conglutinata est ei amoris uinculo indissolubili, et per excessum mentis extra claustra corporis euolans, haurit poculum premirificum e celis', *Incendium*, ed. M. Deanesly, Manchester, 1915, p. 255.
68. E.g. Ps. 134:7: 'Cloudis are lerers of goddis worde. whom he makes oft syth of synful men'. Rolle tends not to emphasise the mystical interpretation in such passages, although elsewhere he indicates the yearning of the mystic for God in his separation from God: Ps. 12:1: 'How lange delays thou me fra the syght of ihu crist, that is right endynge of myn entent: and how lange turnes thou thi face fra me. that is when will thou gif me perfite knawynge of the'. *The Psalter or Psalms of David*, ed. H. R. Bramley, Oxford, 1884, p. 45.
69. See J. A. Alford, 'Biblical *Imitatio* in the Writings of Richard Rolle', *English Literary History*, 40 (1973), 1–23. On p. 23, Alford notes Rolle's stylistic debt to the Victorines 'and to Richard in particular'.
70. *Contra Amatores Mundi, op. cit.*, p. 89. (Italics mine).
71. Riehle, *op. cit.*, p. 92, claims that the English mystics blur the distinction between *extasis* and *raptus*; the former in Bonaventure denotes *elevatio* towards God, the stage immediately prior to entry into the cloud, the latter term is used by Aquinas to denote violent ecstasy. The confusion is perhaps rather in modern English use of the word *ecstasy* to mean what in Middle English was called *ravyshing*.
72. Noted by Clark, *op. cit.*, p. 127.
73. P. Theiner, *op. cit.*, p. 41.
74. Cf. *Contra Amatores Mundi*, ch. 5, p. 90, ll. 244ff.: 'Sed alii sunt qui . . . dicunt . . . quod viderunt clare celestia. Asserant qui hoc noverunt; ego id non expertus sum, nec puto experiri dum in carne sum'.
75. *W.A.*, p. 109.
76. The pronoun shifts in ch. 5 do not seem to me to reflect Rolle's concern to present himself as the passive receiver of mystic rapture (third person narrative), emerging as the transmitter to pupils of his great gift (first person), as Theiner claims for other parts of this work, *op. cit.*, p. 22.

77. Tr. Theiner, *op. cit.*, pp. 175:1. 360; 177:435f.
78. 'Richard Rolle's Carmen Prosaicum, An Edition and Commentary', ed. G. M. Liégey, *Medieval Studies*, 19 (1957), pp. 15–36; p. 22, 1. 36.
79. 'Ego Dormio', *E.W.*, p. 70, l. 311.
80. *Ibid.*, p. xxxiv. For more favourable comments on Rolle's Latin style, see e.g. G. M. Liégey, *op. cit.*, esp. 25f., and 'The *Canticum Amoris* of Richard Rolle', *Traditio*, 12 (1966), 369–91; Arnould, *Melos*, pp. lvii–lvx; Theiner, *Contra Amatores Mundi*, pp. 29f. Criticism of his English style has always been more favourable: e.g. J. P. Schneider, *The Prose Style of Richard Rolle of Hampole with especial reference to its Euphuistic Tendencies*, Baltimore, 1906; R. W. Chambers, 'On the Continuity of English Prose', in *Harpsfield's Life of Thomas More*, Early English Text Society, 186, 1932, p.ci; A. Olmes, *op. cit.*, where some of the Latin works are instanced; R. M. Wilson, 'Three Middle English Mystics', *Essays and Studies*, 9 (1956), 89–96; Phyllis Hodgson, *Three Fourteenth Century English Mystics*, Writers and their Work, 196, London, 1967. But recent criticism has shown that the English prose works are as highly worked and have as many surface and sub-textual patternings as the Latin, e.g. in: Alford, *op. cit.*, *The Passio Domini Theme in the Works of Richard Rolle*, ed. M. F. Madigan, Salzburg, 1978, pp. 118–75; L. K. Smedick, 'Parallelism and Pointing in Rolle's Rhythmical Style', *Medieval Studies*, 41 (1979), 404–67; M. F. Wakelin, 'Richard Rolle and the Language of Mystical Experience in the Fourteenth Century', *Downside Review*, 97 (1979), 192–203; Gillespie, *op. cit.*, esp. 218–24.
81. Liégey, '*Canticum Amoris*', *op. cit.*, p. 382, also 'Carmen Prosaicum', *op. cit.*, p. 20.
82. Olmes, *op. cit.*, pp. 93ff, who cites Gregory and Anselm. Alford, *op. cit.*, points to Rolle's adoption of some of the sentence structures of favourite texts, as well as the phraseology of the Bible.
83. Wakelin, (*op. cit.*, p. 201), however, still terms Rolle's prose 'deeply individualistic'.
84. See Riehle, *op. cit.*, esp. p. 77.
85. By R. M. Wilson, *op. cit.*, p. 93. Supported with some qualification by Madigan, *op. cit.*, pp. 112 & 115.
86. Clark, *op. cit.*, p. 122.
87. *Melos Amoris*, dated (under the title *Melum Contemplativum*) by Allen as an early work, *W.A.*, esp. p. 125, is now accepted as a work of the middle period: e.g. S. deFord, 'Mystical Union in the *Melos Amoris*', in *The Medieval Mystical Tradition in England*, ed. M. Glasscoe, Exeter, 1980, p. 195. Clark, *op. cit.*, p. 112 (and n. 35, p. 134) cites the opinion of Gillespie that *Melos* may postdate *Incendium* and have been written to articulate the experience described there.
88. Allen, *W.A.* pp. 253–4.
89. Riehle, *op. cit.*, p. 77, implies that Rolle is more daring and expressive in Latin. Rolle's figurative language 'only attains its full development in his Latin mysticism'.
90. Allen, *W.A.*, p. 203.
91. E.g. by Madigan, *op. cit.*, p. 143.
92. *Incendium*, *op. cit.*, ch. 22, p. 209. Richard of St Victor on the first degree of love may be compared here: 'Desiderio ardet, feruet affectu, estuat, anhelat, profunde ingemiscens et longa suspiria trahens . . . post modicam interpolationem, estuans ardor feruentior redit, animumque jam fractum acrius incendit et vehementius urit'. P.L. 196, col. 1209. Passages from Richard and Rolle cited by Clark, *op. cit.*, pp. 125–6.
93. *Melos Amoris*, ch. 28, *op. cit.*, p. 82.
94. *Contra Amatores Mundi*, ch. 7, *op. cit.*, p. 105.
95. *Ibid.*, ch. 4, p. 82.
96. *Emendatio Vitae*, MS., Cambridge University Library, Dd. v. 64, f. 13^r.
97. Perhaps for the same reason, Rolle also uses other consonantal inflexions for *similiter cadens*, e.g. comp., superl., 3rd pers. sg.: 'It woundes in lufe, and fulfilles of charite', 'The Form of Living', *E.W.*, p. 108.
98. 'Ego Dormio', *E.W.*, p. 67.
99. 'The Form of Living', ch. 10, *E.W.*, p. 111.
100. 'Ego Dormio', *E.W.*, p. 61.
101. 'The Form of Living', ch. 5, *E.W.*, p. 100.
102. 'The Form of Living', ch. 8, *E.W.*, p. 105.

103. 'Meditations on the passion' Text 2, *E.W.*, p. 30.
104. *Selections from the English Wycliffite Writings*, ed. Anne Hudson, Cambridge, 1978, p. 68. As Hudson points out (notes to text, p. 175), the resolutions are not as unambiguous as the writer implies, since using a finite verb expresses a definite, causal or temporal, relation which may be undefined in the Latin, where the participial construction may simply imply attendant circumstances.
105. But Alford, *op. cit.*, p. 12, notes that the principles of commentary writing, by association, substitution, and amplification, were carried over as principles of composition into Rolle's prose writing.
106. See Riehle, *op. cit.*, p. 70: 'verbal nouns, which are decisive for the dynamic effect of the language of German mysticism, occur with comparable frequency in English texts too, almost as a stylistic element'.
107. *Showings*, *op. cit.*, p. 481.
108. R. A. Browne, *British Latin Selections, AD 500–1400*, Oxford, 1954, Introd., p. xxx. In marked distinction from Classical Latin, it is used to denote action completed relatively to the main verb, where Classical Latin would use an ablative absolute. In Medieval Latin, the present participle no longer solely connotes action contemporaneous with the verb with which it is associated, but is used as in modern English.
109. e.g. Verum cum, vernantes in virtutibus [comparabili] constancia vanitates visibilium prediorum pro invisibilis veritatis precepto perpetuo perfecteque postponimus, devote diligentes absque ambiguitate ad saporem celestis suavitatis ab insipido scelerosoque solacio ad eternum amorem ardenter aspicientes, per transitum a terrenis tute transmigramus'. *Melos Amoris*, *op. cit.*, ch. 10, p. 31.
110. 'The Form of Living', ch. 5, *E.W.*, pp. 97–98.
111. Heinrich Roos, *Forschungen zur Geschichte der Sprachlogik im Mittelalter*, Beiträge zur Geschichte der Philosophie des Mittelalters, Vol. 37, Heft 2, Müunster, 1961.
112. *Ibid.*, p. 146. For Martin, the verb is defined as 'modus fieri distantis', the noun, as in Aristotle and medieval logicians, 'modus esse', defined more closely by Martin, and followed by all the *modistae*, as 'modus habitus et quietis et determinatae apprehensionis', replacing the older identifications of quality and substance in the noun.
113. See: *The Grammatica Speculativa of Thomas of Erfurt*, ed. G. L. Bursill-Hall, London, 1972, pp. 20–2.
114. *Ibid.*, p. 23.
115. *Ibid.*, p. 52.
116. The lack of a systematic organisation in Rolle's writing seems evidence of a lack of formal scholastic training beyond the *trivium*; Clark, *op. cit.*, p. 132, n. 14., gives the plausible explanation that there has been confusion between Richard Rolle and the Scot, Richard of St Victor by fifteenth-century scribal interference in the apparent evidence for Rolle's study in Paris. But for contrary views see N. Marzac, *Richard Rolle de Hampole, Vie et Oeuvres, Suivies du Tractatus Super Apocalypsim*, Paris, 1968, pp. 22–5; Riehle, *op. cit.*, p. 7; and now *The Fire of Love and the Mending of Life by Richard Rolle*, tr. M. L. Del Mastro, New York, 1981, p. 12.
117. *Office*, Lectio prima, simply says that he was maintained when older by Neville at Oxford, leaving 'decimo nono vitae sue anno', Allen, *W.A.*, p. 55.
118. Lynn Thorndike, *Speculum*, 15 (1940), 405 cites an ideal educational scheme from MS. Vatic. Palat. lat. 1252, f. 99^v which suggests this order of study, recommending precociously early ages for gifted children to follow them.
119. Thomas of Erfurt, *op. cit.*, p. 153, tr. Bursill-Hall. The Latin is: 'Et ut sciamus, a qua rei proprietate iste modus significandi sumatur, notandum est, quod in rebus invenimus quasdam proprietates communissimas, sive modos essendi communissimos, scilicet modum entis, et modum esse. Modus entis est modus habitus et permanentis, rei inhaerens, ex hoc quod habet esse. Modus esse est modus fluxus et successionis, rei inhaerens, ex hoc quod habet fieri. *Ibid.*, p. 152.
120. 'Proprietas habitus et permanentis, quae primo et principaliter in substantia reperitur' *Ibid.*, p. 154.
121. *Ibid.*, p. 162.
122. 'Verbum ergo est pars orationibus significans per modum esse distantis a substantia'. *Ibid.*, p. 214.

123. '. . . et licet aeternitatis sit tota simul et perfecta possessio, secundum Boëtium; tamen, quia intelligimus ex istis inferioribus, ideo imaginamur ibi successionem et durationem aeternitatis per diversa spatia temporis'. *Ibid.*, p. 210.

124. *Incendium*, ch. 17, *op. cit.*, p. 194.

125. *Contra Amatores Mundi*, ch. 2, *op. cit.*, p. 70.

126. *Incendium*, ch. 17, *op. cit.*, p. 195.

127. 'The Form of Living', ch. 3, *E.W.*, p. 94.

128. *Incendium*, ch. 35, p. 245; Meditations on the passion', Text 2, *E.W.*, p. 36. See also M. M. Morgan, 'Versions of the Meditations on the Passion Ascribed to Richard Rolle', *Medium AEvum*, 22 (1953), pp. 102f.

129. See Liégey, 'Canticum Amoris', *op. cit.*, pp. 376–9, and 'Carmen Prosaicum', *op. cit.*, pp. 18–19.

130. The paradox is pointed out by Theiner, *op. cit.*, p. 25, and noted, less critically, by Liégey, 'Canticum Amoris', p. 378.

131. Theiner, *op. cit.*, p. 26.

132. *Melos Amoris*, ch. 36, *op. cit.*, p. 109.

133. *Ibid.*, ch. 39, p. 119, ch. 15, p. 46.

134. *Contra Amatores Mundi*, ch. 6, *op. cit.*, p. 96.

135. 'The Form of Living', ch. 10, *E.W.*, p. 110.

136. 'De Wohunge of Ure Lauerd', ed. W. Meredith Thompson, Early English Text Society, O.S, 241, London, 1958, p. 21, ll.36f.

137. *Ibid.*, p. 34, ll.514–7.

138. *Ibid.*, p. 22, ll.71–2.

139. *Ibid.*, p. 22, l.96f.

140. 'Meditations on the Passion', Text 1, *E.W.*, p. 21.

141. *On Lofsong of Ure Lefdi*, ed. W. M. Thompson, Early English Text Society, O.S, 241, London, 1958, p. 17, ll.40f.

142. Noted by Riehle, *op. cit.*, p. 71.

143. 'Meditations on the Passion', Text 2, *E.W.*, p. 33.

144. 'The Form of Living', ch. 3, *E.W.*, p. 94.

145. *Incendium*, ch. 17, *op. cit.*, p. 195, cited in Riehle, *op. cit.*, p. 211, n. 70.

146. *Ibid.*, p. 196.

147. 'Luf es lyf þat lastes ay', 'Lyrics', *E.W.*, p. 44.

148. Lyric at end of ch. 8 in 'The Form of Living', *E.W.*, p.107.

149. Richard of St-Victor, *De Quattuor Gradibus Violentae Charitatis*, P.L., 196, col. 1217.

150. 'Ego Dormio', *E.W.*, p. 62.

151. E.g., by Madigan, *op. cit.*, pp. 81–2.

152. *Incendium* ch. 35, *op. cit.*, p. 247.

153. *Ibid.*, ch. 34, p. 244.

154. 'The Form of Living', ch. 10, *E.W.*, p. 113 cf. also 'The Commandment', *E.W.*, p. 79. 'swa þat þou may haue rest and savoure in hys lufe'.

155. *Super Apocalypsim*, *op. cit.*, p. 124.

156. Alford, *op. cit.*, p. 10.

157. *Incendium*, ch. 15, *op. cit.*, p. 189.

158. N. F. Blake, 'Middle English Prose and its Audience', *Anglia*, 90 (1972), p. 446 identifies the audience of writers such as the authors of *Ancrene Wisse* and the English mystical writers as 'religious, particularly female religious', which implies that Rolle's later works were for an audience which differed from that of his earlier writing, and for whom the Latin works were not comprehensible.

159. N. F. Blake, 'Varieties of Middle English Religious Prose', in *Chaucer and Middle English Studies in Honor of Rossell Hope Robbins*, ed. Beryl Rowland, London, 1974, pp. 348–356, is too restrictive in referring to Rolle's prose as 'descriptive and lyrical in tone' (p. 350), distinguishing it from texts written as Rules for the conduct of a particular way of life; much of Rolle's writing, even of individual works, would come under several of the headings listed by Blake, since, as Alford (*op. cit.*, pp. 10–11) observes, 'Rolle would have felt the modern division of his work into genres, such as commentaries, treatises, and epistles, to be artificial. His works are a whole, closely related by similarities of tone, purpose, and frequently of style'.

160. *Contra Amatores Mundi*, ch. 5, *op. cit.*, p. 93.
161. *Ibid.*, ch. 3, p. 74, ch. 5, p. 92.
162. *Ibid.*, ch. 7, p. 102.
163. *Ibid.*, ch. 5, p. 86.
164. *Ibid.*, ch. 7, pp. 108–109.
165. *Melos Amoris*, ch. 22, *op. cit.*, p. 65.
166. *Ibid.*, ch. 27, p. 79.
167. *Ibid.*, ch. 24, p. 70.
168. *Ibid.*, ch. 58, p. 191.
169. *Ibid.*, ch. 16, p. 49.
170. *Ibid.*, ch. 4, p. 137.
171. See Alford, *op. cit.*, p. 12. Liégey, 'Carmen Prosaicum', pp. 23–4 emphasises the Gregorian principle involved in the variety of style within the *Melos*, as the arts of speech are used to open up the kernel of the text, in what he identifies as a sequence of *postillae*.
172. 'The Form of Living', *E.W.*, p. 105.

RICHARD ROLLE AND THE RHETORICAL THEORY OF THE LEVELS OF STYLE

RITA COPELAND

RICHARD ROLLE HAS attracted modern critical attention as much for his remarkable literary style as for his mysticism. Increasing critical and historical interest in the development of Middle English prose has favoured Rolle's reputation as a brilliant stylist who synthesises various currents of the early traditions of rhetorical prose in Latin and in the English vernaculars, and who fully exploits the potential of native formal devices. While his figurative language shares much with that of contemporary mystical writers who, like him, strive to contain transcendent experience in human speech, the distinctive tendencies of both his Latin and English styles identify him particularly with the strong Latin tradition of rhetorical stylistics. Indeed, Rolle's exuberant plundering of rhetorical convention, of tropes and figures and of the rhythmical forms of ornamental Latin prose, is the most noticeable feature of his style and has elicited considerable critical attention.[1]

His distinctive affinity with the rhetorical tradition needs investigation, however, not only in terms of stylistic effect, but also in terms of the theoretical assumptions about literary style that governed his practice. Rolle, like contemporary mystical and devotional writers, inherits a tradition of Christian-ecclesiastical rhetoric which grows from Augustine's formulation of a theory of Christian oratory in the *De Doctrina Christiana*. But while the ecclesiastical model was pre-eminent in the early and later Middle Ages, it has its own source in the classical tradition which was never entirely superseded. One of the most important theoretical issues in Augustine's rhetoric is the question of the levels of style which he takes over from the classical doctrine of decorum. Augustine's concept of a hierarchy of styles directly informs and constitutes the principles of Christian stylistics from the early Latin period to the emergence of the vernaculars in the thirteenth and fourteenth centuries.

It is against the continuity of this theoretical tradition of classical and Christian rhetoric that Rolle's special position among vernacular stylists must be viewed. This study will thus be concerned with the influence of this dual tradition—classical and medieval—of the levels of style upon Rolle's work, and will consider how these traditions provide the foundation of his theoretical assumptions about literary style. The study of the theoretical background of Rolle's literary practice allows us to place his writings not only in the immediate context of the English mystical movement, but in the broader historical context of Christian literary discourse, both in Latin and in the vernacular, which derives its basic aesthetic premises from patristic reformulations of classical rhetoric.

1

The essential terms of the theory of the levels of style set forth in turn by Cicero and Augustine deserve preliminary attention here to establish the major distinctions between pagan and patristic assumptions and dictates.

The most definitive statement from the classical period on the theory of the three levels of style and of oratorical practice is that of Cicero's *Orator*, a mature work written about 44 B.C. This text is Augustine's primary source for his own appropriation and redefinition of Ciceronian stylistic terms. In the *Orator*, Cicero defends his own oratorical style, with its variety and exuberance against the criticism of the Attici, the stylistic purists. His purpose is to define the ideal orator, without necessarily referring to a specific historical practitioner (v, 20).[2] There are three oratorical styles, in each of which certain men have been successful, but few have attained the ideal of being eloquent in all. Cicero sets forth the three styles, the grand, the plain, and the moderate, and proposes that mastery of these three styles and decorous observation of the restrictions that govern their use is correlative with an understanding and fulfilment of the duties of the orator. The ideal orator will master not only the styles but also the duties of oratory:

> Erit igitur eloquens . . . is qui in foro causisque civilibus ita dicet, ut probet, ut delectet, ut flectat. Probare necessitatis est, delectare sauvitatis, flectere victoriae; nam id unum ex omnibus ad obtinendas causas potest plurimum (xxi, 69).

These three duties, *probare*, *delectare* and *flectere*, had already been introduced in the *De Oratore*, written about 54 B.C.[3] In the *Orator*, the *officia oratoris* (duties of the orator) are associated with stylistic decorum, and Cicero briefly suggests a correspondence between the duty at hand and the choice of style:

> Sed quot officia oratoris tot sunt genera dicendi: subtile in probando, modicum in delectando, vehemens in flectendo; in quo uno vis omnis oratoris est (xxi, 69).

This correspondence between intention (duty or function) and style, which assumes fundamental importance in Augustine's rhetoric, receives no further elaboration in Cicero's argument. It is worth noting here, to anticipate the contrast with Augustine's treatment of the subject of style, that Cicero's definition of the first duty as *probare*, proof or demonstration, is linked firmly with the Aristotelian method of logical argumentation (*logos*).

Thus the identification of this function with the plain style does not have the moral-pedagogical implications that it has for Augustine, who replaces *probare* (logical demonstration or proof in a judicial or deliberative inquiry) with *docere* (evangelical teaching).

Cicero's primary concern in his exposition of the three styles is decorum, the proper matching of subject and style. The ideal orator should be able to vary and combine the three styles, not only according to the duty at hand (a connection mentioned only once) but, more importantly, according to the subject:

> Est autem quid deceat oratori videndum non in sententiis solum sed etiam in verbis. Non enim omnis fortuna non omnis honos non omnis auctoritas non omnis aetas nec vero locus aut tempus aut auditor omnis eodem aut verborum genere tractandus est aut sententiarum (xxi, 71).

It is inappropriate to use the grand style when arguing a trivial matter, such as property rights, before a single speaker, or to use a humble style when addressing a large audience about a great matter, such as the Roman nation (xxi, 71–xxii, 74). Thus in what consists the ideal orator?

> Is est enim eloquens qui et humilia subtiliter et alta graviter et mediocria temperate potest dicere. . . . Is erit igitur eloquens, ut idem illud iteremus, qui poterit parva summisse, modica temperate, magna graviter dicere (xxviii, 100).

This insistence upon the correlation between subject matter and style— defined as decorum—is the foundation of any treatment of style itself. Subject matter is itself variable, and it is the decorous presentation of the subject that makes a speech admirable (xxxiv, 122). The achievement of such decorum, however, does not depend simply upon adapting the subject matter (that is, the facts themselves, the *res*) to the rules of art (xxxiv, 122), but also upon the ethos of the orator himself, of his active realization of his role within a threefold function of speaker, speech or text, and audience.[4] The man of eloquence, then, needs not only to master the sciences of logic and philosophy, so that his understanding of the nature of things (*res*) will impart depth to his exposition (*verba*), but must also be skillful in accomodating his material to the audience:[5]

> Volo enim prius habeat orator rem de qua dicat dignam auribus eruditis, quam cogitet quibus verbis quidque dicat aut quo modo (xxxiv, 119).

In sum, eloquence is the fitting of speech to all conceivable circumstances, and the application of a style which is 'proper' and 'adequate' to the subject (xxxv, 124). It is the nature of the subject itself that must take priority in the speaker's preparation of his delivery. The injunction to vary the mode and level of expression within one speech (xxii, 74) is in effect an injunction to recognize the different substantive levels within one argument as the gravity of the matter increases or lessens.

2

In the *De Doctrina Christiana* Augustine translates Ciceronian theory into Christian terms and reorients pagan rhetoric to serve the aims of evangelical preaching. He redefines rhetoric against the terms provided by Cicero, appropriating the basic terms of inquiry: *an sit, quid sit, quale sit* (*Orator* xiv, 45).⁶ The structure of the *De Doctrina Christiana* derives from two of the five parts of rhetoric enumerated by Cicero: discovery or *inventio*, which takes up Books 1–3, and statement or *elocutio*, which is treated in Book 4 as the *modus proferendi.* ⁷

When Augustine proposes the guidelines of a didactic Christian rhetoric in Book 4, he begins with Cicero's prescription for persuasive oratory (*Orator* xxi. 69), that is, the duties of the orator, and assigns this precept a new value in a Christian context:

> Dixit enim quidam eloquens, et verum dixit, ita dicere debere eloquentem ut doceat, ut delectet, ut flectat. Deinde addidit: *Docere necessitatis est, delectare suavitatis, flectere victoriae.* Horum trium quod primoloco positum est, hoc est docendi necessitatis, in rebus est constituta quas dicimus, reliqua duo in modo quo dicimus (xii, 27).

This distinction between the 'things that we say' and the 'way in which we say them' corresponds to the two-part structure of *modus inveniendi* and *modus proferendi* of the *De Doctrina Christiana*: 'what we say' is the discovery of truth in Scripture, and 'how we say it' is the teaching or statement of that discovered truth. Instruction takes priority over delight and persuasion, as the listener cannot be moved or take delight before he has learned (xii, 28). But delight has no small place in Christian eloquence, for the victory of persuasion lies not only in the hearer's acknowledgement of a truth which he has learned, but in the implementing of that truth:

> Ille quippe iam remanet ad consensionem flectendus eloquentiae granditate, in quo id non egit usque ad eius confessionem demonstrata veritas, adiuncta etiam suavitate dictionis (xiii, 29).

Augustine returns to the *Orator* to suggest a corollary to Cicero's main premise concerning stylistic decorum:

> Ad haec enim tria—id est ut doceat, ut delectet, ut flectat—etiam illa tria videtur pertinere voluiess idem ipse Romani auctor eloquii, cum itidem dixit: *Is erit igitur eloquens, qui poterit parva summisse, modica temperate, magna granditer dicere,* tamquam si adderet illa etiam tria, et sic explicaret unam eandemque sententiam dicens: 'Is erit igitur eloquens, qui ut doceat poterit parva summisse, ut delectet modica temperat, ut flectat magna granditer dicere' (xvii, 34).

He takes up these distinctions between the low, moderate and lofty styles, but he associates them definitively with the three duties of the orator. In this way he reshapes classical theory to bring it into accordance with Christian precept. Whereas Cicero distinguishes between base subjects, such as pecuniary matters, which decorum dictates be treated in a lowly or plain style and the lofty subjects of human welfare and life which merit the grand style, the Christian orator makes no such absolute distinctions in subject matter. His eloquence (*verba*) is always defined and determined by the truth or reality (*res*) of Christian revelation.

Like Cicero, Augustine treats of 'things' (*res*) and 'signs' (*signa* or *verba*).[8] But in Augustine's use, rhetorical language has been adapted to a statement of theology; and the use of eloquence is dependent on the structure of reality, that is, on the eternal *res* or truths which are to be sought and formulated, and which are permanent truths to be loved and enjoyed.[9] Cicero insists upon the necessary unity of eloquence and wisdom to produce a good orator; but this unity is accomplished in the ethos of the orator, in his very act—informed by his philosophical knowledge—of fitting words to things.[10] But this also implies then that 'things' do not determine 'words', for truth is conveyed and accepted through the appropriate choice of words.[11] Moreover, there are various subjects, various 'things' of which eloquence treats, and hence various styles.

But Augustine's rhetoric is defined in relation to a dialectical framework in which the wisdom and eloquence of the world are to be contrasted to eternal wisdom and eloquence. As there are two kinds of *res*, temporal and divine, so there are two kinds of *verba* or signs: temporal or conventional, and eternal, divine eloquence, which is that which is found in Scripture.[12] This divine eloquence is not of human making:

> Neque enim haec humana industria composita, sed divina mente sunt fusa et sapienter et eloquenter, non intenta in eloquentiam sapientia, sed a sapientia non recedente eloquentia (vii, 21).

It is an eloquence which cannot be separated from its source, wisdom, as this kind of eloquence is, as it were, conceived in wisdom. Thus of sacred authors he argues that their verbal style is integral with their meaning, indeed is determined by their subject:

> Nam ubi eos intellego, non solum nihil eis sapientius, verum etiam nihil eloquentius mihi videri potest. Et audeo dicere omnes qui recte intellegunt quod illi loquuntur, simul intellegere non eos aliter loqui debuisse (vi, 9).[13]

Augustine's concern in Book 4 is thus not so much with the precepts of rhetoric as 'with an eloquence in which the words are supplied by the things and by wisdom itself and the speaker is unlearnedly wise'.[14] In divine eloquence, *res* and *verba* are not distinguished: Christ reveals his truth through the divine eloquence of Scriptures, and it is the business of conventional human rhetoric to interpret and express these truths.

Thus because the Christian orator treats of divine realities, his subject matter is immutable and all subjects are fundamentally the same. Matters which in temporal terms are small—say, questions of equity or of conduct—take on great importance, and great matters may be spoken of in lofty fashion, even as God elected to become the humblest of men, and even as the Scriptures may treat the most lofty themes in the humblest style:[15]

> In istis autem nostris, quandoquidem omnia, maxime quae de loco superiore populis dicimus, ad hominem salutem nec temporariam, sed aeternam referre debemus, ubi etiam cavendus est aeternus interitus, omnia sunt magna quae dicimus, usque adeo ut nec de ipsis pecuniariis rebus vel adquirendis vel amittendis parva videri debeant quae doctor ecclesiasticus dicit, sive sit illa magna sive parva pecunia (xviii, 35).

For Augustine the level of style is determined, not according to a hierarchy of themes, but by the immediate context and function of the discourse: that is, which of the threefold duties the speech is to serve, *docere*, *delectare* (also *vituperare sive laudare*), or *flectere*. Thus the doctrine of the three duties of the orator has been conflated with that of the three levels of style:

> Et tamen cum doctor iste debeat rerum dictor esse magnarum, non semper eas debet granditer dicere, sed summisse cum aliquid docetur, temperate cum aliquid vituperatur sive laudatur. Cum vero aliquid agendum est et ad eos loquimur qui hoc agere debent nec tamen volunt, tunc ea quae magna sunt dicenda sunt granditer et ad flectendos animos congruenter. Et aliquando de una eademque re magna et summisse dicitur si docetur et temperate si praedicatur et granditer si aversus inde animus ut convertatur impellitur.
> Quid enim deo ipso maius est? (xix, 38).

Indeed, the conflation of the doctrines of duties and styles is so complete that the three styles are understood as three interdependent means to the achievement of one purpose; and the three tasks or purposes of eloquence are in essence three aspects of one task, so that even in the use of one style the orator attends to all three duties and fulfills a threefold purpose (xxv, 55–xxvi, 56).[16]

Thus choice of style is contingent entirely upon intention or function—teaching, praise or blame, or impelling to action—rather than upon the nature of the matter itself. Meaning is achieved, not in particular signifiers, but in the knowledge of God;[17] *res* or meaning remains immutable, and language, whose function is anchored in the knowledge of God, is the changeable element. Paradoxically then, style and matter become here, in practice, separable, independent entities, rather than, as in classical use, mutually defining correspondents, a sublime theme signified by an elevated, figured style. Stylistic use is determined according to intentional context, and this is conditioned by the spiritual state of the audience, whether it requires simple instruction or forceful persuasion.

3

The *De Doctrina Christiana* synthesises pagan and Christian rhetoric by transforming the functions of the public orator, who deals in civic and legal affairs, into those of the preacher, who deals in the spiritual matters of salvation. It also provided the later Middle Ages with a statement of some of the primary stylistic principles of Ciceronian rhetoric outside of the *De Inventione* and the *Ad Herennium*. This is of some importance: until the fifteenth century, the *Orator* was known only in a partial form which did not include the full text of Cicero's argument on the levels of style.[18] The *Orator*, moreover, was not widely read, even in partial form.[19] Augustine, unlike his late medieval successors, was in possession of the greater Cicero, and his work thus provided indirect access to theoretical matters beyond the scope of those contained in Cicero's early treatise, the *De Inventione*. [20]

In the early Middle Ages, before the Carolingian period, the influence of Augustine's rhetoric declined, although the *De Doctrina Christiana* remained a primary influence in the tradition of theological exegesis. As a directive for preaching, Gregory's *Cura Pastoralis* superseded Augustine's rhetorically oriented text in influence.[21] But although Augustine's synthesis of preaching and rhetoric was not widely current, it was not unrecognized. Bede, for example, revived a concern for the application of rhetoric to preaching; and while his source is not Augustine, but the grammarian Donatus, he appears to have owned a copy of the *De Doctrina Christiana* and to have transcribed large portions of it.[22]

With Hrabanus Maurus (776–856), student of Alcuin, abbot of the monastic school at Fulda, and Archbishop of Mainz, the interest in the terms of rhetorical preaching established by Augustine reappears, and the *De Doctrina Christiana* itself comes to join Ciceronian texts in importance as a model of rhetoric and the *Cura Pastoralis* as a model for preaching.[23] Hrabanus' treatise *De Instutione Clericorum* (819) was an influential sourcebook on preaching and priestly duties in the post-Carolingian period.[24] Its importance for the tradition of rhetoric lies in Book 3, where Hrabanus takes up the subject of speaking. Here, in the section devoted to rhetoric among the liberal arts (ch. xix), and in the sections on Christian oratory (chs. xxviii–xxxix), Hrabanus directly quotes lengthy passages from the *De Doctrina Christiana*, Book 4. Along with the rhetorical writings of Bede and Alcuin, Hrabanus' text attained great currency;[25] and as it served to promote the popularity of the *De Doctrina Christiana* as a rhetorical model, so it served also to popularise Augustine's appropriation of Ciceronian terms.

The latter portion of Book 3 of the *De Institutione Clericorum* is built almost entirely of direct quotation of long passages from Augustine, with some additional material taken from Gregory. Hrabanus clearly intended to provide a digest of Augustine's text, as his selections follow the sequential order of the *De Doctrina Christiana*.[26] Nevertheless, Hrabanus is selective in his appropriation of Augustine's text; thus it is significant that when he offers a model of general rhetorical principles, he locates in the *De Doctrina Christiana* and quotes the very passages which argue the distinction between classical and Christian rhetoric, and which propose the synthesis of the two. In chapters xxxi-xxxiii he gives the section in which Augustine quotes from the *Orator* on the duties of the orator and on the three levels of style, and in which Augustine synthesises style and duty. In ch. xxxiii he quotes the key passage in which Augustine replaces subject with intention as the stylistic directive:

> Et aliquando de una eademque re magna et submisse dicitur, si docetur; et temperate si praedicatur; et granditer si aversus inde animus ut convertatur impellitur (xix, 38).

Hrabanus' selective arrangement highlights these passages, and by isolating them from the difficult qualifying material that surrounds them in Book 4 of the *De Doctrina Christiana* he assures the impact of these primary arguments. Hrabanus is better known for re-establishing the primacy of the exegetical tradition of Augustine;[27] but in his role as clerical educator he also confirmed the currency of Augustine's rhetorical dictates in contemporary learning.

4

Because the *De Doctrina Christiana* gained importance in the schools, through the influence of Hrabanus, as a rhetorical model for preaching, the impact of its principles is evident in vernacular religious writings. Indeed, the importance of Augustine's Christian definition of eloquence is reflected in the tradition of vernacular Christian apologetics, as the most subdued stylist, professing his simplicity, may become the eloquent purveyor of the most sublime truths.[28] Augustine's rhetorical premises can justify the rendering of lofty matters from grand stylistic registers into the often subdued strains of the vernacular. This is the continuous theoretical assumption in the tradition of Old English and Middle English prose and prose translation, from Alfred's versions of Boethius and Augustine to Nicholas Love's rendering of the *Meditationes Vitae Christi* in the fifteenth century.

In this connection, Augustine's definition of the grand style has important implications for an understanding of vernacular stylistics. In the same way in which style and subject are not absolute correspondents, so style is not necessarily defined by degree of ornamentation. The grand style, through which the task of persuasion is accomplished, differs from the moderate and subdued manner, not in quantity of verbal figures but in degree of force:

> Grande autem dicendi genus hoc maxime distat ab isto genere temperato, quod non tam verborum ornatibus comptum est quam violentum animi affectibus. Nam capit etiam illa ornamenta paene omnia, sed ea si non habuerit, non requirit. Fertur quippe impetu suo et elocutionis pulchritudinem, si occurrerit, vi rerum rapit, non cura decoris adsumit (xx, 42).

This notion, that the grand style is fed with force of conviction and spirit rather than with excessive figures and *copia verborum*, is not exactly a departure from classical precedent in theory or in literary practice.[29] But in the later Latin rhetorical tradition of the schools, from the sixth- and seventh-century commentators and compilers to the flourishing of the *ars dictaminis* in the thirteenth century, the high style comes to be equated with a lavish adornment of figures. The strongest line of stylistic continuity in Christian literature, however, is that of the *sermo humilis*, what Auerbach has called 'blending of two realms, the sublime and the lofty.'[30] Here the plainest and most accessible of didactic styles, expressing the most lofty of concerns, that is, the Passion of Christ and eternal salvation, can attain to the most elevated dignity by its force and conviction. This tradition does not exclude rhetorical technique: indeed, within the use of the theological *sermo humilis* in the Middle Ages, the writing of Bernard of Clairvaux represents a direct link with the classical rhetorical tradition through Augustine.[31] But because this is a conception of a high style which does not rely only upon rhetorical mannerisms and which sometimes eschews them, it provides for late vernacular writers, striving to awake literary expression in the national tongues, a ready avenue of credibility for the terms of a native *sermo humilis*. If grandeur can be achieved through spiritual conviction and emotional power, if its effects upon an audience are discerned 'non clamore potius quam gemitu, aliquando etiam lacrimis, postremo vitae mutatione' (xxiv, 53), and if it needs no recourse to elaborate systems of rhetorical colors, then the vernacular writer may have at his disposal a literary discourse as powerful, significant, and in some respects as authoritative as that of his Latin precedents.

   With the efflorescence of Middle English devotional prose in the thirteenth century, we can begin to speak of certain established stylistic traditions in English which have their roots in Anglo-Saxon religious prose. Broadly speaking, earlier Middle English prose texts can be divided into two groups with respect to stylistic precedents and also to later developments for which they serve as models. It is now recognized that the devotional prose 'lyrics' of the *Wohunge* group should be identified with a tradition of designedly elaborate prose writings in Anglo-Saxon, exemplified by the highly rhetorical and semi-metrical mode of Aelfric's *Lives of Saints* or of some of the homiletic writings of Wulfstan.[32] The ornamental prose style of the thirteenth century directly anticipates the mannered and high rhetorical practice of certain fourteenth-century writers, notably Rolle in his most lyrical English prose and the anonymous author of *A Talking of the Love of God*.[33]

But Anglo-Saxon prose also has a strong plain style vein, exemplified by the tradition of homiletic translation and Bibilical rendering, as well as in the *Homilies* of Aelfric.[34] With this second tradition of a homiletic plain style in prose the *Ancrene Riwle*, *Sawles Warde* and *Hali Meiþhad* may be identified.[35] This more moderate stylistic tradition in Middle English prose constitutes a second line of continuity between Old English and developments in later Middle English prose, represented by Walter Hilton, the anonymous *Cloud of Unknowing*, Julian of Norwich, some of the work of Rolle (notably his *Psalter*), and Nicholas Love.[36]

This stylistic division in the continuous tradition of Anglo-Saxon and Middle English prose has its theoretical correspondent in the division Augustine establishes between the duties of teaching and of triumphant persuasion.[37] Writings in the heightened rhetorical manner aim, not to teach the basics of doctrine nor to provide an attractive exposition, but to move the informed reader to pious response, or as Augustine writes, '. . . persuadet in grandi ut agantur quae agenda esse iam sciuntur nec aguntur . . .' (xxv, 55).[38] The aims of the plain style, on the other hand, are reformulated by Aelfric in one of the prefaces to his *Homilies*:

> . . . interpretare, non garrula verbositate, aut ignotis sermonibus, sed puris et apertis verbis linguae hujus gentis, cupientes plus prodesse auditoribus simplici locutione quam laudari artificiosi sermonis compositione, quam nequaquam didicit nostra simplicitas. . . .[39]

In accordance with the Augustinian premise, the plain style is the medium of teaching, and for so clearly designated a purpose, the high, 'artificial' style would be merely a literary vanity.

5

In this continuous tradition of English homiletic and devotional writing, the work of Rolle is exceptional for its manifest departure from the stylistic dictates of Augustine. Where the practice of his English contemporaries points to Augustinian theory on style as the norm, Rolle's practice has a distinctly classicizing tendency. How and from where Rolle derived his peculiar synthesis of classical and Christian stylistic theory must be a matter of conjecture. It is not clear that his stylistic procedure represents a deliberate favoring of Ciceronian theory or a reversion to classical norms; but the theoretical categories that appear to govern his stylistic choices have much greater affinity with classical than with patristic dictates.

Rolle's formal education at Oxford was, of course, very limited.[40] In his brief stay there, as well as in his earlier studies, he would have covered rhetoric as an adjunct to dialectic and grammar. Augustine and Gregory were still the primary authorities in the study of preaching; but in the fourteenth century study of Cicero advanced with new commentaries on the *De Inventione* and the *Ad Herennium*.[41] The rich classical erudition of certain largely Dominican circles at Oxford, and the consequent opening of new avenues to classical texts and scholarship certainly contributed to the greater prominence of Cicero as a literary model.[42] But the extent to which this growing interest in classical antiquity encouraged new consideration of Ciceronian rhetoric *qua* Cicero rather than through the traditional medium of Augustine's Christian synthesis is unclear. The *Orator* was known only in *mutili* until the fifteenth century, and there is no evidence that the new enthusiasm for classical studies would have promoted a thorough re-examination of Ciceronian rhetorical theory on its own terms.[43] With the evidence that we have, then, about the nature of rhetorical studies at Oxford in the fourteenth century and thus about Rolle's exposure to Ciceronian rhetoric, his particular stylistic tendencies are not readily explicable on historical grounds. As a stylist he is unique among his contemporaries; perhaps this singularity in itself should suggest that his rhetorical orientation was not a direct product of any revised direction of rhetorical studies in the schools. Undoubtedly what he knew of the classical theory of the levels of style he knew through the *De Doctrina Christiana*.

Rolle's concept of stylistic procedure is bound up not only with his own pious and ecstatic mysticism but, in a more complex way, with his understanding of the function of literary discourse in its highest rhetorical form as an effusion of *canor*. In *The Form of Living* he assigns the experience of *canor* to the highest degree of love.[44] Fervent song is itself, ultimately, an ineffable entity, and thus he describes it in the *Incendium Amoris*:[45]

> Istud namque dulce canticum spirituale quidem et speciale ualde, quia specialissimis datum est; cum exterioribus canticis non concordat, que in ecclesiis uel alibi frequentatur. Dissonat autem multum ab omnibus que humana et exteriori uoce formantur, corporalibus auribus audienda: sed inter angelicos concentus armoniam habet acceptabilem admiracioneque commendatum est ab hiis qui cognouerunt (ch. 33, p. 239).

> Mundi quippe amatores scire possunt uerba uel carmina nostrarum cancionum, non autem cantica nostrorum carminum; quia uerba legunt, sed notam et tonum ac suauitatem odarum addiscere non possunt. O bone Ihesu ligasti cor meum in cogitacione nominis tui, et illud iam non canere non ualeo! (ch. 42, p. 278).

This extended figure of thought in which song is at once the form of expression and the thing expressed, the celebration of love and the profusion of a love which is divine and mysterious in its origins, is perhaps the most complex rhetorical strategy that he puts into practice in his writings. As others have noted, for Rolle the 'inexpressibility topos' is not merely a literary posture: he is genuinely 'caught in the linguistic incapacity trap—the inability of a fallen language to articulate and express an experience of perfection and beauty which persistently refuses to allow itself to be categorised in terms of human sense perception as articulated by the limited potential of either Latin or the vernacular'.[46] Yet Rolle does not eschew description, either of song itself, or of the highest degree of mystical love of which such song is both experience and signifier:

> þan þe sange of lovynge and of lufe es commen, þan þi thoght turnes intil sang and intil melody. . . . swa þat þe saule es anely comforted in lovyng and lufying of God, and til þe dede com es syngand gastly til Jhesu, and in Jhesu, and Jhesu, noght bodyly cryand wyth mouth—of þat maner of syngyng speke I noght, for þat sang hase bath gude and ill; and þis maner of sang hase nane, bot if þou be in þis thyrd degre of lufe, til þe whilk degre it es impossibel to com, bot in a grete multitude of lufe. ('Form of Living', *English Writings*, pp. 105–06).

Unlike the author of *The Cloud of Unknowing*, who meets the paradoxical problem of having to express transcendent spirituality through the medium of earthly language by insisting on a kind of verbal minimalism,[47] Rolle designs a style which is reserved for mimetic representation of the highest degree of love. In Rolle's writings the apprehension of this love is always recorded in a rhetorically heightened style.

The patristic formulation of the three levels of style and their functions in a Christian rhetoric is not commonly applied to Rolle's works, which—with the possible exception of his *English Psalter*—are generally classed as affective mystical writings in a tradition of elaborate composition.[48] But the old stylistic distinctions do correspond to Rolle's procedure in English, although they have different implications for his conception of literary discourse. In various parts of his writings, and systematically in the *Ego Dormio*, he gives a practical designation of the three stages of mystical love.[49] The style he assigns to each stage corresponds almost precisely with the prescription for each level of style in the *De Doctrina Christiana*. But in Rolle's writing each style, simple, moderate, and grand, is equated, not with a particular task of preaching (teaching, admonishment, or persuasion), but with a grade in the development of mystical compassion. Rolle distinguishes his own calling from that of the preacher, observing in the *Melos Amoris* that the mystic and contemplative who is too preoccupied to preach may yet undertake certain labours:[50]

> Doceat, exhortetur, suadeat omnes ad charitatem, ut vivant in concordia et castitate, in mansuetudine et paciencia.

These three functions correspond with those three tasks of the preacher which Augustine designates. But whereas for Augustine the purposes of the speaker with regard to his audience, rather than the subject at hand, determine the three divisions of style, for Rolle the inverse is true. In his writings the task, or nature of the intention, is always the same, to exemplify the compelling mysteries of love. What changes is the nature of the subject, that is, the degree and quality of love which is exemplified. In one sense, of course, love is always the subject; but the degrees of love are so sharply distinguished that they effectively form different subjects. To each of the three degrees of love, Rolle assigns a particular level of style: the highest degree of love is represented by an ecstatic high style, and the first or lowest degree of love is never represented by anything but a simple or restrained style. It seems that in Rolle one may trace a return—in effect, if not in theoretical purpose—to the classical rhetorical principle, in which expression corresponds to the gravity of subject rather than to the aims of the speaker with regard to his audience.

Rolle's practical definition of the levels of style in relation to the stages of mystical love and compassion are established in the *Ego Dormio* which, like his other English epistles, was composed for the benefit of pious women.[51] At the start of the *Ego Dormio* he describes himself not as a teacher but as a 'messenger' of God's love:

> For þi þat I lufe, I wow þe, þat I myght have þe als I walde, noght to me, bot to my Lorde. I will become þat messenger to bryng þe to hys bed, þat hase made þe and boght þe, Criste, þe keyng sonn of heven. For he wil with þe dwelle, if þou will lufe him: he askes þe na mare bot þi lufe (*English Writings*, p. 61).

He identifies his own role as writer metaphorically as that of a go-between for the Lover and the beloved. This ingenious conceit in which the mystical writer becomes a wooer on behalf of Christ (noght to me, bot to my Lorde') suggests that Rolle's rhetorical intentions are not of a basic didactic order, that he does not formally set out to teach the tenets of the faith. W. A. Pantin observes generally that mystical literature addressed to the devout laity 'presupposes a thorough grounding in dogmatic and moral instruction'.[52] The application of this to Rolle would suggest that his didacticism is of a relatively high order. He assumes a reader enlightened, educated, and passionately suggestible. When in the *Ego Dormio* he moves from a level of metaphorically sustained writing to a humble and direct manner, it is in order to set forth in mimetic stylistic terms the humility and self-restraint which define the preliminary stage of love:

> þe fyrst degre of lufe es, when a man haldes þe ten commandementes, and kepes hym fra þe seven dedely synnes, and es stabyl in þe trowth of hali kyrke; and when a man wil noght for any erthly thyng wreth God, bot trewely standes in his servyce, and lastes þarin til his lyves ende (*English Writings*, p. 63).

This manner has something in common with the balanced prose of the more moderate fourteenth-century stylists, exemplified in *The Cloud of Un-*

knowing or the *Deonise Hid Diuinite*.[53] The interpolated lyric which illustrates this first stage of love in the *Ego Dormio* is a well-wrought but not elaborate moralizing lyric. By contemporary standards the poem is distinctive, but by the standards of Rolle's poetic canon it is an uncomplicated production, using as its only ornamental device the alliteration which is the hallmark of Rolle's lyric writing:[54]

> Alle perisches and passes þat we with eghe see
> It wanes into wrechednes, þe welth of þis world.
> Robes and ritches rotes in dike,
> Prowde payntyng slakes into sorow,
> Delites and drewryse stynk sal ful sone,
> þair golde and þaire tresoure drawes þam til dede.
>
> (*English Writings*, p. 64, ll. 104–09).

In overall effect and tone this lyric is not very different from the severe mortality epigrams of the *Fasciculus Morum*.[55]

The severe stylistic restraint and literalism of this part of the epistle in which Rolle treats restraint of worldly passion (purgation) gives way, with the transition to the second stage of love (illumination), to an eloquent metaphoric style, in which certain key affective terms make their first appearance in the work: 'lyghtly,' 'gastly', 'swetnes', 'joy', 'byrnand', and 'lufe'.

> þan enters þou into þe toþer degre of lufe, þat es, to forsake al þe worlde, þi fader and þi moder, and al þi kyn, and folow Criste in poverte. . . . Perfite life and gastly es, to despise þe worlde, and covete þe joy of heven, and destroy thorow Goddes grace al wicked desyres of þe flesch, and forgete þe solace and þe lykyng of þi kynredyn, and lufe noght bot in God: whethir þai dy or lyfe, or be pore or riche, or seke, or in wa or in hele, thank þou ay God, and blisse hym in al þi werkis. . . . For thorow gode thoghtes and hali prayers þi hert sal be made byrnand in þe lufe of Jhesu Criste, and þan sal þow fele swetnes and gastely joy bath in praying and in thynkyng (*English Writings*, pp. 64–66).

The quality of this prose, and especially the sudden abstract and figurative turn that it takes, is commensurate with the progression of the subject matter. The style has a greater hortatory and affective intensity, although it is not ecstatic. The corresponding lyric interpolation is a meditation on the Passion ('My keyng, þat water grette and blode swette') which incorporates an older Passion poem, the 'Candet nudatum pectus,' in its descriptive scheme.[56] The lyric changes in style midway, at the statement of a paradox: 'A wonder it es to se, what sa understude,/How God of mageste was dyand on þe rude', and leaves behind the affective physical description to anticipate, in a more abstract and intellectual language, the themes and verbal motifs associated with Rolle's most ecstatic writing:

> Jhesu, receyve my hert, and to þi lufe me bryng;
> Al my desyre þou ert, I covete þi comyng. . . .

Kyndel me fire within, þat I þi lufe may wyn,
And se þi face, Jhesu, in joy þat never sal blyn.
(English Writings, p. 68, ll. 239–43).

The emergence into the final degree of love (union, or 'singuler lufe') is marked by a tonal change produced by sustained cola and rhymed endings. The emphatic alliterative accents commonly associated with his most lyrical prose (e.g., 'Gastly Gladnesse') are not prominent here:

> And þan enters þow into þe thirde degre of lufe. . . . þis degre es called contemplatife lyfe, þat lufes to be anely, withowten ryngyng or dyn or syngyng or criyng. At þe begynyng, when þou comes þartil, þi gastly egh es taken up intil þe blysse of heven and þar lyhtned with grace and kyndelde with fyre of lufe in þi hert ever mare and mare, liftand þi thoght to God, and feland lufe, joy, and swetnes so mykel þat na sekenes, anguys, ne schame, ne penance may greve þe, bot al þi lyf sal turne intyl joy (English Writings, p. 69).

The lyric which accompanies this section is one of Rolle's most rhetorically intense products, and also one of his finest for its control. In metrical terms it is less precisely constructed than the lyrics which are found independently in MS. Cambridge University Library Dd.5.64.[57] But this interpolated lyric, like the independent pieces, shows how Rolle favours a long line in which a strong caesura signals a break in alliterative pattern:

> My sange es in syhtyng, my lyfe es in langynge,
> Til I þe se, my keyng so fayre in þi shynyng. . . .
> Jhesu, my dere and my drewry, delyte ert þou to syng,
> Jhesu, my myrth and melody, when will þow come, my keyng?
> (English Writings, pp. 70–71, ll. 313–14, 341–42).

Where the prose of this section is comparatively restrained, the poem takes on all of the features of Rolle's impassioned lyric style, a mode with which he may have first experimented in the early alliterative Latin poem to the Virgin, the 'Canticum Amoris':[58]

> Claret carnis castitas; flos feruens fundaris
> Nectat nos nobilitas; amatrix amaris.
> Niuea nigredinem digne detestaris,
> Habens altitudinem summan singularis. (ll. 57–60).

In Rolle's English and Latin writings, such a style is always used as a suggestive transcription of ecstatic spirituality, and of the compulsion of a love which is violent and overpowering, as opposed to the natural affection exemplified in the poetic tradition of the Dulcis Jesu Memoria.[59] Rolle's heightened rhetorical manner seems an embodiment of Augustine's dictum that the sublime style is the eloquence of conviction which gathers up ornament in its powerful wake rather than contriving its grand effects:

> Satis enim est ei propter quod agitur ut verba congruentia non oris eligantur industria, sed pectoris sequantur ardorem. Nam si aurato gemmatoque ferro vir

fortis armetur, intentissimus pugnae agit quidem illis armis quod agit, non quia
pretiosa, sed quia arma sunt (*De Doctrina Christiana* 4, xx, 42).

This dictum has a close, although certainly not deliberate correspondent in
Rolle's own account of the spontaneous origins of song, in which the soul
becomes an instrument of divine music. This in a sense supplies Rolle's
operative critical theory:

> Sed non est hec gracia omnibus passimque concessa, sed anime sancte, sanctissime
> imbute, cui lucet excellencia amoris, et hympni amorosi familiariter in ea Christo
> inspirante eruperunt, et quasi iam hympnidica effecta in conspectum Conditoris sui
> ineffabiliter personat iubilando (*Incendium Amoris*, ch. 37, p. 254).

It is worth noting in this connection that in Rolle's mystical terms the
attainment of the highest degree of love is beyond the volition of the devout
aspirant:

> . . . if þow may get grace to com þartill. For I say noght þat þou, or another þat
> redes þis, sal do it all; for it es at Goddes will to chese wham he will, to do þat here
> es sayde, or els another thyng on another maner, als he gifes men grace til have
> þaire hele. . . . Wha sa es in þis degre, wisdom he hase, and discrecion, to luf at
> Goddes will ('Ego Dormio', *English Writings*, p. 69).

Rolle's applied definition of an effusive grand manner is in a sense a formal
extension of this spiritual premise: in a style whose exuberance belies its own
artifice he seeks to realize the intensity of his otherworldly *canor*, his
infusion with 'gastly' love.

The pattern of a stylistic shift from subdued to high style in relation to
subject matter emerges the most clearly in the *Ego Dormio*. In Rolle's other
English writings, including *The Commandment* and the *Meditations on the
Passion*, this pattern is not as prominent. But the adjustment of level of style
to degree of love does recur in *The Form of Living*, although here the
contours of the pattern are somewhat obscured by the greater length of this
text compared to the *Ego Dormio*, and by its greater structural com-
plexity.[60]

The *Form of Living*, like the *Ego Dormio*, is an instructive and
illustrative text, rather than an actual devotional text like the *Meditations on
the Passion*. In terms of its subject it divides roughly in half at the seventh of
its twelve chapters. The initial chapters are chiefly instructive and hortatory,
a preparatory guide to the *via contemplativa*. The latter sections, beginning
with the 'Amore langueo' of chapter 7, while still didactic in aim, are largely
illustrative and descriptive of the actual experience of love. Verbal
ornamentation and rapturous style are concentrated in chapters 8, 9, and 10,
which describe the three degrees of love, the devotion to the Holy Name,
and the five questions about love.[61] These sections do not consistently
maintain a heightened style; but in the passage which actually concerns the

experience of love at its most advanced level, all the signatures of Rolle's high rhetorical, ecstatic style are present.

Chapter 8, which begins 'thre degrees of lufe I sal tell þe, for I walde þat þou moght wyn to þe heest' (*English Writings*, p. 104), sketches briefly the terms of the first two degrees ('insuperabel' and 'inseparabel'), and then takes up the third degree at length. The stylistic change here is sudden and remarkable: language merges with matter in a mimetic transcription of inward experience:

> Bot þat fire, if it be hate, es swa delitabell and wondyrful þat I kan noght tell it. þan þi sawle es Jhesu lufand, Jhesu thynkand, Jhesu desirand, anly in þe covayties of hym anedande, til hym syngand, of hym byrnand, in hym restand. þan þe sange of lovyng and of lufe es commen, þan þi thoght turnes intil sang and intil melody, þan þe behoves syng þe psalmes þat þou before sayde, þan þou mon be lang abowte few psalmes, þan þe wil thynk þe deed swettar þan hony, for þan þou ert ful syker to se hym þat þou lufes; þan may þou hardely say: 'I languysch for lufe'; þan may þou say: 'I slepe, and my hert wakes' (*English Writings*, pp. 105–06).

The 'inexpressibility topos' ('I kan noght tell it') signals a shift in focus from meaning signified and registered by the common conventions of language to language itself as affective tool and as sensual medium which can produce intimations of spiritual experience.[62] This passage is replete with the heightened rhetorical devices most characteristic of Rolle's rapturous style, both in Latin and in English: alliteration, anaphora, *similiter cadens*, *isocolon*, *adjunctio*, punning through *adnominatio* ('lovyng,' i.e., praising, and 'lufe'), and subtle play upon prepositions in parallel clauses ('til him syngand, of hym byrnand, in hym restand').

The features of this style extend even into the comparatively hortatory chapter on devotion to the Holy Name (chapter 9):

> 'And when þou spekes til hym, and says 'Jhesu', thurgh custom, it sal be in þi ere joy, in þi mouth hony, and in þi hert melody' (*English Writings*, p. 108).

The metaphors here, 'joy', hony', and 'melody', as throughout Rolle's writings, represent a merging of tenor and vehicle. 'Hony' and 'melody' are not simply affective terms employed as sensual icons for a meaning that defies discursive expression: the experience of love *is* supernatural sweetness and song, and the thought of God is transformed into song as God emanates music and is experienced through music:[63]

> Cumque uero, in illis tribus [in feruore, in canore, et in dulcore] que sunt signa perfectissimi amoris, summa perfeccio christiane religionis sine omni ambiguitate inueniatur. . . . Canorem uoco quando iam in animo, abundante ardore, suscipitur suauitas laudis eterne ac cogitatus in canticum conuertitur, et mens in mellifluum melos immoratur (*Incendium Amoris*, ch. 14, p. 185).

In Rolle's metaphorical language the terms are dialectically doubled. There are linguistic signs, denoting sensual experience, by which we are brought towards an understanding of spiritual experience; but these same terms, when removed from a sensual sphere and placed in a transcendent sphere, constitute the experience itself. The domain of such linguistic manipulation, in which the dual terms of metaphor unite and the verbal image assumes literal force, is exlusively that of the highest degree of love.

The main signatures of Rolle's grand style are displayed to best advantage in his Latin prose. From his stylistic practice in Latin devolve the characteristic features of his English writing, and the same critical principles inform his practice in both languages. Of this stylistic communication between his Latin, which is his primary literary language, and his English, the most direct evidence is his translation of sections from the penultimate chapters of the *Incendium Amoris* in the lyric which begins 'Luf es lyf þat lastes ay', which is found among the group of lyrics attributed to Rolle in MS. Cambridge University Library Dd. 5. 64.[64]

The *Incendium Amoris* is somewhat more restrained in terms of alliterative detail and rhythmic parallelism than the earlier *Melos Amoris*. In general, the verses of 'Luf es lyf' (of which only the first sixty lines are a translation) follow the content of chapters 41 and 42 of the *Incendium Amoris* quite closely, but their stylistic organization seems to be modelled upon the striking parallelism of the *Melos Amoris*. A passage from the *Incendium Amoris* and the corresponding English verses may illustrate this:

> Est enim amor uita sine fine permanens, ubi in Christo figitur et solidatur, quando iam ipsum amorem secundum amorosum affectum in celestibus radicatum nec prospera nec aduersa ualebunt immutare, quemadmodum sapientissimi conscripserunt. Tunc nimirum noctem uertit in diem, tenebras in lucem, molesciam in melodiam, punicionem in amenitatem, laboremque in suauissimam requiem. . . .
> Et siquidem si isto modo, ut ostendi, amaueris, cum optimis et honorabilibus in regno Dei ipsi uisioni uiuifice assistes gloriosus (ch. 40, pp. 267–68).

This is a fine example of controlled and subtle parallelism, in the rhythmic cadences and the *similiter cadens*. The English verse takes on a more condensed rhythmic form heightened by more frequent and regular alliterative accents:

> Luf es lyf þat lastes ay, þar it in Criste es feste,
> For wele ne wa it chaunge may, als wryten has men wyseste.
> þe nyht it tournes intil þe day, þi travel intyll reste,
> If þou wil luf þus as I say, þou may be wyth þe beste.
>
> (*English Writings*, p. 43, ll. 1–4).

This poetic structure, with its accentual alliterative links and parallel cola, seems to duplicate to some extent the dense composition characteristic of the *Melos Amoris*:

O dulce, delectabile et desiderandum osculum quod tantum confert gaudium, gignit devotos, nutrit ferventes, perficit pios! Dum enim intra nos eterni amoris delicias canentes supra nos rapimur, secundum affluenciam divinitus degustatam, in miro amoris gaudio granditer gratulamur (*Melos Amoris*, ch. 2, p. 7).

This illustrates Rolle's mastery of the rhetorical techniques which are so felicitously transferred to verse: the rhythmic parallelism of *isocolon* and of grammatically suspended cola, and the rhyming effects produced not only by alliteration but also by careful assonance and *similiter cadens*. These effects are taken over in the verse by the precision of the leonine rhymes and by a surprising regularity of cadenced endings. The anaphora which Rolle adopts as the main principle of strophic organization throughout the poem, and which allows him to achieve a cumulative high-pitched tone (e.g., stanza 2: 'Lufe es thought . . . Lufe I lyken . . . Lufe us clenses . . . Lufe þe keynges hert may wyn . . .') has its most direct echoes in the alliterative prose of the thirteenth century, as well as in the fourteenth century *A Talking of the Love of God*, which closely resembles the earlier prose texts of the *Wohunge* group: e.g., 'Ihesu soþ God, Godes sone; Ihesu soþ God soþ mon. . . . Ihesu myn holy loue. . . . Ihesu mi Makere þat me madest of nou3t. . . . Ihesu my Buggere þat bou3test me so deore. . . .'.[65] In the *Ego Dormio* anaphora also signals the transition into the third degree of love:

þan es Jhesu al þi desyre, al þi delyte, al þi joy, al þi solace, al þi comforth; al I wate þat on hym ever be þi sang, in hym all þi rest (*English Writings*, pp. 69–70).

A great part of the poem (lines 17–44), however, takes over closely linked rather than scattered passages of the *Incendium Amoris*. These verses offer the best evidence of precise compositional reordering by appropriating the rhetorical design of the prose.

O bone Ihesu qui mihi uitam tribuisti eciam in tuum amorem, deduc me ad ipsum suspirantem, totam intencionem meam cape tibi, ut tu sis totum desiderium meum, nec ultra te aliquid affectet cor meum! Dolor et duricia abscederent a me, ueniret quoque quod concupisco, si anima mea audisset acceptissetque canticum laudis tue (ch. 41. p. 272).

This is condensed easily into one verse:

Jhesu, þat me lyfe hase lent, intil þi lufe me bryng.
Take til þe al myne entent, þat þow be my 3hernyng.
Wa fra me away war went, and comne war my covaytyng,
If þat my sawle had herd and hent þe sang of þi lovyng.
                              (*English Writings*, p. 44, ll. 21–24).

From the Latin to the English there is little loss of figurative verbal impact. Rolle achieves the same word play and antitheses, and borrows from the Latin the method of setting off a paradox in parallel clauses.

These resemblances would suggest that Rolle does not perceive his English verse as occupying a lower rhetorical sphere than his Latin prose.

His English verse is addressed to an audience which, if not necessarily conversant with the actual Latin treatise, is responsive to its formal properties. He does not appear to distinguish markedly between the formal capacities of Latin and those of English, nor in this case does he seem to expect from his English audience a lesser degree of aesthetic appreciation and literary sophistication than he would expect from a clerical audience. The distinctions he makes with regard to stylistic level seem to correspond to his sense of the degree of mystical 'education' in his readers and their progress in the *via contemplativa*.

It is significant that Rolle expressly directs the *Incendium Amoris*, one of his most impassioned and rhetorically elaborate works, to the 'simple and unlearned':

> Istum ergo librum offero intuendum, non philosophis, non mundi sapientibus, non magnis theologicis infinitis quescionibus implicatis, sed rudibus et indoctis, magis Deum diligere quam multa scire conantibus. Non enim disputando sed agendo scietur, et amando. Arbitror autem ea que hic continentur ab istis questionariis et in omni sciencia summis, sed in amore Christi inferioribus, non posse intellegi (Prologue, p. 147).

The distinction between the *sermo humilis* and the *sermo altus et superbus* depends upon the intensity of spiritual experience under consideration; it would be inappropriate to simplify rhetorically any treatment of so sublime a subject, even if expression is undertaken in English as an alternative to Latin, as a concession to a non-clerical audience. In Rolle's hands the vernacular becomes as important a medium for communicating the joys of spiritual fervour as Latin, which is his first and more natural literary language. Within Rolle's usage, then, one can teach in the grand style to a 'simple and unlearned' audience, in English verse as well as in Latin prose, if one is teaching of the highest degree of love.

This sense of stylistic propriety, or decorum, informs the literary tradition which Rolle's work generated. Richard Misyn's English translation of the *Incendium Amoris* (ca 1435) is obviously designed, like so many English versions of central devotional texts, to popularise the treatise by extending the perimeters of its circulation to include a vernacular audience. Yet this translation makes no apparent distinction between the rhetorical impact that can be achieved in an English text and that which is desirable in a Latin text. There is nothing about Misyn's version that suggests a simplification of Rolle's style and fervour. Misyn's treatment of the passage quoted above as the source of stanza 1 or Rolle's 'Luf es lyf' may illustrate this:[66]

> Luf certan is lyfe abydinge with-owt end qwher it is seet, qwhen þe lufe after lufely desyre in hevyns rotyd prosperite ne aduersite may chaunge, als wysist men has writtyn. þen no meruayll þe nyght to day he sall turne, Dyrknes to lyght, heuynes to melody, noy to solas and labyr to sweet rest. þis lufe truly is not of ymaginacion

or fenyd, bot trw and parfytte and to criste with-outt partynge gywyn, aungel songe
with melody to Ihesu ȝeeldand. And forsothe if þou lufe in þis maner as I haue
sayd, with þe best and worþiest in þe kyngdome of god to þat qwhikly syght þou
salt be nere full glorius (p. 95–96).

It is significant that Misyn regards the style of Rolle's text as integral with its
proper meaning, so that he reproduces its technique to the extent that his
own talents will allow. For some of Rolle's more elaborate passages, heavy
with alliteration, assonance, and rhythmic closures, Misyn offers as close as
equivalent as intelligibility can permit:

Porro perfecti qui in hanc excellencie abundanciam eterne amicicie assumuntur, in
preclaro calice caritatis melliflue dulcore indelibili iam imbuti uiuunt, atque in
almiphono amenitatis archano in animum suum hauriunt felicem ardorem. Quo
iocandati iugiter inestimabilem habent eterni electuarii confortacionem
(*Incendium Amoris*, ch. 2, pp. 151–52).

Parfyte forsoth þat in-to þis passynge plente of endeles frenschyp ar takyn, taght
with swetnes þat sall not waste new lyffe in þe clere chales of full swete charite, and
in holy consaill of myrth þai drawe in to þere saules happy hete, with þe whilk þai
gretely gladdyd, has gretter comforth þen may be trowyd of gostely letwary (p. 7).

As in Rolle's own 'Englishings' of the *Incendium Amoris*, there is some
inevitable condensing and diffusion, but without substantial loss to the
figurative fabric of the text. The deliberate diction of the English attests to
Misyn's concern with the affective tone of Rolle's Latin.

Misyn's own prologue may also suggest his regard for the integrity of
style and matter. He proposes his translation, in a conventional way, for the
edification of many:

. . . to þe askynge of þi desyre, Syster Margarete, . . . þat curiuste of latyn
understandes noght, I . . . þis wark has takyn to translacion of lattyn to englysch,
for edificacyon of many saules. . . . The whilk boke, in sentence ne substance I
þink to chaunge, bot truely aftyre myn understandynge to wryte it in gude
exposicione (p.1).

Although the 'Margarete' of this address represents a reader less educated
than Rolle had intended for his Latin text, Misyn makes no reference to a
concern for simplicity or plain accessibility in the vernacular version. The
voicing of such a concern is one of the oldest commonplaces of homiletic
translation theory. I have noted earlier how Aelfric condemns 'garrulous
verbosity' and artificiality in a vernacular translation, as Wycliffe was later to
do.[67] But such conventional claims, both to the openness of language and to
the translation according to sense rather than to word, which represent
utilitarian, didactic aims, are conspicuously absent from Misyn's statement
of principle. Evidently for Misyn as for Rolle, the emphasis in composition,
whether in Latin or in the vernacular, is on the unity of sentence and
substance, the decorous matching of style and matter. Under Rolle's distant

tutelage, Misyn's concept of fidelity in translation is defined in artistic and rhetorical as well as in substantive terms.

Rolle's aims are similar to those of Augustine, in that, for both, the spiritual state of the audience determines the function or task of oratory (rhetoric). But Rolle's realization of this aim is distinguished from Augustine's rhetorical model in that to the same audience, and within the same text, Rolle will speak in subdued, sublime, or moderate terms, depending on the nature of his immediate contextual concern, that is, his subject, the degree of love in question. This is *not* to argue that for Rolle, as for Cicero, subject matter is variable, that *res* do not determine *verba*, nor that the orator can match various words to various things, ends, and circumstances. For Rolle, as for any Christian evangelist, the truth that is signified in the discourse is constant and immutable. But in stylistic—hence rhetorical—application, Rolle has, in a sense, returned to the Ciceronian concern with decorum, with fitting the appropriate style to the appropriate subject. Like Cicero, his sense of fulfilling the three duties of the orator is to make subject and style accord with each other.

But as I have suggested with regard to Rolle's literary transcription of the experience 'singuler lufe' in *The Form of Living*, it is not simply decorum that moves him to transcribe fervent love in fervent style. The metaphorical and stylistic terms that he uses to communicate this highest experience constitute the essence of the experience itself. 'Melody,' 'honey', or 'fire', and other metaphorical and affective elements of Rolle's rhapsodic style are not arbitrary, conventional, linguistic signs. In an elusive and paradoxical way, these are the essence of love, and the means by which love is experienced and understood. It is impossible to signify otherwise the essence of love. This is, then, a realisation of Augustine's own arguments about divine eloquence, in which verbal style is perceived as integral with, and inseparable from, meaning. This is, also, the highest achievement of decorum. Paradoxically, then, while Rolle's applied rhetoric seems to gravitate towards the terms of the Ciceronian model with its emphasis upon decorum, he is actually operating within Augustine's dialectical framework of a temporal as opposed to a divinely inspired eloquence. What Rolle achieves is a redefinition of the concept of classical decorum in a transcendental Christian context.

NOTES

1. Among critical appraisals of Rolle's figurative language, the recent study by W. Riehle, *The Middle English Mystics*, tr. B. Standring, London, 1981, (orig. publ. in German, Heidelberg, 1977), is outstanding. Important recent studies of Rolle's rhetorical style include: A. Olmes, *Sprache und Stil der englischer Mystik*, des Mittelalters, Halle Saale, 1933; M. Schlauch, 'Chaucer's Prose Rhythms', *Proceedings of the Modern Language*

Association, 65 (1950), 568–89; M. Morgan, '*A Talking of the Love of God* and the Continuity of Stylistic Tradition in Middle English Prose Meditations', *Review of English Studies* 3, n.s. 10 (1952), 97–116; G. L. Liegey, 'The Rhetorical Aspects of Rolle's *Melos Contemplativorum*', Ph.D. diss., Columbia Univ., 1954; E. Salter, *Nicholas Love's 'Myrrour of the Blessed Lyf of Jesus Christ'*, Analecta Cartusiana 10, Salzburg, 1974, ch. 6, 'The English Tradition of Prose translation'. Among stylistic studies of a more general nature should be noted that of N. Blake, '*The Form of Living* in Prose and Poetry', *Archiv für das Studium der Neueren Sprachen und Literaturen*, 211 (1974), 300–08. The first major study of Rolle in the context of Middle English prose is of course that of R. W. Chambers, 'On the Continuity of English Prose from Alfred to More and his School', in *Harpsfield's Life of More*, ed. E. V. Hitchcock, Early English Text Society 186, London, 1931.

2. The text of the *Orator* used here is the Loeb edition, with notes and translation by H. M. Hubbell, Cambridge, Mass., 1939, revised, 1971.

3. The three *officia oratoris* correspond to Aristotle's three modes of proof, *logos*, *ethos*, and *pathos*. See G. A. Kennedy, *Classical Rhetoric and its Christian and Secular Tradition from Ancient to Modern Times*, Chapel Hill, North Carolina, 1980, pp. 68–69, 100.

4. For discussion of the speaker-language-audience model in classical and patristic rhetoric, see R. O. Payne, 'Chaucer's Realization of Himself as Rhetor', in *Medieval Eloquence: Studies in the Theory and Practice of Medieval Rhetoric*, ed. J. J. Murphy, Berkeley, 1978, 270–87; and see G. A. Kennedy, *op. cit.*, pp. 69–81.

5. Cf. *De Oratore* I.v.17, and *De Inventione*, I.i.1.

6. I use the text of the *De Doctrina Christiana* in the Corpus Scriptorum Ecclesiasticorum Latinorum, 80, ed. W. M. Green, Vienna, 1963. For the adaptation of basic terms from the *Orator* see R. McKeon, 'Rhetoric in the Middle Ages', *Speculum*, 17 (1942), 1–32, pp. 4–5.

7. See *De Doctrina Christiana* I.i.1. See also R. McKeon, *op. cit.*, 5, and J. A. Mazzeo, 'St. Augustine's Rhetoric of Silence', *Journal of the History of Ideas*, 23 (1962), 175–96, p. 176 and note 5.

8. See L. D. McNew, 'The Relationship of Cicero's Rhetoric to Augustine', *Research Studies of the State College of Washington*, 25 (1957), 5–13, p. 9.

9. See R. McKeon, *op. cit.*, 6–7, and J. A. Mazzeo, *op. cit.*, 176.

10. See *De Inventione* I.i.1.

11. L. D. McNew, *op. cit.*, pp. 8, 10.

12. See R. McKeon, *op. cit.*, pp. 6–7, and McNew, *op. cit.*, pp. 8–9.

13. Cf. also vi.10: 'Et in quibus forte locis agnoscitur a doctis, tales res dicuntur, ut verba quibus dicuntur, non a dicente adhibita, sed ipsis rebus velut sponte subiuncta videantur, quasi sapientiam de domo sua, id est, pectore sapientis intellegas procedere et tamquam inseparabilem famulam etiam non vocatam sequi eloquentiam'.

14. R. L. McKeon, *op. cit.*, p. 6. See also J. A. Mazzeo, *op. cit.*, p. 187. Mazzeo points out that Augustine's true rhetoric is the silent, internal, verbal signs by which Christ teaches truth, and that in this divine eloquence words and realities are inseparable.

15. See E. Auerbach, *Literary Language and its Public in Late Latin Antiquity and in the Middle Ages*, tr. R. Mannheim, New York, 1965 (orig. publ. in German, Bern, 1958), ch. 1, '*Sermo Humilis*'. Auerbach's investigation of the semantic background of the word *humilis* is the foundation of his argument.

16. See also C. S. Baldwin, 'St. Augustine and the Rhetoric of Cicero', *Proceedings of the Classical Association*, 22 (1925), 24–46.

17. See M. Colish, *The Mirror of Language: A Study of the Medieval Theory of Knowledge*, New Haven, 1968, pp. 61–2.

18. See H. M. Hubbell, Introduction to text of *Orator*, *op. cit.*, p. 299.

19. R. R. Bolgar, *The Classical Heritage and its Beneficiaries*, Cambridge, 1954, rpt. 1977, p. 396. The principles of the *Orator* and the *De Oratore* were known to some extent through the compendium of Julius Victor, which Alcuin knew, as well as through Augustine. See J. J. Murphy, *Rhetoric in the Middle Ages*, Berkeley, 1974, p. 80 and note 132.

20. M. Colish, *op. cit.*, p. 63; and C. S. Baldwin, *Medieval Rhetoric and Poetic*, New York, 1928, pp. 54–5.

21. G. A. Kennedy, *op. cit.*, pp. 175–80.

22. See C. B. Kendall, 'Bede's *Historia ecclesiastica*: the Rhetoric of Faith', in *Medieval Eloquence*, ed. J. J. Murphy, *op. cit.*, 945–72, p. 149.

23. J. J. Murphy, 'St. Augustine and Rabanus Maurus: the Genesis of Medieval Rhetoric', *Western Speech*, 3 (1967), 88–96, p. 94. See also G. A. Kennedy, *op. cit.*, p. 184.

24. *Patrologiae Latina*, ed. J. P. Migne, Paris, 1844–1902, 107. The relevant sections of Book 3 are in columns 396 ff.

25. G. A. Kennedy, *op. cit.*, p. 190. See also D. Bethurum, 'Wulfstan', in *Continuations and Beginnings: Studies in Old English Literature*, ed. G. E. Stanley, London, 1966, pp. 210–46. Bethurum notes the availability of rhetorical treatises, including Ciceronian texts, the *De Doctrina Christiana*, and the manuals of Bede, Alcuin, and Hrabanus Maurus, for a writer like Wulfstan who demonstrates a familiarity with rhetoric.

26. See J. J. Murphy, 'St. Augustine and Rabanus Maurus', *op. cit.*, p. 93.

27. B. Smalley, *The Study of the Bible in the Middle Ages*, Oxford, 1952, rpt. Notre Dame, 1964, pp. 58–60, 65–66, passim.

28. See E. Auerbach, *op. cit.*, p. 51. See also J. J. Murphy, 'St. Augustine and the Debate about a Christian Rhetoric', *Quarterly Journal of Speech*, 46 (1960), 400–10.

29. See E. Auerbach, *op. cit.*, pp. 192–94 for a discussion of this background; and cf., for example, *Orator* v. 20.

30. *op. cit.*, p. 65.

31. Jean Leclerq, 'L'Art de la composition dans les sermons de S. Bernard', *Studi Medievali*, series terza, 7 (1966), 128–53.

32. See D. Bethurum, 'The Connection of the *Katherine* Group with Old English Prose', *Journal of English and Germanic Philology*, 34 (1935), 553–64; and E. Salter, *Nicholas Love's 'Myrrour'*, *op. cit.*, pp. 193–208.

33. See E. Salter, *Nicholas Love's 'Myrrour'*, *op. cit.*, p. 210; and E. Zeeman (Salter), 'Continuity in Middle English Devotional Prose', *Journal of English and Germanic Philology*, 55 (1956), 417–22. See also M. Morgan, '*A Talking of the Love of God*', *op. cit.*, and M. Morgan, 'A Treatise in Cadence', *Modern Language Review*, 47 (1952), 156–64. For evidence of one fifteenth-century descendent of this tradition, see P. Hodgson, '*A Ladder of Foure Ronges by the Whiche Men Wele Clyme to Heven*: a Study of a Middle English Translation', *Modern Language Review*, 44 (1949), 465–75.

34. E. Salter, *Nicholas Love's 'Myrrour'*, *op. cit.*, pp. 193–94.

35. D. Bethurum, 'The Connection of the *Katherine* Group', *op. cit.*, pp. 553–57.

36. E. Zeeman, 'Continuity in Middle English Prose', *op. cit.*, pp. 418–19.

37. See R. Copeland, 'Translation and Literary Style in Medieval English Religious Texts', unpubl. Ph.D. diss., Univ. of California, Berkeley, 1982, pp. 82–149.

38. See also *De Doctrina Christiana* IV.xix.38: 'cum vero aliquid agendum est et ad eos loquimur qui hoc agere debent nec tamen volunt, tunc ea quae magna sunt dicenda sunt granditer et ad flectendos animos congruenter'.

39. *The Homilies of the Anglo-Saxon Church, or Homilies of Aelfric*, ed. B. Thorpe, London, 1846, 2, Preface 2, 1.

40. See *The English Writings of Richard Rolle*, ed. H. E. Allen, Oxford, 1931, Introduction, pp. xv–xvi. All quotations from Rolle's English writings are from this edition, and page and line references are incorporated in the text.

41. See J. O. Ward, 'From Antiquity to the Renaissance: Glosses and Commentaries on Cicero's *Rhetorica*', in *Medieval Eloquence*, ed. J. J. Murphy, *op. cit.*, pp. 25–67.

42. See B. Smalley, *English Friars and Antiquity in the Early Fourteenth Century*, Oxford, 1960; and also J. Coleman, 'English Culture in the Fourteenth Century', in *Chaucer and the Italian Trecento*, ed. P. Boitani, Cambridge, 1983, 33–63, pp. 46–49.

43. See J. J. Murphy, 'Rhetoric in Fourteenth-Century Oxford', *Medium Aevum*, 34 (1965), 1–20; and J. J. Murphy, 'Literary Implications of Instruction in the Verbal Arts in Fourteenth-Century England', *Leeds Studies in English*, n.s. 1 (1967), 119–35.

44. See V. Gillespie, 'Mystic's Foot: Rolle and Affectivity', in *The Medieval Mystical Tradition in England*, ed. M. Glasscoe, Exeter, 1982, 199–230, p. 213; and see 'The Form of Living' in *English Writings*, ed. H. E. Allen, p. 106.

45. *The Incendium Amoris of Richard Rolle of Hampole*, ed. M. Deanesly, Manchester, 1915.

46. V. Gillespie, *op. cit.*, 215. See also W. Riehle, *op. cit.*, pp. 120–21. For a related treatment

of inexpressibility, see A. C. Watts, '*Pearl*, Inexpressibility, and Poems of Human Loss', *Proceedings of the Modern Language Association*, 99 (1984), 26–40.

47. See W. Riehle, *op. cit.*, pp. 8–9.
48. For a recent classification of this sort see N. Blake, 'Varieties of Middle English Prose', in *Chaucer and Middle English Studies in Honor of R. H. Robbins*, ed. B. Rowland, London, 1974, 348–56. For an illuminating approach to classification see V. Lagorio, 'Problems in Middle English Mystical Prose', in *Middle English Prose: Essays on Bibliographical Problems*, ed. A. S. G. Edwards and D. Pearsall, London, 1981, pp. 129–48.
49. For a brief account of the background of the *via contemplativa* see H. E. Allen, *Writings Ascribed to Richard Rolle, Hermit of Hampole, and Materials for his Biography*, London, 1927, pp. 201–03. For a comparative treatment of these three stages as defined by contemporary mystics (purgation, illumination, and union), see J. E. Milosh, *The Scale of Perfection and the English Mystical Tradition*, Madison, Wisconsin, 1966, pp. 37, 40–41, 43, 67.
50. Text from *The Melos Amoris of Richard Rolle of Hampole*, ed. E. J. F. Arnould, Oxford, 1957, ch. 48, p. 154. See H. E. Allen's general remarks on this passage, *Writings Ascribed to Richard Rolle, op. cit.*, p. 149, and on the work as a whole, pp. 113–29.
51. See H. E. Allen, *Writings Ascribed to Richard Rolle, op. cit.*, p. 60. Allen regards the English epistles as late works; see pp. 89, 186 for dating in relation to the early Latin works.
52. W. A. Pantin, *The English Church in the Fourteenth Century*, Cambridge, 1955, p. 191.
53. See *Deonise Hid Diuinitee*, ed. P. Hodgson, Early English Text Society, O.S., 231, London, 1955, pp. xlvii–lvii.
54. I assume here that the lyrics contained in his epistles are Rolle's own, and that some of the poems contained in MS. Cambridge University Library Dd.5.64 should also be ascribed to him. For a full account of his lyric canon, see R. Woolf, *The English Religious Lyric in the Middle Ages*, Oxford, 1968, pp. 380–82, and H. E. Allen, *Writings Ascribed to Richard Rolle, op. cit.*, pp. 287–306. The lyrics incorporated in the English prose writings contain echoes of passages in the *Incendium Amoris* and *Melos Amoris*; and among the lyrics found in Cambridge University Library Dd.5.64 there are versions of lyrics found in prose epistles. Most of the lyrics from this MS. are found in *Religious Lyrics of the Fourteenth Century*, ed. C. Brown, Oxford, 1924, nos. 77–86.
55. E.g., 'When þe hed quakyth/And þe lyppis blakyth/And þe nose sharpyth . . .' in S. Wenzel, *Verses in Sermons: Fasciculous Morum and its English Poems*, Cambridge, Mass., 1978, p. 197.
56. It is worth noting that in the mystical thought of Rolle, meditation on the Passion had a limited place in the intermediate stage of the *via contemplativa*. Meditation on the Passion is recommended as an early exercise, but Rolle does not return to it to signify the highest reaches of love, either in his Latin or in his English writings. The exhortation in the *Ego Dormio*, 'thynk oft on his passyon' (p. 67), pertains to a preliminary or intermediate stage. See also R. Woolf, *op. cit.*, pp. 160–61.
57. See above, note 54. A version of 'My sange es in syhtyng' is found in MS. Cambridge University Library Dd.5.64: see C. Brown, *Religious Lyrics of the Fourteenth Century*, no. 83, lines 21 ff.
58. For the text and critical remarks on this poem see G. M. Liegey, 'The *Canticum Amoris* of Richard Rolle', *Traditio*, 12 (1956), 369–91.
59. R. Woolf, *op. cit.*, p. 161.
60. See D. Rygiel, 'Structure and Style in Rolle's *Form of Living*', *Fourteenth-Century English Mystics Newsletter*, 4 (1978), 6–15.
61. *Ibid.*, 8. See also S. K. Smedick, 'Parallelism and Pointing in Rolle's Rhythmical Style', *Medieval Studies*, 41 (1979), 404–67, esp. pp. 406–10, for a close stylistic analysis of the first part of ch. 10, 'þe fyrst askyng es: what is lufe?'
62. Cf. V. Gillespie, *op. cit.*, p. 211.
63. See W. Riehle, *op. cit.*, p. 120.
64. The evidence for the ascription of this poem to Rolle is no more fixed than that for the other poems in the same manuscript. H. E. Allen accepts the authenticity of those lyrics which exhibit the same formal features as those incorporated in the epistles. See *Writings Ascribed to Richard Rolle, op. cit.*, p. 299, and *English Writings, op. cit.*, p. 37.

65. Text in *Yorkshire Writers: Richard Rolle of Hampole and His Followers*, ed. C. Horstman, 2, London, 1896, p. 346.

66. Text from *The Fire of Love and the Mending of Life, Translated by Richard Misyn*, ed. R. Harvey, Early English Text Society, 106, London, 1896. All page references are incorporated in the text.

67. Cf. another of Aelfric's formulations from the *Homilies* (text in *The Homilies of the Anglo-Saxon Church*, ed. B. Thorpe, London, 1844, 1, Preface I, 1): 'Ideoque nec obscura posuimus verba, sed simplicem Anglicam, quo facilius possit ad cor pervenire legentium vel audientium, ad utilitatem animarum suarum, quia alia lingua nesciunt erudiri, quam in qua nati sunt. Nec ubique transtulimus verbum ex verbo, sed sensum ex sensu, cavendo tamen diligentissime de deceptivos errores, ne inveniremur aliqua haeresi seducti seu fallacia fuscati'. Wycliffe's theoretical statements are contained in the Latin *Sermones* and are illustrated in the Biblical renderings within his *English Sermons*.

THE MANUSCRIPTS AND EARLY PRINTED EDITIONS OF RICHARD ROLLE'S *EXPOSITIO SUPER NOVEM LECTIONES MORTUORUM*

MALCOM MOYES

THE WORK with which this paper is concerned, the *Expositio super Novem Lectiones Mortuorum*, has received scant attention from scholarship beyond brief bibliographical citations, and it is to Miss Allen's short chapter that one must turn for an introductory survey of the manuscripts and printed editions, and also, for an elementary analysis of the text.[1] There is no critical edition available, despite the fact that there are over forty extant manuscripts of the full text and that it has been printed more times than any other work by Rolle.

The *Expositio* is unquestionably an authentic Rolle work: whenever the text appears in manuscript, whether in the form of a quotation or complete, it is accompanied by an ascription to Rolle; and conversely, no manuscript or early bibliography attributes the work to any other writer but Rolle. The internal evidence for Rolle's authorship is equally convincing: there are parallels and reminiscences of other works known to be by Rolle,[2] and, at one point in the text, Rolle refers his audience to two of his other works, one of which is certainly the *Melos Amoris*,[3] whilst the other, *De Vita Heremitarum*, seems to be either a lost work, or an extant work known under another title.[4] The quatrain found at the end of nineteen manuscripts of the complete text, which Miss Allen termed 'a verse signature' on the strength of its similarity to the highly personal and self-referential last stanza of the *Canticum Amoris*, and on the testimony of two fifteenth-century manuscripts, may be accepted as Rolle's own valedictory verses only with reservation.[5]

The date of composition is, like the chronology of Rolle's work in general, difficult to establish with any certainty. An attempt to give some kind of chronological definition to the Latin corpus was undertaken by Miss Allen, but her work on the problem must be queried: an overall impression of the Rolle canon, with its repetitiveness, self-quotation and consistent attempts to encapsulate the same experiences in different modes of discourse, suggests that Miss Allen's definition of maturity was a highly subjective reaction against certain kinds of Latin verse and prose styles, rather than any objective criterion for establishing chronology;[6] further, later researches have clearly demonstrated just how unreliable Miss Allen's terms of reference could be.[7]

The *Expositio* is, strictly speaking, a liturgical not a Scriptural commentary: a distinction that Miss Allen not only failed to consider, but explicitly went some way towards denying.[8] It comments upon the nine sets of readings from the book of *Job*, which form part of the recitation of the *Office of the Dead;*[9] the work thus falls naturally into nine sections, observed by all the manuscripts of the text, with the exception of Lincoln Cathedral MS. 218.[10] This is an elementary description, but it is one that needs to be insisted upon, in the light of occasional mistaken and misleading manuscript,[11] bibliographical[12] and editorial entries[13] suggesting that Rolle, like Peter of Bath in his *Compendium in Job*, has commented selectively on the book of *Job*. Miss Allen was aware of the nature of the verses which Rolle expounds, but her convenient abbreviation of the title of *Job* only misled later writers on Rolle, as did her abbreviation of the *Commentary on the First Verses of the Cantica Canticorum*, to *Canticles*.[14]

In terms of the number of extant mansucripts, the *Expositio* was one of the most frequently copied of Rolle's Latin prose works and the best known of the exegetical works. There are forty-four manuscripts of the full text (three of which are imperfect), dating possibly from the last quarter of the fourteenth century to the second quarter of the sixteenth century; in addition, there are two manuscripts of large-scale *excerpta*, which Miss Allen mistakenly listed as complete texts, and three compilations drawing on Rolle works which utilise long citations from the *Expositio*; only the *Incendium Amoris* and the *Emendatio Vitae* survive in comparable numbers of manuscripts.[15] None of the surviving manuscripts, with the possible exceptions of Lincoln Cathedral MS. 218 and Huntington MS. 504, was written on the Continent; although the *Expositio* is cited in more books printed on the Continent than any other single work in the Rolle canon.[16]

The citations of the *Expositio* in Continental printed books draw on both manuscript and printed sources. The quotation used by the Dominican polemicist Anthony Rescius, in his compilation *De Sacrificio Missae pro Defunctis*,[17] is almost certainly from the 1536 edition of Rolle's works, edited by Johann Faber of Heilbron, who was similarly a Dominican friar: Rescius employs the cognomen *Pampolitanus* and the accompanying title of *Dominus* used by Faber (and later Continental biographers) and he also repeats the erroneous title of *Enarratio* utilised by, and unique to, Faber's edition of the *Expositio*; interestingly, Rescius lists Ricardus Pampolitanus as a twelfth-century writer in his index of authorities. The quotation from the *Expositio* in the popular compilation *Summa que Destructorium Viciorum appelatur*, cannot have had a printed text as its source, as its date of completion, 1429, antedates the first printing by fifty years. All the known editions of the *Summa* were printed on the Continent, at Cologne,

Nuremburg and Paris, but the compiler, Alexander Carpenter, was an Englishman, who seems to have had ready access to a number of English manuscripts, for his vast compilation draws extensively on English writers of the later Middle Ages.[18]

The question of whether the *Expositio* was circulated on the Continent alongside other works in the Latin corpus is confronted when the problem of Faber's manuscript source for his editions of Rolle is discussed. Both the 1535[19] and the 1536 editions were prepared for publication during Faber's period of study at the University of Cologne, and it was to the medieval library of that University (and also of Augsburg Cathedral where Faber was, for a time, a preacher), that Miss Allen had recourse in a vain attempt to discover the manuscript, or manuscripts, used by Faber.[20] That Faber prepared his editions in the interests of theological orthodoxy[21] at Cologne is significant: Cologne in the fourteenth and fifteenth centuries was a centre for the dissemination of German mysticism, represented primarily by Tauler, Eckhardt and Suso; it later became a stronghold of orthodoxy against the apostasy of Luther. The two aspects of sixteenth-century religious life were embodied by the German Charterhouses, and in particular by the Charterhouse of St Barbara in Cologne. We have evidence to suggest that the Cologne Carthusians were active in assisting publications in the interests of the contemplative life and theological orthodoxy, both through the loan of manuscripts from the substantial library[22] and by way of the editorial efforts of its own monks.[23] In the light of this kind of literary activity, it is probable that Faber did not draw on the University of Cologne, as Miss Allen thought, but on the resources available from the Cologne Carthusians for his editions of Rolle. The Charterhouse of St Barbara, if we can depend upon the extant library catalogue, did not possess any Rolle manuscript itself, but did own manuscripts from Charterhouses known to have received copies of Rolle's work from England.[24] The presence of an important Rolle manuscript on the Continent containing a full text of the *Expositio* receives further confirmation from the bibliographer Eysengrein, who in drawing up his entry for Rolle's works, which includes the *Expositio*, was working independently of both Faber's Cologne editions and English bibliographies.[25]

If the *Expositio* was copied more often than most of Rolle's other Latin works, it also appears in a greater diversity of medieval contexts. It is cited, alongside other miscellaneous extracts, as a piece of anti-clerical propaganda, by a Lollard scribe in Cambridge, Trinity College MS. 333; the same passage was partially cited in the sixteenth century by the Protestant bishop of Ossery, John Bale,[26] whose use of the *Expositio* for the same self-justifying ends as the scribe of the Lollard manuscript forms a line of continuity for the reputation of Rolle's work in non-Catholic circles; the image of Rolle the anti-cleric fell easily into place alongside that of the advocate of vernacular Scripture, a misrepresentation also perpetrated by Lollard scribes,[27] and embraced by Protestant apologists and anti-quarians.[28]

The Lollard distortion of the spirit in which the citation concerning clerical laxity was written is to a certain extent redressed by the quotation of the same passage in the *Summa que Destructorium viciorum appelatur*, which despite its sometimes virulent language, is an orthodox manual.[29] Carpenter cites the same passage twice, firstly in *Pars* 4, ch.xxii, to censure priests '. . . qui libere veritatem non predicant' (Carpenter's phrase in his introductory summary of contents), and again, in *Pars* 6, ch.iv, as an interdict forbidding the involvement of the clergy in secular affairs.

A further dimension to the seeming infinite variety of the *Expositio*, is the citation by Rescius of Rolle's words on the necessity and efficacy of praying for our dead, quoted in the interest of anti-Reformation polemics. The context is surprising, and, at the same time, unique in our knowledge of the fortunes of Rolle's work on the Continent; although our surprise should be tempered by the fact that Rescius' book was published bound up with one of Johann Faber's own polemics on the Mass,[30] and is found in close connection with Faber's literary-polemical activity in other contexts.[31]

The case for a wide diffusion of the *Expositio* cannot be argued on the basis of isolated quotations alone (and in two examples the same quotation), and must be supplemented by the evidence of ownership of complete texts and large-scale compilations. That the *Expositio* was frequently copied, especially in the first three-quarters of the fifteenth-century, is undeniable; but the extent of manuscript diffusion is a different proposition from a mere numerical account, demanding discussion in terms of the sections of medieval society, as distinct from individuals, involved in the copying and circulation of the *Expositio*, and their relationship to each other.

The section of medieval society for whom the *Expositio* would have an obvious and immediate appeal, and who at the same time were responsible for the copying and circulation of many Rolle manuscripts,[32] were the clergy.

The evidence of clerical wills in the Diocese of York between the late fourteenth and early sixteenth centuries, and allowing for the possibility of duplication, reveals that the *Expositio*, whilst never as widely owned as William of Pagula's *Pars Oculi*[33] and John of Burgh's *Pupilla Oculi*,[34] appears in bequests in comparable numbers to the *Legenda Aurea* and *Summa Summarum*. Two bequests of the *Expositio* were made by un-beneficed chaplains 'in Ecclesia Ebor', and one by the sub-treasurer of York Cathedral. The extant evidence from legal documents goes some way towards connecting these owners of the *Expositio* with other owners of Rolle-manuscripts in fifteenth-century York and with each other: William Gate and Thomas Pynchbeck were both attached to St Peter's Cathedral, as was

Robert Est, owner of an autograph of Rolle's *Latin Psalter*;[35] Robert Semer, the sub-treasurer of the cathedral followed in the footsteps of another high-ranking official of the cathedral, John Newton, in his enthusiasm for Rolle.[36] At the same time, Semer and Pynchbeck, like Robert Wasselyn, the scribe of the extensive compilation for Rolle's works in Cambridge University Library MS. Ff.I.14, and possibly the Norton family connected with Oxford, Magdalen College MS. 71, were all members of the Corpus Christi Guild,[37] one of the richest and most prestigious of the York Guilds, which included the royal persons of Richard III and Cicely, Duchess of York (herself with a taste for devout reading),[38] in its register of members. These connections are strengthened by the appearance of owners of Rolle works in each other's wills, as either beneficiaries or executors.[39] The clear evidence of these connections points firmly towards a milieu of educated clergy and ecclesiastical officials in fifteenth-century York, converging on the Cathedral, with a particular devotion towards Rolle and his works, and with a keen interest in sophisticated spiritual reading in general;[40] the reason for the relative popularity of the *Expositio* amongst the clergy will be discussed below.

A fourth manuscript of the *Expositio*, discovered amongst the wills of the York Probate Register, is listed in the inventory of the possessions of William Duffield, canon residentiary of York, Southwell and Beverley, whose life is well documented, and whose career connects him with several owners of the *Expositio*. Duffield was a graduate of Merton College and was, at one time, proctor of the University (1407); his highly successful career included not only his Yorkshire canonical holdings, but also in his early years after graduation, the office of keeper of the temporalities of Rochester and Chichester (1419/20), and subsequently, the archdeacon-ship of Colchester (1425).[41] His will connects him with various members of the York clerical milieu discussed above, as does his membership of the Corpus Christi Guild;[42] at the same time he is connected with other successful ecclesiastics, particularly of the University of Oxford, whose ownership of the *Expositio* emerges as a significant factor in a survey of the extant manuscripts. The career of the scribe and owner of Oxford, Bodley MS. 52, John Maynesforth, for example, forms an intriguing parallel with that of Duffield: both men were graduates of Merton College and both held office in Yorkshire; further, the younger man also held ecclesiastical office in Colchester, where he was sub-dean c.1454: both also gave books to the medieval library of Merton.[43] Three of the more handsome volumes containing the *Expositio* were also owned by high-ranking ecclesiastical dignitaries, who were also graduates of Oxford: William Smith, one time bishop of Coventry and Lichfield, owned British Library Royal MS. 7.E.ii, whilst John Stevens, chaplain to Henry V, was the owner of Oxford, Bodley MS. 315; William Gray, bishop of Ely and nephew of Cicely, Duchess of

York, whose ownership of Oxford, Balliol College MS, 224A is surrounded by speculation, was also a graduate of the University of Oxford.

The strong connection between the *Expositio* and fifteenth-century Oxford University seems to be confirmed by the printing of the text by Theodoric Rood c.1483, who with his partner Thomas Hunt printed a small number of books during the last quarter of the fifteenth century at Oxford.[44] Rood's publications fall into two distinct areas: firstly, unlike contemporary printers in his native Cologne, who published almost exclusively in the interests of Thomist and Albertist orthodoxy,[45] Rood was involved in the dissemination of early humanistic literature. He published Leonardi Bruni's Latin text of Aristotle's *Ethics*, a book much in demand in contemporary Oxford,[46] and also, significantly, the *Epistolae* of Pseudo-Phalaris (in the Latin of Francesco Griffolini) edited by Pietro Carmeliano, teacher of rhetoric at Oxford. The connection with the University of Oxford is strengthened by the fact that Rood also printed the *Compendium Totius Grammatice* by John Anwykell, teacher of grammar at Magdalen College School, a work summarising the treatises of Valla and Perotti.[47] Secondly, Rood like other printers of the period issued books designed to appeal to a wider and more conservative audience (and perhaps a more reliable market), such as John Lathbury's *Liber Moralium super Threnis Ieremiae* (c.1482) and John Mirk's *Liber Festivialis* (1486) and it is to this group of publications that the *Expositio* belongs. The elaborate title given to the *Expositio*, which is not found in any manuscript that can be dated with certainty before c.1483, suggests in its pretension to a scholastic comprehensiveness, a printer's recommendation for academic study; it may be, in view of the above connections with the University and the number of Oxford men owning manuscripts of the text in the fifteenth century, that Miss Allen was correct in her suggestion that the *Expositio* had achieved some kind of academic reputation.[48]

A parallel context may be observed for the first Continental printing of the *Expositio*, in Paris, by Berthold Rembolt (1510). This edition is almost certainly a reprint of Theodoric Rood's first edition. Rembolt's version maintains the title of the Oxford printing and diverges only occasionally in the text, probably arising out of editorial interference or misreading; Rembolt also appends the sermon by St Augustine to the *Expositio*, also found in Rood's edition. The text would have been made accessible to Rembolt by way of the general trading relationship which had been established between Oxford and Paris printers in the late fifteenth century and early sixteenth-century due to the printing of books for the English market by Parisian printers[49] and, also, the importation of early French printed books by Oxford booksellers.[50] Rembolt, like Rood, was a printer of early humanistic texts, as were many Parisian printers from the 1470s onwards, under the influence of Italian and Byzantine humanism;[51] again, like Rood, Rembolt printed books intended to meet the requirements of the clergy and of traditional theological studies, printing on a large scale, pastoral manuals, commentaries and book on canon-law.[52] Both Rembolt and his early partner Ulrich Gering were closely associated with the University of Paris, with which the latter consulted on the question of publications.[53]

The third area of medieval society known to have owned the *Expositio* are the religious houses of England, although the responsibility for its transmission and dissemination varies from order to order.

The place of the English Benedictines in the pre-Reformation transmission of the classics of fourteenth-century English spirituality is seemingly a small one, paralleled by the Order's lack of spiritual writers and directors, until Augustine Baker and the exiled Cambrai Nuns, in the first three-quarters of the seventeenth century.[54] This general observation is not contradicted by the particular picture of the fortunes of the *Expositio* in the Benedictine houses of England presented by the available evidence. The work was owned by the two great abbeys of Bury St Edmunds and St Mary's, York: we cannot discuss the Bury manuscript with any confidence as it appears to be lost and we are wholly dependent upon a brief catalogue entry for our knowledge of it. The extant St Mary's MS, Oxford, Corpus Christi MS. 193, is the work of one scribe, Fr John Hanton, and as such suggests the devotion of one man to Rolle's work in general, rather than the interest of the house to which that man was attached; this is supported by the fact that the few annotations of the manuscript are scribal, and by our present knowledge of St Mary's library, which does not include any other Rolle manuscript.[55] In both of the Benedictine manuscripts, the *Expositio* appears in a large volume of the Latin corpus merely as one other work by Rolle. In the other extant Benedictine manuscript, Oxford, St John's College MS. 147, from Westminster Abbey, the *Expositio* does appear as a text independent of Rolle's Latin corpus, but the manuscript was the commission of an individual monk to the metropolitan scribe William Ebesham, rather than a production of the Westminster scriptorium.

The extant catalogue of the library of the Brigettine brethren of Syon Abbey, compiled c.1504–26, leaves us in no doubt that the *Expositio* was valued as a text on its own terms. In the library of the Brigettine brothers alone (which the catalogue records), there were four manuscripts of the work, more than the recorded number of the Benedictine congregations of England *in toto*; in addition one of the extant manuscripts, Cambridge, Trinity College MS. 792, was owned by the Syon priest John Steyke, and may have been donated to the sisters' library. Only one of the four manuscripts listed in the catalogue was *ex dono*, whilst the other three possibly, though not necessarily, originated in the Syon scriptorium; further, and in contradistinction to the Benedictine collections of Bury and York, the *Expositio* appears in manuscripts containing works other than those by Rolle: in other words, whilst being read as part of a special devotion to Rolle, it was also valued in the Brigettine community for itself, and as such was included in, and was part of, collections of standard theological and ascetical materials.

Manuscripts connected with the Charterhouses of Sheen and London, it is well known, found their way into Syon, probably as part of a scheme of loan and exchange of manuscripts between the two Orders, for purposes of reading and copying.[56] We can therefore speculate with some confidence that exemplars of the *Expositio* were sent out from one house to the other, and by extension, that the Charterhouses of Sheen and London owned manuscripts of the *Expositio*. Unfortunately, the only Carthusian manuscript that we can identify with certainty is British Library, Royal MS. 8.A.vii, which was annotated by James Grenhalgh; at the same time there are several tantalizing probabilities: Cambridge, University Library MS. Dd.iv.54 contains large extracts from the *Speculum Spiritualium*, the large spiritual compendium with Carthusian associations;[57] British Library, Sloane MS. 2275 and Paris, Bibliothèque Nationale MS. 15700, themselves closely related, are both connected with the lost Syon MS. M.5 in kind –they are all three large compendia of the formative devotional, ascetical and theological texts of fifteenth- and sixteenth-century English spirituality – and in their duplication of texts. The texts of *Expositio* in British Library, Additional MS. 11304 and MS. Sloane 2275 are close enough to be either dependent on or derived from the same exemplar; both, in turn, are related to Pierpont Morgan MS. 872, again, probably a Carthusian production of the Rolle cult.

Connections between the religious houses owning Rolle's work and the general clerical milieu propagating and transmitting that work in the north of England, and especially in and around York, are available, and form a highly suggestive, albeit incomplete, series of links in the transmission of the *Expositio* outwards into the larger religious context of medieval England. Robert Alne, the examiner-general of the York diocese, who bequeathed his copy of the *Melos Amoris* to the University of Cambridge,[58] had a brother, John Alne, who was a monk of the London Charterhouse;[59] Nicholas Hulme, receiver-general and later treasurer under Bishop Thomas Langley of Durham, and holder of various benefices in York-shire,[60] who bequeathed a manuscript of the *Emendatio Vitae* to a York cleric,[61] died in the Benedictine Abbey of St Mary's, York;[62] whilst the scribe and owner of the York Abbey manuscript, John Hanton, is found in at least one context, in close association with both the household of Bishop Langley and the clerical milieu of York.[63]

The connection between the secular clergy of York and the Brigettine house of Syon is a less direct one, through the medium of the Scrope family and Lord Henry Fitz-Hugh, related to the Scropes by marriage, who was a benefactor of the newly-formed community.[64] Miss Allen discovered evidence in the wills of the Scrope family that they had from the 1380s onwards taken an interest in the Hampole cult and in the solitaries inspired (and once possibly directed) by Rolle.[65] Lord Henry Scrope (ob. 1415), brother-in-law of Fitz-Hugh, owned an autograph of the *Judica me Deus*, and in his will bequeathed books to the abbess of Syon Monastery, a bequest which may have included Rolle works. Several of the clerics and cathedral officials owning Rolle texts, or known to have an interest in sophisticated spiritual reading, are connected with the Scropes, in particular by way of the martyred archbishop. John Newton and Robert Wolveton, treasurers of the Cathedral, worked under the archbishop, being appointed as his deputies during his absence.[66] Magister Thomas Dauntre, a lawyer connected with the clerical milieu of York through his brother, Robert de Alta Ripa chantry priest at the altar of the blessed Virgin in Holy Trinity, Goodramgate,[67] and by his obvious cultured and discriminating reading tastes,[68] bequeathed to his son 'librum parvum vocatum Scropp' – either an original work by the archbishop,[69] or a personal possession that had acquired the importance of a relic;[70] Dauntre also appears with Fr. John Hanton on the schedule of Thomas Langley discussed above.[71] Robert Semer, the sub-treasurer of the Cathedral appears, as he does in many important wills of the late fourteenth- and early fifteenth-centuries as an executor of the will of Stephen Scrope, archbishop of Richmond and late chancellor of Cambridge University.[72]

It is undeniable that the *Expositio* found its way into the religious communities of England as part of the Rolle canon and, more specifically, as part of the Rolle cult: it appears in such large and important collections as Oxford, Bodley MS. 861, Pierpont Morgan MS. 872 and Laud Misc. MS. 528, and also in smaller volumes exclusively devoted to Rolle; for example, Cambridge, Trinity College MS. 14, Cambridge, Corpus Christi College MS. 365 and Lincoln Cathedral MS. 209. The interest in, and devotion to, Rolle is made overt in these manuscripts by the various annotations of passages in the *Expositio* which are explicitly self-referential.[73] However, the phenomenon of the Rolle cult is an inadequate explanation of the extraordinary success of the *Expositio*, for the work appears in manuscripts exclusive of the cult, and further, some works by Rolle never found a wider audience than the adherents of that cult.[74] In order to define more clearly and precisely the nature of the appeal of the *Expositio* (and therefore, in part, the nature of the work itself), we must consider contemporary responses to the work, both in the kinds of compilations drawn out of the *Expositio* and the sections of the text most consistently annotated by medieval readers.

The compilation found in Cambridge, University Library. MS.KK.vi. 20, drawing upon the *Emendatio Vitae, Melos Amoris, Incendium Amoris*,

Commentary on the First Verses of the Cantica Canticorum and the
Expositio, is an excellent example of early fifteenth-century devotion to the
Holy Name in England and of the association of Rolle with that particular
devotion. The compiler's use of the material from the *Expositio*, his choice
of passages for inclusion in the compilation and the kind of text which he
consequently produced, illustrate another facet of the *Expositio's* transmission by way of the Rolle cult, but at the same time, as part of the spiritual
climate which his works, in their devotional aspect, did so much to create.
The organizing principle employed by the compiler in his selection of
materials from the complete text, is one of extracting passages from the
Expositio which move towards and enact colloquy with both Jesus and God
the Father, combining them with larger and more general addresses to
construct short *preces*, or private prayers, which are in mood both
contritional and confessional. It is difficult to be precise in defining the exact
process of construction, in our ignorance of the exemplar available to the
compiler;[75] on the evidence of the extant manuscripts of the full text, the
compiler can be seen to have made some slight adjustments to his text, which
although minor, are significant in terms of the compiler's interests and the
devotional climate in which he was writing. The extracts from the *Expositio*
open with the address 'O bone Ihesu . . .'; in the manuscripts and printed
editions we do not find this direct mode of speech, but merely the adverb
'Hinc'; further, many manuscripts where the compilation has the invocation
'Ihesu' have the less intimate reading of 'domine'. The substitution of words
and phrases by the scribe of a derivative text which slightly alters the spirit in
which the primary text was written is, of course, not unique to the present
compiler: it is well known, for example, that the compiler of the fourteenth-
century *Orison of the Passion*[76] altered his model Passion account by
substituting 'Jesu' for 'Love' and the second person pronoun for the third,[77]
for the overt devotional ends of intimacy and compassionate involvement of
the reader's emotions in the Crucifixion. The ease with which these
penitential materials from the *Expositio* move into the realm of private
prayer is to be seen in the use of these same passages in formal meditation by
the compiler of the *Liber meditationum de vita domini et salvatoris nostri
Ihesu Christi ac venerabilis mater eius virginis Marie*, found in British
Library, Royal MS.8.C.xiv and Oxford, Bodley MS, 417; interestingly, the
compiler adds the epithet 'dulcissime' to his text and thus makes his own
contribution to the metamorphosis of this section of the *Expositio*. The
compiler of Cambridge, University Library. MS.KK.vi. 20 has similarly
adapted his materials to the needs of private prayer, not only by altering
words and in the rearrangement of passages, but also by the very process of
compilation: these sections of the *Expositio* in their original context of the
exegesis grow out of a process of explanation in motion and as such enhance
and enlighten our understanding of the exegetical point: they supplement

the discursive methods of exegesis employed by Rolle. When the compiler brings them together, however, these passages, hitherto defused by their respective contexts, acquire a meditative expressiveness denied to them in the context of the exegesis.

We have established that the compiler has constructed a series of private prayers; but it must be pointed out that they are constructed and assembled under the title *Orationes excerpte de diversis tractatibus quos composuit beatus Ricardus heremita ad honorem nominis Ihesu*, and so purport to be a definite kind of prayer. An analysis of the constituent elements extracted from the *Expositio* in terms of devotion to the Holy Name reveals that the expressions which carry the most significance for the compiler are the commonplaces of medieval Latin devotion, found in such widely circulated texts as the *Stimulus Amoris* and the *Meditationes Vitae Christi*. These passages, which the compiler has understood as significant invocation of and to the Holy Name in the *Expositio*, were also important for other medieval readers: the scribe of Bibliothèque Nationale. lat. MS. 543 has annotated the passage 'Igitur o domine non sim de illorum quibus parcis in presenti et punis in futuro . . .' (f. 6^r) with the word 'Oratio'; it is this recognition of materials useful for prayer which has probably prompted the 'nota' signs annotating these passages in other manuscripts.[78] But for the compiler of Cambridge, University Library. MS.KK.vi.20 the words have acquired a significance beyond commonplace rhetorical possibilities; his more complicated response is paralleled in the mid-fifteenth-century Oxford, Magdalen College MS.71, a volume connected with the Rolle cult and written by a scribe devoted to the Holy Name, where the name of Jesus is distinguished from the body of the text throughout the entire work by a rubricated script.[79] Two comparatively late manuscripts, Oxford, Bodleian. th.d.15 and Lyell 38, like the preceding manuscript, originate in a special devotion to Rolle and both have interesting sets of annotations in response to the passages used in the Cambridge compilation. Robert Parkin, the scribe of the former manuscript, annotates the address 'O bone *Ihesu* . . .' (f.18^v), (the word is underlined in the manuscript), with the note 'Verba divi Ricardi heremite' and the petition 'O pater misericors . . .' (f.25^v), in *Lectio* II, with the words 'Supplicatio divi Ricardi'. The reading of these commonplaces as if they had hidden depth charges of meaning has its apotheosis in the annotations of John Coleman, in Oxford, Lyell MS, 38, who annotates the same passages as Parkin with the unique 'contemplatio' (ff,55^v and 64^r). The conclusion suggested by these brief observations is that in the eyes of some medieval readers, the mere repetition of the word 'Ihesu' in the context of a Rolle work evoked a response denied to the same words in another writer's work. The response is one of an adherent of the Rolle cult which defined the Holy Name, as Rolle himself had done, as central to the hermit's spirituality (and which encouraged similar affective and rhapsodic invocations by later writers).[80] Moreover, it is also the response of a mind familiar with the most important works, in terms of his personal spiritual history, in the Rolle canon: a writer's greatest work poses perhaps the greatest danger to the reader approaching that same writer's less distinguished works, by its insistence, concomitant upon its own particular power and impressiveness, that all other works be read through it. The citations used by the compiler of the Cambridge manuscript, from the *Incendium Amoris*, *Melos Amoris* and, in particular, the fifth section of the *Commentary on the First Verses of the Cantica Canticorum*, often employ the address 'O bone Ihesu . . .' as does the *Expositio*, but their respective contexts in works preoccupied (albeit not exclusively), with devotional and contemplative themes, indicate that the commonplace is being made to work beyond its usual capacity in the interests of a specific and special kind of devotion. In the *Oleum Effusum* section of the *Canticle* commentary, which is almost a hymn to the Holy Name, the significance of the evocations is determined both by the explicit references to the 'nomen Ihesu' and by the verse of Scripture being expounded.[81] In the *Expositio* there is no such justification for reading the sections in question in terms of devotion to the Holy Name specifically; it is significant that the scribe appends to the extracts from the *Expositio* an interpolation which, in a sense, directs the reader's response to the foregoing passages.[82]

The use of these passages which enact the drama of contrition and confession has its counterpart in the reading and annotation of the *Expositio* as a discursive manual of the penitential life in its various aspects, and as such took its place in the manuscripts alongside manuals of vices and virtues and also, alongside the standard ascetical works of the later Middle Ages, in particular the pseudo-Augustinian *Speculum Peccatoris*, Innocent III's *De Miseria Humane Conditionis* and the Pseudo-Bernadine *Meditationes Piissime*.

The compilation found in both Cambridge, University Library. MS. Ff.i.14 and Oxford, Hatton MS.97 is a collection of segments extracted mainly from the Latin works of Rolle and especially the *Expositio*. They do not form any consistent and ordered manual of the penitential life, but rather they remain a series of well-wrought extracts which pose the great medieval questions placed over the value of existence, that had found their formulation in the penitential themes of *de contemptu mundi* and *memento mori*: the transitoriness and uncertainty of life, the certainty of death and judgement. The citations from the *Expositio* are essentially restatements of the ascetical and penitential axioms inherited by the Middle Ages from patristic commentaries and treatises, which had found their way into almost every genre of religious literature, from the popular vernacular sermon to learned Latin treatises on the contemplative life. These sections of the *Expositio* receive thorough annotation in many of the extant manuscripts and are not restricted to any one class of owner.

Intimately related to these ascetical attitudes and equally well annotated, are Rolle's expositions of vices and virtues: the scribe of Cambridge, University Library MS. Ff.v.36, for example, like the annotators in several of the manuscripts, has constructed a marginal index, either for his own use or for that of a future reader, of Rolle's explications of both particular vices and virtues, such as 'humilitas', 'caritas', 'patientia' (f.2^v) and 'cupiditas' (f.11^v), and also of more general definitions, for example, 'virtutes' (f.3^r). Miss Allen remarked of the *Expositio* that the theological and scholastic aspects of the text outweigh and overwhelm the mystical.[83] As a general statement about the *Expositio* we can concur with this analysis and, at the same time, suggest that this kind of bias to the work may, in part, account for the success of the work amongst fifteenth-century Oxford men: it is significant that in their manuscripts British Library, Royal 7.E.ii, Oxford, Bodley 52, Bodley 315 and Magdalen College 6 (although excepting Oxford, Balliol College 224A whose origins are surrounded by speculation), there is no other Rolle work accompanying the *Expositio*. More than in any other work, with the possible exception of the *Latin Psalter*, Rolle attempts to clarify in precise, albeit uncomplicated scholastic language, his theological positions; he ranges over a wide area of topics, defining vices and virtues, more general conceptual lists and elementary dogmatics of penitential theology, such as the three marks of true contrition (annotated more than any other single passage) and the impossibility of being without sin.

Connected with these penitential materials is the idea central to Christian experience, of the suffering and deprivation of the just man, and his consequent temptation to deny God. It is this aspect of the *Expositio* which seems to have been taken up by the Westminster monk Thomas Lynne, who may have commissioned Oxford, St John's College MS. 147, and which has subsequently influenced his choice of texts: the *Expositio* is followed by a short English text on the fruits of tribulation, the *Vita* and *Passio* (especially the latter) of fourteen Christian martyrs who suffered persecution for the early Church and, finally, by the Passion sections of the *Meditationes Vitae Christi*. Once again Rolle restates traditional attitudes towards tribulation, found in such earlier expositors as Peter of Bath in his *Compendium in Job* and also, more fully, in *De XII Utilitatibus Tribulationis*.

The application of these penitential materials is relevant to the everyday business of virtuous Christian living and would therefore have an obvious relevance to the clergy as practitioners of exemplary virtue, and as teachers of those virtues—they are straightforward and basic enough concepts to be generally available through the medium of the pulpit, to a popular audience. At the same time, the teachings are essential, and were expounded as such by Rolle in his own manuals, as a prelude to the contemplative life. The orientation by Rolle of these penitential themes towards the pursuit of contemplative perfection is minimal, unlike, for example, the use of similar materials in the opening chapters of the *Emendatio Vitae*, where they are defined and given a specific point of reference by subsequent chapters. The adoption and use of these penitential teachings in the *Expositio* as useful for the instruction of the contemplative, by some medieval readers and scribes, is suggested by the presence in some manuscripts of more specialised texts such as Hilton's *Scale of Perfection* and Suso's *Horologium Sapientiae*.

Whichever way the didacticism of Rolle's penitential materials were taken up and interpreted, it is clear that his medieval readers were attached to the stiff, formal theological rationalizations and to the restatements of well-worn ascetical wisdom as much as to the more distinctive, rhapsodic and devotional rhetoric, which modern commentators have emphasised as the source of Rolle's success and appeal. At the same time, it is true that the two share an intimate and mutually dependent relationship, peculiar and perhaps even necessary to every exponent of highly affective spirituality: the definition and the truism having acquired a freshness and conviction in the light of the extraordinary experiences embodied in the rhapsodic, and belief in the latter being vindicated by its foundation in the well-known and traditional: both, in turn, having their justification in the miracles and sanctity surrounding the cult of St Richard Hampole.[84]

If the *Expositio* was valued for its instructions on the spiritual life of both the active and contemplative, it was also valued as a source of *dicta* on the sacerdotal office. The sanctity of the priest and his function was a constant theme of Rolle's work, co-existent with, and connected to, the theme of personal sanctity, as it had been for the best European spiritual writers.

The compilation found in Dublin, Trinity College MS. 277, with the title *De Pastoribus* is not unique in the way that it draws upon Rolle's work. Ely Priory, the owner of at least one Rolle manuscript,[85] also owned a compilation *De Mercenariis Sacerdotibus*, which utilised extracts from the *Judica me Deus*;[86] discussion of sacerdotal ideals, drawn from the *Melos Amoris*, is also found in a collection of extracts from Rolle's works in Heneage MS. 3043, prefacing quotations from the *Incendium Amoris* and further selections from the *Melos Amoris*.[87]

The passages from the *Expositio* utilised by the compiler of *De Pastoribus* in the Trinity College manuscript examine the areas of clerical morality and duties, in both general and specific terms, which are expounded more fully and in greater detail in the orthodox pastoral manuals of the period. Primarily homiletic in tone, these extracted blocks of passages range between a discursive and cool analysis of the basic necessities of instructing the laity, both by the word of the sermon and the example of personal sanctity, and the oratorical vehemence of the denunciation of clerical abuse and ignorance. That these commonplaces embedded in the *Expositio*, as they are in the *Judica me Deus*, draw in part of William of Pagula's *Oculus Sacerdotis*, perhaps the most widely read pastoral manual of the fourteenth and fifteenth centuries,[88] suggests that the *Expositio's* own popularity (and by extension other works by Rolle), is inseparable from the clerical audience created by the dictates of the 4th Lateran Council in 1215, English Councils growing out of these, and by mid-thirteenth-century English Synodolia[89]—in other words, an audience receptive to manuals of elementary pastoral instruction, giving explications, pared down to the essentials, of the theology of the Seven Deadly Sins, Creeds, Pater Noster, Articles of Faith and the Sacraments (especially penance), in an easily grasped form, which in turn could be imparted to the laity by the priest. On the other hand, as with the devotional life, Rolle created the means by which his own work flourished: his intense and earnest concern for the sanctity of the priesthood, which formulated, or more exactly re-formulated, the teachings of contemporary *pastoralia*, is coloured by Rolle's explicit encouragement of the contemplative life as part of his programme for virtuous sacerdotal living. If Rolle's English prose and lyrics made highly specialised modes of religious feelings and emotions more generally available, consequently raising the level of some vernacular devotional verse,[90] he also encouraged the pursuit by the clergy of a rigour of religious life which hitherto had been the prerogative of the cloister and raised the expectations of the religious experiences available to the parish priest. In literary terms his work encouraged the movement of the pastoral manual into the realm of the contemplative treatise, to meet (while at the same time encouraging) these new expectations. In the *Manuale Sacerdotis* which has been attributed to John Mirk,[91] a commonplace treatise drawing upon patristic and medieval sources for information on pastoral duty, we can observe this kind of excursion into the contemplative treatise: the work, in five parts, ends with a final capitulum, *De Contemplatione Celestium Gaudiorum*, celebrating the vision of God in an adaptation of the words of the pseudo-Bernardine *Meditatio V*.[92] The fruit of Rolle's encouragement of the secular clergy in the pursuit of contemplative perfection can still be observed over two hundred years after his death, in the life and literary work of his spiritual descendant, Robert Parkin, curate of Adwick-le-Street, scribe and owner of Oxford, Bod,lat.th.d.15.

NOTES

ABBREVIATIONS

W.A.   *Writings Ascribed to Richard Rolle and Materials for his Biography*, ed. H. A. Allen,
        New York and London, 1927.
Y.W.   *Yorkshire Writers, Richard Rolle of Hampole and his Followers*, ed. C. Horstman,
        2Vols, London, 1895–6.
M.A.   *The Melos Amoris of Richard Rolle of Hampole*, ed. E. J. J. Arnould, Oxford, 1957.
S.A.   *Richard Rolle of Hampole, Super Apocalypsim*, ed. N. Morzac, Paris, 1968.

All quotations from the *Expositio* are made from Balliol College, Oxford MS.224A

1. *W.A.*, pp. 136–44; see also *M.A.*, *Introduction*, pp. liv-lv, n. 35.
2. Compare, for example, the opening of the *Expositio*, 'Exprimitur autem in his verbis
   humane condicionis instabilitas, que non habet in hac miserabili valle manentem
   mansionem . . .' (f. 63vb), with ch. 4 of the *Melos Amoris*,' Corporalem namque in hac
   miseria nec mansionem habeo nec manentem inquiro . . .', *M.A.*, p. 11, and with the
   parallel phrase in the *Commentary on the First Verses of the Cantica Canticorum*,
   'Peregrinus igitur ego sum et advena, sicut omnes patres mei, dum in hac presenti miseria,
   nec mancionem manentem habeo . . .', 'Le Commentaire de Richard Rolle sur les
   Premiers Versets du Cantique des Cantiques', ed. O. Madon, *Mélanges de Science
   Religieuse*, 2 (1950), 313–25, p. 315.
3. Compare, 'sed querite de hac materia in libello de vita heremitarum & Eciam *in libro de
   perfeccione & gloria sanctorum* . . . (f. 75vb), with, '. . . inspirante spiritu qui prebet
   potenciam, *de gloria et perfeccione sanctorum* precellencium postillas proferam . . .', *MA*,
   p. 15.
4. *Y.W.*II, *Introduction*, p. xxxvii, identified this work with the anonymous *Regula
   Heremitarum*, found in Cambridge, University Library, MS. Mm, vi 17, ff. 70^{v}–76^{v},
   preceded by three parts of the *Judica Me Deus*; Horstman's suggestion was treated
   sceptically by both Miss Allen in *W.A.*, pp. 325–9, who lists the work under *Dubia*, and P. L.
   Oliger, 'Regulae Tres Reclusorum et Eremitarum Angliae saec xiii–xiv', *Antonianum*, 3
   (1928), 151–190, pp. 162–5, who edits the text in question, *ibid*, 299–320.
5. Lincoln Cathedral, MS. 209, offers an interesting alternative to Miss Allen's interpretation. The contents of the MS., which include the *Officium* and *Miracula* of Rolle
   strongly suggests a production connected with the Rolle cult; further, the scribe John
   Wodeburgh, was both familiar with the literary biography of Rolle (annotating the phrase
   'de perfeccione & gloria sanctorum' with the marginal 'liber illa dicitur melos amoris'—
   subsequently incorporated into the text of the *Expositio* in some MSS) and with Rolle's
   mysticism (he writes the interpretative 'cordis' next to '. . . cum hoc in canorum iubilum
   Christo amante surgit . . .', f. 66^{r}). This personal devotion to Rolle, as well as the verses
   composed by Wodeburgh after the *Commentary on Psalm XX*, suggests that the scribe may
   also have written the quatrain appended to the *Expositio*.
6. Our only certainty in terms of the chronology of the Latin works appears to be that the
   Expositio was composed after the *Melos Amoris*; although even this small foothold has
   been challenged by Arnould, *M.A.*, *Introduction*, pp. lxvi–lxvii, who speculates (uncon-
   vincingly) that both the *Melos Amoris* and the *De Vita Heremitarum* were only in
   preparation at this time, the latter having never been completed.
7. See L. Boyle, 'The *Oculus Sacerdotis* and some other Works of William of Pagula',
   Transactions of the Royal Historical Society, Fifth Series, 5 (1955), 81–110, pp. 90–91 n. 3,
   dates the *Pars Oculi* c. 1327–9: Miss Allen dated the Judica B2, which apparently draws on
   the *Pars Oculi*, as ante 1322.
8. *W.A.*, p. 350, concerning the *Missa de Nomine Jhesu*: 'Rolle showed a general indifference
   to liturgy that would forbid our ascribing to him a work like the present'. Miss Allen's large
   statement must be placed alongside that of W. A. Pantin, *The English Church in the*

Fourteenth Century, Oxford, 1955, p. 245, whose remarks present a more acceptable view: 'It seems clear that it was the more systematic and practical of Rolle's works that had the greatest popularity, those that served as a general directory of the spiritual life or as commentaries on those parts of Scripture that were in everyday liturgical use . . .'.

9. Job 7: 16–21; 10: 1–7; 10: 8–12; 13: 22–28; 14: 1–6; 14: 13–16; 17: 1–15; 19: 20–27; 10: 18–22. C. Wordsworth and H. Littlehales, *The Old Service Books of the English Church*, London, 1904, p. 111, note that the *Officium Defunctorum*, from around 1200, had become appended to the *Psalter*.

10. The text, breaking off at *Lectio* viii, is divided in 21 *capitula*.

11. See Oxford, Bodley MS. 315, f. 28ra, 'Explicit tractatus Ricardi heremite de hampool super Job'.

12. The error was especially perpetrated by continental bibliographers, see G. Eysengrein, *Catalogus Testrium Veritati Omnium Orthodoxe Matris Ecclesiae Doctorum*, Dillinger, 1563, f. 159^{v}; C. Gesnero, *Bibliotheca Instituta et Collecta*, Tiguri, 1583, p.725. The titles utilised by modern commentors on Rolle's works are equally misleading, see *Le Feu de l'Amour, Le Modèle de La Vie Parfaite, Le Pater*, ed. M. Noetinger, Tours, 1928, Introduction, p. lvii, n. 2; E. Ph. Goldschmidt, *Medieval Texts and their First Appearance in Print*, supplement to the Bibliographical Society's Transactions no. 16, 1943, p. 130 (following earliest printed text); *M.A., Introduction*, p. xvi; P. Hodgson, *The Fourteenth Century English Mystics*, British Council Pamphlet, 1967, p. 14; *Contra Amatores Mundi*, ed. P. Theiner, California, 1968, Introduction, p. 53 etc.

13. See J. Faber's vague title in the 1536 edition of the *Expositio*, '. . . in aliquot capita Iob prophetae Enorratio', (f. 89^{r}).

14. See Sr. E. M. Murray, *Richard Rolle's Comment on the Canticles, edited from MS. Trinity College, Dublin 153*, (unpublished Ph. D. Dissertation, Fordham University, 1958); the erroneous title used here should be placed alongside that employed by O. Madon, *op. cit.*

15. Manuscripts of the *Incendium Amoris* are listed *W.A.*, pp. 213–25 and manuscripts of the *Emendatio Vitae* are listed *W.A.*, pp. 231–40, 245. To the former add Prague Cathedral MS. 695, noted *S.A., Introduction*, p. 56; to the list of extracts add British Library, Additional MS. 34, 807, f. 40^{r} (bottom margin): 'Ricarda heremita de Hampull. O mors ubi moraris, cur tam tarde venis . . . gaudiorum'; to lost manuscripts add the following: that listed by Prior Richard Roche of London Charterhouse, as one of the consignment sent to Coventry Charterhouse (2° non habeo), cited by E. M. Thompson, *The Carthusian Order in England*, London, 1930, p. 326; that manuscript in the list of Witham Charterhouse books found in Oxford, Laud Misc. MS. 154, f. 7^{v}, cited *ibid*, p. 321 (2° superferundi); that manuscript listed in the inventory of Robert Braybrook, bishop of Lincoln, dated 1404, found in St Paul's Dean and Chapter Muniments A, Box 67 N° 58, item N° 30, 'Item de Incendio amoris' (2° tis), cited by R. H. Bartle, *A Study of Private Book Collections in England . . . with special reference to books belonging to Ecclesiastical Dignitaries*, (Oxford, B. Litt. thesis, 1956, shelf number d. 612), Note 9, p. xxiv.

To the list of manuscripts of the *Emendatio Vitae* add Cambridge, Gonville and Caius College MS. 223/238, pp. 423–50 (lacking capitulum 1); Oxford, Lyell MS. 38, ff. 1–34^{r}; Windsor S. George MS. E.I. i, noted by H. E. Allen, *Times Literary Supplement*, N° 1399, Nov. 22, 1928, p. 910; Munich, King's Library MS. 8094 (1829), ff. 226–46, 'ex bibliotheca coenobii Franciscorum in kelheim', described in C. Halm, G. Thomas and G. Meyer, *Catalogus Codicum Manuscriptorum Bibliothecae Regiae Monacensis*, Munich, 1873, 3(iii), p. 221; Chicago, Newberry Library MS. Ry. 8, ff. 39–66^{r}, listed in S. de Ricci, *Census of Medieval and Renaissance Manuscripts in the United States and Canada I*, New York, 1935–40, p. 542, and Washington, Library of the Catholic University MS. 114, ff. 5–30^{v}, listed *ibid*, pp. 454–5. To the list of lost manuscripts add that found in the (probably) Carthusian booklist edited by R. Bressie, 'MS. Sloane 3528, Folio 158', *Modern Language Notes*, 54 (1939), 246–56, p. 251, 'Item xij capitula ricardi hampole in uno quaterno', and also that found in the library of All Soul's College, Oxford, cited by N. R. Ker, *Records of All Soul's College Library, 1437–1600*, Oxford Bibliographical Society Publications, New Series, 16, 1971, p. 6, item 82(66), 'Liber de Emendacione vite', (2° cuncta que).

16. *W.A.*, pp. 11, 263 and 406 notes citations from Rolle's works found in the *Speculum*

Spiritualium, to which could be added Rolle's *Commentary on the Pater Noster*, drawn on by the compiler in Book 3, ch. 27, 'De Oratione Dominica et eius brevi expositione'.

Rolle's *Latin Psalter* is quoted extensively in A. Lipsius, *Catena in Psalmos*, Rome, 1585, pp. 31, 48, 62–3, 71, 103, 110, 121, 130, 135, 156, 159, 185, 205, 209–10, 215, 220, 233, 236, 239, 244, 261, 276, 279, 319, 325, 332, 344, 357, 364, 398–9, 405, 409, 424, 441–2, 481, 505, 511, 521, 536, 539, 559, 568, 577. The source of the quotations is quite clearly Faber's 1536 edition, the index of authorities prefacing the text referring to 'Ricardus Pampolitanus Anglosaxo'.

17. The work is found with a translation into Latin of Johan Faber's *Grundliche und christliche . . .*, one of his several vernacular polemics in response to Lutheran apostasy: J. Faber, *De missa envangelica et de veritate Corporis et Sanguinis in Eucharistia, sacrameto libri V . . . Quibus adiectus est libellus, in quo sacrae scripturae testimoniis, sanctorum Patrum Conciliis, Summorum pontificum decretis, per celebrium Doctorum ac interpretum sententias, Ecclesiasticique historiis, sancrosanctum Missae sacrificium pie defunctis prodesse ostenditur (per Anthonium Monchiacenum Democharem Ressonaenum, doctorem, Sorbonicum)*, Paris, 1558.

18. See G. R. Owst, *The Destructorium Viciorum of Alexander Carpenter. A Fifteenth-Century Sequel to Literature and Pulpit in Medieval England*, London, 1952, p. 23, listing Robert Holcot, Richard Rolle, John of Ayton, Richard Fitzralph, William of Nottingham, Richard Wynkley, John of Burgh, John of Mirfield, John Waldeby, John Bromyard and Philip Repingdon. The citations from John Waldeby include a hitherto unnoticed quotation from the lost *Commentary on the Apolcalypse*.

19. *W.A.*, p. 12; Faber, in the *Prefatory Letter*, to his edition, gives notice of Rolle's works not included in following pages, which were subsequently included in the 1536 edition.

20. *W.A.*, p. 13.

21. *W.A.*, p. 12, cites the *Prefatory Letter* of the 1535 edition, which extols the orthodoxy of Rolle's works and makes clear that his edition was intended as a weapon in the Counter-Reformation. The efficacy of the two editions in Reformation polemics was obviously taken seriously by Thomas Cranmer, who owned two copies of the 1536 edition, in which he annotates both the text and Faber's marginal commentary; both copies are now located in the British Library.

22. The Charterhouse of St Barbara owned Darmstadt MS. 84, which was used for the 1536 edition of St. Gertrude's *Insinuationes*, cited R. B. Marks, *The Medieval Library of the Charterhouse of St. Barbara in Cologne*, Salzburg, 1975, 2, p. 280.

23. The most oustanding figure in this context is Lurence Surius, who after joining the Cologne Carthusians, edited both Henry Suso and Jan van Ruysbroeck, as well as bringing out new editions of standard theological writers and joining in current controversies more directly, by way of polemical pamphlets, see P. Polman, *L'Element Historique dans la Controverse Religieuse du XVIe siècle*, Gembloux, 1932, p. 395 and n. 1, R. B. Marks, *op. cit.*, I, p. 130; the literary works of Surius are incompletely surveyed by T. Petreius, *Bibliotheca Cartusiana*, Cologne, 1609, pp. 276–82. It may be significant for a discussion of the proposed connection between the Carthusians of Cologne and Faber that Surius translated the latter's *Der Recht Weg* into Latin, as *Via Regia quo Itinere Fidelis Debeat Ambulere*, Cologne, 1536.

24. R. B. Marks, *op. cit.*, 2, pp. 193, 253; St Barbara owned Berlin, Theol. lat. Quart. MS. 369, from Mainz Charterhouse and Cologne, Historisches Archiv. MS. W. 124, from Trier Charterhouse. L. Hendricks, *The London Charterhouse*, London, 1889, Appendix VII, pp. 366–8, presents evidence for literary contact between the London and Cologne Charterhouses.

25. G. Eysengrein, *op. cit.*, p. 159^v; the Continental bibliographers of Rolle, largely ignored by Miss Allen on the presumption that they merely followed English bibliographers, deserve a careful study for their testimony to the Continental manuscript traditions of Rolle's work: Eysengrein, for example, writing over fifty years before Pitts (see *W.A.*, p. 425), cites Rolle as the author of a commentary on the *Ambrosian Creed*; he also credits Rolle with the authorship of the *Commentary on Six Old Testament Songs*, found appended to Rolle's *Latin Psalter* in all but three MSS, where they are alone (*W.A.*, pp. 166, 167, to which add York Cathedral MS. XVI. I.5, ff. 193–196^r, found appended to Peter Lombard's *Psalter*),

but does not list the *Latin Psalter*; had he seen Prague University MS. 681, containing only the *Epilogue* to the *Psalter* and the *Commentary on Six Old Testament Songs*?

26. *W.A.*, p. 425, gives a slightly simplified (and inaccurate) description of the passage; the citation is not a quotation of the anti-clerical passage in *Lectio VII*, used by the Lollard scribe: the passage, 'Heu . . . amiserunt', is a juxtaposition of two clauses, taken out of their respective contexts, from *Lectio VI*; whilst the passage which follows is a selective paraphrase, rather than an exact citation, from *Lectio VII*.

27. For a discussion of Lollard interpolations in the *English Psalter*, see D. Everett, 'The Middle-English Prose Psalter of Richard Rolle of Hampole', *Modern Language Review*, 17 (1922), 217–27, 337–50; 18 (1923), 381–93.

28. *W.A.*, p. 401.

29. G. R. Owst, *op. cit.*, pp. 6–14, discusses affinities between the work of Wycliffe and the *Summa* of Carpenter.

30. See note 17 above; for the fullest list of Faber's works, and the various translations of them, which supercedes and corrects the entry in *The Catholic Encyclopedia*, 5, New York, 1909, p. 742, see art. 'Johann Faber de Heilbron', in *Dictionnaire de Spiritualité, Ascétique et Mystique, Doctrine et Histoire*, Paris, 1964, c. 22–3.

31. *Via Regia quo Itinere Fielis Debeat Ambulare*, Cologne, 1563, trans. L. Surius, Dedicatory Epistle: 'Porro quod has suas pro Catholica fide lubricationes Germanico idiomate conscripsit, non alia ratione eum fecisse patet, quam ut Germaniae intestinis bellis et in religione dissidiis mire et misere id temporis tumultumati, succurreret. Verum cum praestantissimus vir *D. Antonius Rescius* Theologiae Doctor, illius pestis extera quoque regna pervasisse et infecisse, animadverteret, obtulit mihi absolutissimi huius viri D. Johannis Fabri . . .' (p. 9).

   The importance of Rescius as a link between the English and Continental Carthusians and Faber is suggested by the few facts concerning his life and literary activity that have come to light: the two main sources are the 'Dedicatory Epistle' to Maximilian, Archduke of Austria, written by Simon Weisser, monk of Wurzburg Charterhouse, which prefaces his edition of Maurice Chaucy's narrative of the Carthusian martyrs, *Innocentia, et Constantia Victrix, sive Commentariolus; de vitaratione, et Martyrio 18 Cartusianorum; qui in Anglice Regno . . .* , 1608, and Antony à Wood, *Fasti Oxonienses*, I, p. 155. Weisser's preface reveals that Rescius was Suffragan Bishop of Wurzburg, a close friend of Bl. John Houghton, who was present at his martyrdom, subsequently relating the events to Weisser; Wood's notice, shows that Rescius was one of the Friars appointed to counter the doctrines of Peter Martyr and others, which had been introduced into Oxford in the reign of Edward IV. Wood's supposition that he was the Friar Richard, present at Cranmer's execution in 1556, with another Spanish friar, John de Villa Garcia, reported by John Foxe, remains purely conjectural; for the latter, see *The Acts and Monuments of John Foxe*, ed. S. R. Cattley, London, 1839, 8, p. 89.

   P. Poleman, *op. cit.*, p. 392, cites Rescius, alongside Gravius, Nannius and Masius, in connection with Counter-Reformation researches into patristic texts for doctrinal proofs, in particular the works of S. Basil; the *Catalogue Général des Livres Imprimés Bibliotheque Nationale*, Paris, 1938, 149, p. 608, notes an edition of S. Anselius *Opera*, Venice, 1547, edited by Antonius Democharis Ressonaeus.

32. W. A. Pantin, *op. cit.*, p. 248–9, emphasises the close relationship between the mundane and didactic literature directed towards the secular clergy, and the mystical and devotional treaties written by Rolle, and before him, S. Edmund.

33. *Testamenta Eboracensia* 1, p. 209; 2, p. 209; to which could be added the wills of: Henry Barneby, chaplain of York, proved 1401, Borthwick Institute, Probate Register 3, f. 72^r; Robert of Newland, Chaplain of Skelton, proved 1404, Probate Register 3, f. 215^v; Robert Newton, rector of Stokesley, proved 1438, Probate Register 3, f. 523^r; William Garland of Malton, vicar-choral of St Peter's York, proved 1408, Dean and Chapter, Register of Wills L.2 (4), f. 116^r.

34. *Testamenta Eboracensia* 1, p. 320; 2, pp. 51, 83 and 219; 3, p. 279; to which could be added the wills of: Richard Plane, rector of Middle Church, parish of Gedelyng, proved 1454, Probate Register, 2 f. 312^r; Roger Morcand, rector of Laxton, proved 1428, Probate Register, 2, f. 547^r; John of Maltby, rector of Rither, proved 1432, Probate Register, 2

f. 617^r; John Fernell, chaplain, (buried All Saints Church, Peasholme Green), proved 1466, Probate Register, 4, f. 67^r.

35. *W.A.*, p. 415.

36. *Testamenta Eboracensia*, 1, p. 366; Newton bequeathed to the York Chapter 'Libros Johannis Howeden, Ricardi Herenitax, domini Walteri Hilton canonici, Willielmi Rymyngton et Hugonis de Institucione Noviciorum, in uno volumine', cited *W.A.*, p. 414.

37. *The Register of the Guild of Corpus Christi in the City of York*, Surtees Society 57, 1872, p. 59 (Wasselyn), p. 66 (Pynchbeck), pp. 84, 85, 90, 106 (several Nortons), p. 246 (Semer's obiit).

38. *A Collection of Ordinances and Regulations for the Government of the Royal Household*, Society of Antiquaries, 1790, p. 37: '. . . during the time whereof she hath a reading of holy matter, either Hilton of Active and Contemplative, Bonaventure De infancia Salvatoris, the Golden Legend, St Maud, St Katherine of Siena, or the Revelations of St Brigit'.

39. Robert Alne, Examiner-General, of the York Diocese, bequeathed a Manuscript to Robert Semer, sub-treasurer of the Cathedral, *Testamenta Eboracensia*, 2, p. 79; the latter was an executor in the will of William de Waltham, Canon of York (ob. 1418), along with William Gate, whilst Thomas Beelby (who owned a manuscript of Rolle's *Psalter*), was a beneficiary in the same will, *Testamenta Eboracensia*, 3, p. 58; Semer was also an executor in the will of John Newton, *Testamenta Eboracensia*, 1, p. 308.

40. The wills published in the *Testamenta Eboracensia* are witness to the high standard of reading tastes amongst this circle of clerics: John Newton, the sub-treasurer of York Cathedral (ob. 1414), bequeathed a fine library to the York Dean and Chapter, *Testamenta Eboracensia* 1, pp. 365–6; Robert Alne left a copy of the *Melos Amoris* to the medieval library of Cambridge, and to his brother John Alne, a monk of the London Charterhouse, Suso's *Horologium Sapientiae*, *Testamenta Eboracensia*, 2, p. 78; Robert Wolvedon, treasurer of York Cathedral (ob. 1432), left to John Lantoft 'unum librum de—votum factum per Walterum Hilton', *Testamenta Eboracensia*, 3, p. 91: the reference is especially interesting as Wolvedon's brother (and executor) was prior of Thurgarton; Robert Semer left manuscripts of St Bridget and Suso's *Horologium Sapientiae*, *Testamenta Eboracensia*, 3, p. 91; William Gate bequeathed a volume of the *Meditationes* of St Anselm to Richard Drax, *Testamenta Eboracensia*, 3, p. 58 n ; Robert Est bequeathed the *Horologium Sapientiae* and a manuscript of Hilton to Robert Bewmond and also a *Collationes Sanctorum Patrum*, which a relative John Est had written, *Testamenta Eboracensia*, 3, p. 159; Thomas Symson 'persona in ecclesia Ebor' (ob. 1491), who was an executor in the will of Robert Est, left a manuscript of the *Revelationes* of St Mechtild, *Testamenta Eboracensia*, 3, p. 160 n; John Hoperton, chaplain of the chantry of St Nicholas in Holy Trinity, Goodramgate, left the *Speculum Ecclesiae*, *Testamenta Eboracensia*, 1, p. 196. To these could be added the wills of Robert Ottelay, vicar of St Martin, Coneystrete, who bequeathed to Robert Pay in 1420 the *Révelationes* of St Bridget, Dean and Chapter, Register of Wills L.2(4), f. 199^v; and of Richard Tolleston, chaplain of York, who bequeathed the same to Richard Russell, after whose death it would revert to Kirkstall Abbey, proved 1435, Probate Register, 3, f. 428^{r-v}.

41. A. B. Emden, *A Bibliographical Register of the University of Oxford, to A. D. 1500*, Oxford, 1957–9, 1, pp. 601–2.

42. *Ibid.*, p. 40.

43. M. Powicke, *The Medieval Books of Merton College*, Oxford, 1931, pp. 67, 100, for Duffield's books.

44. E. Gordon Duff, *A Century of the English Book-Trade*, London, 1903, p. 139, for a list of Rood's publications.

45. The press of Ulrich Zell, for example, established in 1404, had printed 1300 titles by the turn of the century, of which more than half were treatises in the Albertist and Thomist tradition, in accordance with the strict scholastic orthodoxy of the University of Cologne, which was in active opposition to advancing humanism, see S. H. Steinberg, *Five-Hundred Years of Printing*, London, 3rd edition, 1974, pp. 62–3.

46. *Collectanea* I, Oxford Historical Series, 1895, pp. 141–3, publishes a list made by Thomas Hunte, Rood's partner, of the most highly sought after books in Oxford, which includes Bruni's Latin edition of Aristotle, as well as other humanistic literature, such as Lorenzo

Valla's *De Vera Bona* and Perotti's *Rudimenta Gramaticae*.
47. R. Weiss, *Humanism in England during the Fifteenth Century*, Oxford, 1941, p. 169, notes that the *Compendium Totius Gramaticae* is not, strictly speaking, a purely humanistic text, but rather a fusion of both medieval and humanistic systems of Latin grammar, abridging Valla's *Elegentiae* and Perotti's *Rudimenta Gramaticae*, and combining the result with Alexander of Villedieu's standard *Doctrinale*. The *Compendium Totius Gramaticae*, of which only fragments remain, is prefaced by two poems by Pietro Carmeliano.
48. *W.A.*, p. 130.
49. Rembolt, for example, printed a *Sarum Manuale* (with Ulrich Gering) in 1498 and a *Sarum Missale* in 1513, cited E. Gordon Duff, *op. cit.*, p. 134.
50. J. Veyrin-Forrer, Caxton and France', *Journal of the Printing Historical Society*, II (1976), 33–47, p. 39, records a consignment of 66 books to Thomas Hunte, including Ulrich Gering's edition of Petrus de Osomas's *In Symbolum S. Athanasii* (c. 1475) and of the *Summa de Quattuor Virtutibus Cardinalitus et Vitiis illis Contrariis* (1480).
51. *Ibid.*, p. 34.
52. See B. Moreau, *Inventaire Chronologique des Éditions Parisiennes du XVI siècle* I, Paris, 1972, *passim*.
53. Both Gering and Rembolt attached epithets to their names, signifying their connections with the Sorbonne: Gering styled himself 'Imprimateur de Livres et Ecolier étudiant en l'Université de Paris; whilst Rembolt Cresswell, *Annals of Parisian Typography . . . compiled principally to shew its general character; and its particular influence upon the early English Press*, London, 1818, p. 31.
54. See P. Spearritt, 'The Survival of Medieval Spirituality among the exiled English Black Monks', *American Benedictine Review*, 25 (1974), 287–316.
55. N. R. Ker, *Medieval Libraries of Great Britain*, London 2nd edition, 1964, p. 217.
56. E. M. Thompson, *op. cit.*, p. 332; the problem of deciding on the provenance of manuscripts of contemplative and devotional texts which share the same textual transmission, by way of either Syon or Sheen, further indicates this close literary filiation between the two houses; see M. Sargent, 'The Transmission by the English Carthusians of some late Medieval Spiritual Writings', *Journal of Ecclesiastical History*, 27 (1976), 225–40, *passim*. The English *Commentary on the Pater Noster*, translating Pars III, ch. 27 of the *Speculum Spiritualium*, found in Cambridge, University Library MS. Ff. vi. 33, exemplifies the connection between Syon and Sheen: it was written (and translated?) by William Dorker, monk of Sheen, for the use of the Syon nuns. The text is currently being edited for publication by the present writer.
57. York Cathedral, MS. XVI. I. 9, perhaps the most important manuscript of the work, and British Library, Harley MS. 237, are from Mount Grace Charterhouse; Magdalen College, Oxford, MS. 141, was owned and partly written by John Dygoun, recluse of Sheen Charterhouse see also note above.
   Copies of the printed book published in 1510 in Paris by Wolfgang Hopyl, at the expense of William Bretton of London, can be traced back to Carthusian libraries: the copy in the Brotherton Library, Leeds, comes from Coblentz Charterhouse, see J. A. Symington, *Early Printed Books in the Brotherton Library*, Leeds, 1931, p. 170 and plate; and that copy sold as Lot 250 at Sotheby's sale, November, 1978, bought by Quevado Bookshop, was from the Charterhouse of Buxheim.
58. see note 39 above.
59. *Ibid.*
60. Nicholas Hulme succeeded John Newton, Master of Sherbourn Hospital (who bequeathed to him the MS. of the *Emendatio Vitae*, as receiver-general to Langley in 1421, having been treasurer (again, having succeeded Newton) of the Langley household since 1419; Hulme was ordained 1413, holding numerous benefices in Durham as well as in Yorkshire, before finally becoming a canon of Ripon, see R. L. Storey, *Thomas Langley and the Bishopric of Durham*, London, 1961, pp. 5, 74–5, 78–9, for information on Hulme's career.
   The close connection between the officials of the Langley household and the clerical milieu in York, in terms of literary interests, is strengthened by the fact that Thomas Hebbedon (ob. 1434), the spiritual chancellor of Thomas Langley (who had himself been

Dean of York), bequeathed his copy of the *Melos Amoris* to Robert Alne, examiner-general of the York diocese; for a review of his career under Langley, see *The Register of Thomas Langley* I, Surtees Society 164, 1949, ed. R. L. Storey, *Introduction*, p. xv.

61. *W.A.*, p. 415; the benefactor was Nicholas Blakwell.
62. *Ibid.*
63. R. L. Storey, *op. cit.*, p. 69. Langley's *schedula* for the visitation of the Durham convent in 1408, includes a John Henton, monk of St Mary's, who is almost certainly the owner and scribe of Corpus Christi College, Oxford MS. 193: 'Quibus sic gestis et actis, ammoveri fecimus omnes clericos et laicos religiosos et seculares a capitulo memorato (exceptis) religioso viro fratre Johanne Henton monacho monasterii sancte Marie Ebor ordinis sancti Benedicti . . . .

   It is interesting to note that in Leicester, Wyggeston Hospital MS. 15, a fifteenth-century MS of Rolle's *Emendatio Vitae* and *Expositio super Novem Lectiones Mortuorum*, we find two works *Compendium Amoris* (ff. 72^r – 78^v) and *De Meditationibus* (ff. 78^v – 93^r), attributed to a John Hanneton.
64. G. Aungier, *History of Syon and Isleworth*, London, 1840, p. 55, Fitz-Hugh's *obiit* was celebrated perpetually by the Syon Community.

   The connection between the York and Durham clerical milieux is, in this context, supported by Bishop Langley's name appearing in the Syon *Martyrologie* (British Library, Additional MS. 22285, f. 70^r), under 'Nomina specialium benefactorum et amicorum'.
65. *W.A.*, pp. 413–14.
66. Borthwick Institute, Scrope's Register, ff. 171^v, 172^r, 173^v, 175^r, 175^v, 176^r.
67. *Testamenta Eboracensia*, 2, p. 59 n.
68. *Ibid.*, p. 60, Dauntre bequeathed 'Wilielmo Bernyngham, nuper clerico meo . . . librum vocatum Francisci Petrarchae laureati . . .', and to his son 'librum meum Bonaventurae', possibly referring to Nicholas Love's translation of the *Meditationes Vitae Christi*. Robert Semer, mentioned above, was an executor to Dauntre's will.
69. Henry Savile owned a (lost) MS. of Scrope's works: 'An exposition upon the 7 psalmes. Item upon diverse other psalmes, and upon Esay 8 Ezechiell in English prose by on (*sic*) Scrope. In follio', cited A. G. Watson, *The Manuscripts of Henry Savile of Barke*, London, 1969, p. 67 (MS. 270). The first work, as Watson suggests, may be the work wrongly ascribed to Rolle in Oxford, Digby MS. 18, see *W.A.*, p. 371.
70. J. Raine, *Historians of the Church of York and its Archbishops 3*, Rolls Series, London, 1894, p. 288–91, prints an account of the proceedings against Scrope, attributed to Dauntre. Raine is in agreement that Dauntre owned the book carried by Scrope to his execution.

   The account of Scrope's trial and execution, found in Lincoln College, Oxford, MS. 54 (not MS. 20 as reported by Raine), is written and annotated by Thomas Gascoigne, and is possibly by him, rather than Dauntre, see W. A. Pronger, 'Thomas Gascoigne', *English Historical Review*, 53 (1938), 606–628, p. 608.
71. R. L. Storey, *loc. cit.*
72. *Testamenta Eboracensia*, I, p. 389.
73. The most frequently annotated passages are those professing the eremetical life and of literary biography which immediately follow.
74. *The Commentary on Lamentations*, *Super Apocalypsim* and *Super Psalmum XX*, for example, are found only in manuscripts devoted to Rolle.
75. Possibly Oxford , Laud Misc. MS. 528 and certainly a closely related text.
76. *Meditations on the Life and Passion of Christ*, ed. C. D'Evelyn, Early English Text Society, O.S., 158, 1921, *Appendix*, pp. 60–64.
77. Cf. *ibid.*, *Introduction* p. xxv, and its erroneous judgements.
78. British Library, Royal MS. 8. A. vii and Bibliothèque Nationale, MS. 15700.
79. The *capitula* to the *Emendatio Vitae* (written in red ink) are preceded by the monogram IHC, inscribed boldly in black ink (ff. 4^v, 7^r, 8^v, 10^r *et al*).

   In the compilation found in Oxford, Bodley MS. 417, from Sheen Charterhouse, the name Ihesu is distinguished from the body of the text, having been written in red ink, in the section 'de laude nominis Ihesu', which draws on the *Incendium Amoris* and *Oleum Effusum* (ff. 23$^{ra–va}$).

80. cf. Richard Methley's *Schola Amoris Languidi*, ch. 14, titled, 'De mirabilibus que fiunt per nomen Ihesu', Trinity College, Cambridge MS. 1160, ff. 13^r–14^r.
81. See A. Wilmort, *Le 'Jubilus' dit de St Bernard*, Rome, 1944, *Appendix* VII, pp. 275–80. 'Venerabilis Ricardus de Hampol composuit de Nomine Ihesu'.
82. 'Nam salubriter omnis quicunque invocaverit nomen eius saluus erit . . . ' (f. 18^v).
83. *W.A.*, p. 144.
84. It is significant that in his defence of Rolle against a Carthusian detractor, Thomas Bassett underlines the point that Rolle, and therefore his books, was inspired by the Holy Spirit: 'Quod si quisquam veritatem agnosceret, et ei acquiescere nollet, tunc pocius inimicus veritatis quam amicus dici deberet. Libri ergo venerabilis Ricardi, si feurit in homine spiritus Dei, non faciunt eum iudicium sui, sed cum Spiritus Dei veritas est, *necessario* compellitur consentire vertitati, alioquin nichil sibi et libris Ricardi', cited from *W.A.*, p. 535.
85. St John's College, Cambridge MS. 23.
86. *W.A.*, p. 96: cf. the lost Syon MS. M.5, a Rolle manuscript, which contained a 'Tractatus de sacerdotibus mercenariis'.
87. The compilation follows anti-clerical material from St Jerome, but is not part of it, the words 'Benedictus deus amoris' clearly signalling the end of the Hieronymian text.
88. L. Boyle, *op. cit.*, *Appendix B*, pp. 109–110, lists 52 extant manuscripts of the *Oculus Sacerdotis*; also pp. 94–5 for mention in wills and visitational records.
89. See M. Gibbs and J. Lang, *Bishops and Reform, 1215–1272*, Oxford, 1934, pp. 94–179; and for English Synodal Statutes, C. R. Cheney, *English Synodolia of the Thirteenth Century*, Oxford, 191.
90. D. Pearsall, *Old English and Middle English Poetry*, The Routledge History of English Poetry, 1977, p. 137.
91. See G. R. Owst, *Preaching in Medieval England*, Cambridge, 1926, p. 275.
92. York Cathedral MS. XVI, O. 11, f. 157^v, the author substitutes 'sacerdos' for 'homo'.

THE LATIN *CLOUD*

JAMES HOGG

SINCE THE PUBLICATION of Phyllis Hodgson's critical edition of *The Cloud of Unknowing* and *The Book of Privy Counselling* in Middle-English in 1944,[1] modernised versions and studies of *The Cloud of Unknowing* have multiplied, so that today the bibliography of the *Cloud*-author is considerable.[2] One sphere in which little has been printed[3] since Phyllis Hodgson's edition is that of the Latin versions of *The Cloud* contained in the Cambridge Pembroke College MS. 221 and Oxford Bodleian Library MS. 856, though James Walsh's recent modernised edition of *The Cloud*[4] offers not only a perceptive introductory section on Richard Methley's rendering of *The Cloud* in the Pembroke MS.,[5] but also presents in the footnotes to the text English translations of Methley's glosses,[6] which renders an extended enumeration of these glosses superfluous here.

The Bodleian MS. 856 has received—and deserves—less attention than Pembroke MS. 221. Unfortunately, its provenance is not known.[7] Its content would, however, suggest a religious community committed to the contemplative ideal:

f. 1^r–13^r *Liber Alberti Magni di adherendo Deo* in 16 chapters with the incipit 'Cogitanti michi aliquid . . .'

f. 13^r–77^r *Liber Contemplacionis qui intitulatur Nubes ignorandi* in 75 chapters, with a prologue, list of chapters, and a preface. The prologue begins 'In nomine sancte Trinitatis. Quincunque fueris . . .' and the preface 'Dilecte amice . . .'. The text proper commences 'Amice michi dilectissime. . . .'[8]

On f. 77^r a collection of *Sermones beati Augustini episcopi morales ad fratres suos in eremo* . . . is preceded by a table of contents. The sermons occupy the rest of the volume.

The manuscript, which is written on parchment by a single hand of the mid-fifteenth century,[9] contains 119 numbered leaves of text, [10] with about 29 lines to the page. It is adorned with illuminated capitals in blue and red with elaborate filigree work. Rubrics and underlining demonstrate the care with which the manuscript was compiled.[11] Presented to the Bodleian in 1602 by Sir Walter Cope, one might have postulated a possible Carthusian provenance for it, had not Methley translated *The Cloud* in the Pembroke MS. 221. It seems, however, stretching probability to postulate two Carthusian Latin versions in the English province, when the relation between the individual Charterhouses was close and the circulation of books apparently frequent.[12] There are few annotations or corrections in the volume, though a finger points to the passage in chapter 41 of *The Cloud* beginning: 'Sed non dico quod continuare semper potes in hoc opere equali appetitu et feruore, ...' (f. 40^r),—a passage that Methley also glosses in his version. The scribe was very economical with his parchment, for the Latin *Cloud* starts immediately under the explicit of the work by St Albert on f. 13^r and terminates on f. 77^r at 1. 6 simply with 'Explicit liber iste'. A list of the sermons that were to complete the volume follows immediately. The manuscript has obviously been used, but not to the same extent as Pembroke MS. 221. As both A. I. Doyle[13] and Hodgson[14] remark, the Bodleian Latin version of *The Cloud* is close to the Middle-English found in the British Library London Harley MS. 959, which can be dated as mid-fifteenth century at the earliest. It is not, however, a translation of Harley 959, as it contains passages that the scribe of the Harley MS. omitted, including, as Hodgson notes, the whole of the eleventh chapter.[15]

The Latin text offered in the Bodleian MS. 856 is more of a paraphrase than a strict translation. There is considerable amplification of the Middle-English text by development of the themes and the introduction of supplementary Biblical quotations. Doyle comments on the Bodleian MS. 856, which he dates as late fifteenth century:

> Superfluous interpolation and translation, as they may seem to us, were means and signs of keen study in the circumstances of cloistered religious life and devotion.[16]

Quite a number of the developments indeed correspond to the additional material offered in Harley MS. 959. Hodgson offers two typical examples of the translator's technique that cannot be bettered. In chapter 16 of *The Cloud*[17] where the anonymous author simply has 'for lackyng of loue', the translator writes: 'pro carencia diuini amoris in suauitate spiritus non dum vt libuit habitu quamquam multum inde gustauerat vt probatur ex verbis oris dominici dicentis. Dimissa sunt ei peccata multa. post quod subiunxit non quia plorauit multum set quoniam dilexit multum quam vnquam languebat ob recordationem commissorum suorum' (f. 32^r).[18] The second example displays his dependence on the amplification in Harley MS. 959 or on a manuscript containing the same text. In chapter 19 of *The Cloud*, where Mary is contrasted with Martha, the passage concludes: '& þerfore sche schuld alwey be had excusid' (1. 12), Harley MS. 959 continues: 'but the principalle cavse of hir excusyng is þat þe most gracius and wysest mastyr þat euyr was or schalle be had hyr excused fully'. Bodley MS. 856 duly offers at this point: 'Set excusacionis eius causa principalis hec est, quia ille graciosissimus et sapientissimus magister qui vnquam fuit vel erit vnquam plane ipsam habuit excusatam' (f. 34^r).[19] Here again Methley glosses the same passage.

In her appendix A[20] Hodgson offers the prayer to the Holy Ghost that precedes *The Cloud* in both the Latin versions. The numerous small variants here and the divergences in the author's own prologue[21] to *The Cloud* rule out any possibility that Methley utilised the Bodleian Latin version in compiling his own translation.

The Pembroke MS. 221 is of greater interest to scholars of English mysticism, not only because we know a good deal about the translator whose versions are presented in it, Richard Methley of Mount Grace Charterhouse, but also because it strengthens the possibility that *The Cloud of Unknowing* may well have been written by a Carthusian of Beauvale, though the case should not be overstressed in view of the fact that late medieval English Carthusians also claimed both Hilton and Ruusbroec as members of their order.[22]

The manuscript was copied by William Darker, a professed monk of Sheen Charterhouse, who died in 1512 or early 1513,[23] with all the expertise of a professional scribe, who even copied manuscripts to order for Syon Abbey as well as for his own community. The manuscript, which is written on vellum in double columns of forty lines each, consists of 102 folios, numbered in pencil in recent times, with two fly-leaves at the front and back.[24] Throughout the manuscript the scribe has inserted red or blue paragraph signs before each gloss and the chapter headings are in red. The initials, three in *The Cloud of Unknowing* and twenty-one in *The Mirror of Simple Souls*, in red and blue are the work of a professional illuminator, whose bill is to be found on f. 102[V].[25] Unfortunately, the manuscript was rebound some years ago, but some of the original blind-stamped leather was used for this purpose.[26]

The manuscript was corrected assiduously—maybe over a period of years—not only to eliminate scribal errors but also here and there to adjust Methley's Latin. Colledge and Walsh distinguish three different 'hands' that the Carthusian Grenehalgh employed in this manuscript, besides attributing other emendations to various unidentified scribes. If we accept Sargent's rejection of Grenehalgh's hand here, (see below, note 3), we are faced with a considerable number of annotators, and not with the wisdom of 'the celebrated amateur of mystical theology James Grenehalgh'.[27]

The manuscript was still being used after the suppression of the Charterhouses, for on f. 99[V] an annotator inserted against the title of chapter 21 of *The Mirror of Simple Souls*: 'Quomodo intelligitur quod dicitur saluat se fide sine operibus et de sua vocacione ad hoc.' 'cave hic 1542'. Sargent maintains that the hand is identical with one of those attributed to Grenehalgh by Colledge and Walsh, which would eliminate the possibility of the annotation stemming from Grenehalgh, whose obit is recorded in the Parkminster Charterhouse MS. B. 77 in 1530.[28] On the outer margin of f. 93[r] seemingly the same hand inserted 'Phelip and Jas 1548', presumably a reference to the date: May 1.[29] No evidence is available, but maybe the manuscript remained in the possession of one of the monks, before being incorporated eventually into Pembroke College Library.[30]

Methley's Latin version of *The Cloud* was written specifically for Dom Watson, who was presumably vicar of the Charterhouse of Mount Grace at the time. At the end of his rendering of *The Cloud* Methley writes: 'Ecce nunc o frater mi Thurstine, pro deo, tuoque in eo rogatu, laboraui, institi, perduxi deo me adiuuante, hoc opus ad finem intentum, optatum, adeptum, sicut rogasti me. Anno domini millesimo quadringentesimo nonagesimo primo, secunda die post festum sancti Laurencij. Deo gracias offero, matrique ecclesie catholice hoc opus, si opus est ad discernendum, et omnia que vsquam habeo'.[31]

The translation was thus terminated on 12 August 1491. We know very little about Dom Watson, though his name does occur along with Methley's in the will of the widow of Richard Strangways, knight, Jane, who left both of them ten shillings among numerous bequests to religious houses.[32] He was subsequently transferred to the neighbouring Charterhouse of Kingston-upon-Hull at a date which has not been ascertained. The Carthusian General Chapter of 1505 recorded his death: 'D. Trustanus Watson monachus et vicarius professus domus in Monte Gracie secundo in Hul'.[33] One can only venture hypotheses as to why Dom Watson might have wished to possess a Latin version of *The Cloud*. Theological writings in English had not yet achieved full respectability in conservative circles, and maybe Dom Watson felt that not only would Latin terminology be more precise, but also that such a version would lend the Middle-English author greater standing.[34] Methley's work as a translator was not confined to merely rendering the text into Latin,—he also provided numerous glosses on what he considered difficult or obscure passages, which were placed after each chapter, but these are referred to by letters in the margin of the text itself at the appropriate places. For a non-university graduate his Latinity, despite minor slips, was impressive, and Colledge and Walsh rate him not only a capable translator, but also 'as a sound spiritual theologian, and as an extraordinarily saintly man'.[35]

Obviously, Methley was ideally equipped to translate *The Cloud*. His autobiographical writings and his 'To Hew Heremyte: A Pystyl of Solytary Lyfe Nowadayes' demonstrate his own assiduous practice of contemplative prayer and his stature as a spiritual director.[36] Colledge and Walsh observe:

He is, first and last, a Carthusian, and one of the most able exponents of the life and spirituality of the solitary, and of that kind of sanctity which such a life produces. He is at home in the company of such predecessors as Guigo II, Hugo of Balma, Guigo du Pont, and his contemporary Denis van Rykel; and one feels that St. John of the Cross would have approved, by and large, of his writings.[37]

Methley supplies a lengthy preface to his translation:

(f. 1^v, col. 1) *Incipit prologus translatoris in diuinam caliginem ignorancie, qua anima vnitur deo.*

Qvoniam ignorantibus non solum sophistriam et logicam, sed et ethicam et phisicam, quinimmo sed et theoricam et practicam purissime non dicam speculatiue sed superintellectualis et superspeculatiue scienciam defecatissime et vnificatissime et viuificatissime vnicionis et vnionis inter deum et viatorum animas, difficillime maxime modernis diebus refrigescente caritate, non dicam solum multorum, sed pre nimietate malorum fere omnium christianorum, difficillime inquam intelliguntur libri contemplatiuorum supersplendidioribus theorijs theordoctorum, institi vt potui, et tandem inueni secundum ocium a ceteris scilicet vacare necessarijs, et transferre de anglico in latinum, et vbi necesse fuerit explanare pro capciosis et opiniosis in fine capitulorum quorumdam que quidem difficilia videntur ad intelligendum, transferre autem librum cui nomen caligo; et ne ignores o lector quid sit caligo hec, addidi diuinam eam esse caliginem, sicut et autor ipse qui composuit, ait caliginem ignorancie, quasi diceret, negatiua in diuinis sunt affirmatiua secundum modum superspeculatiue contemplacionis, in qua nimis affectus quis predestinatus et raptus, nichil scit immediate ex humana consideracione ante vel post, et ideo dicitur ignorancie, vnde et Dionisius Ariopagita ait: Sapiencia est diuinissima/[col. 2] dei cognicio, per ignoranciam cognita, secundum vnionem que est super mentem. Nec prophanas vocum nouitates sectabor, sed eas superspeculatiue contemplacioni assuetissimas, secundum quod Paulus gerarcha Dionisium Ariopagitam, Dionisius Timotheum docuisse in scriptis Dionisii patet euidentissime.

Sophistria, logica, ethica, phisica note sunt pluribus melius quam michi qui nunquam penitus aliquam vniversitatem vidi. Quatuordecim quidem aut eo circiter annis exercitatos habens sensus ad discrecionem huius caliginis diuine, ob ignoranciam in actu pro tempore terminos huic sapiencie diuinissime per ignoranciam cognite secundum Dionisium exponam, ne rudes et deuote persone ob defectum litteralis sciencie totum quod absit dimittant. Theoricam quantum ad presens propositum dicimus esse litteralem scienciam, practicam vero ipsum exercicium negacionis omnium encium quantum ad affectiuam cognicionem, pro tempore dumtaxat superspeculatiue contemplacionis. Et notandum quod hoc super, cum dicitur superspeculatiue vel superintellectualis, supersplendidioribus vel aliquid huiusmodi, importat superlacionem, vt sciliet plus intelligatur quam illud quod dicitur. Vnificacio in proposito presenti notat vnionem anime et dei, et ibi fit vnificacio quedam a morte quam incurrimus per Adam. Est autem vnicio actiue ex parte dei, passiue ex parte anime, in purissima coniunccione vt possibile est viatori. Vnio autem est illorum duorum copulacio quorum vtrumque manet in sua substancia. Et hoc contra heresim Begardorum. Sequitur in prologo presenti, Theorijs, id est diuinis illuminacionibus; Theodoctorum, id est a deo doctorum: Ariopagita, id est homo de studio virtutum in quodam pago; Gerarcha, id est sacer princeps. Nunc/[f. 2^r, col. 1] ad destinatum opus manum mittimus. *Explicit prologus.*[38]

It is obvious that Methley feels that the Carthusians are specially called to practice the prayer outlined in *The Cloud*,[39] and in chapter 1 of his translation he comments on the 'foure degrees & fourmes of Cristen mens leuyng; & ben þeese: Comoun, Special, Singuler, & Parfite'[40]:

Communis et cetera vt supra. A. Hoc loco attende lector quod communis status, est laycorum, specialis clericorum, vel religiosorum, singularis solitariorum scilicet heremitarum, anachoritarum, vel, precipue cartusiensium; vnde videtur quod, cuidam cartusiensi hic liber compositus fuit, quia scilicet non solent moderni, de approbata religione, exire ad heremum, vt antiquitus sed ad cartusienses.[41]

Many of his glosses merely seek to clarify what the *Cloud*-author really meant. Thus in Chapter 4 there are a whole row of glosses designated A–K. Among his more interesting comments are his gloss to chapter 2:

Look now forwardes, & lat be bacwardes. & see what þee faileþ, & not what þou haste: for þat is þe rediest getyng & keping of meekness.[42]

Methley comments:

Perpende et cetera vt supra. A. Bonum est frequenter recordari, ad minus semel in die, quid tibi deest perfeccionis, scrutinum faciendo consciencie tue, vt de beneficijs et virtutibus quas habes deo gracias agas, de defectibus et peccatis doleas. Sed vanam gloriam tibi timuit qui dixit: Non quid habes.[43]

In chapter 8:

& riȝt as it is impossible to mans vnderstondyng a man to come to þe hiȝer party of actyue liif, bot if he seese for a tyme of þe lower party: so it is þat a man schal not mowe com to þe hiȝer party of contemplatiue liif, bot ȝif he seese for a tyme of þe lower partye,[44]

Methley glosses:

Et sicut impossibile est et cetera. A. Nota lector quod ait impossible, quia vnum tantum intelligimus in vno instanti vel momento seu puncto. Sed tamen ex speciali gracia, vel habitualiter vel actualiter, cooperante spiritu sancto, eciam aliquid agendo de deo meditari non solum non impossibile sed et facillimum est, quamuis a certis personis, nec in diuino officio, nec in spirituali aliquo exercicio presumendum sit. Hoc excepto, quod quantum in nobis, de deo eciam operando semper et vbique deuote et reuerenter cogitare debemus. Quod vt perfeccius impleamus, perfeccius quo possumus ab operibus mentem abstrahamus eciam operando.[45]

In the same chapter on

For whi loue may reche to God in þis liif, bot not knowing. & al þe whiles þat þe soule woniþ in þis deedly body, euermore is þe scharpnes of oure vnderstonding in beholding of alle goostly þinges, bot most specially of God, ...[46]

Methley observes:

Quia, amor in presenti et cetera. B. Vtinam intellectus nostri acumen, nunquam esset in vanitatibus occupatum, sed semper circa spiritualia, maxime circa deum exercitatum; sed autor iste loquitur pro tempore huius exercicij, quando graciam quidem habemus, sed non tantam eius habundanciam quanta[m] in raptum evolvemus.[47]

In treating the passage:

For by Mary is understonden alle contemplatyues, for þei schuld conforme here leuvng after hirs; & by Martha, actyues, on þe same maner, & for þe same skil in licnes.[48]

Methley comments:

Quia per Mariam et cetera. C. Cave ne velis sic Mariam imitari, vt prius pecces grauiter et postea peniteas fortiter, quoniam qui peccat in spe, manet in morte. Non enim secundum hoc debes te conformare illi sed in quiete.[49]

Methley's enthusiasm is aroused by

Bot þeire specyal preiers risen euermore sodenly vnto God, wiþ-outyn any meenes or any premeditacion in special comyng before, or going þer-wiþ.[50]

He exclaims:

Sed eorum speciales et cetera. A. Practici contemplatiui vtuntur oracionibus vocalibus id est corporali voce dictis, et hoc diuersimode, secundum quod per inspiracionem et infusionem ducuntur vel aguntur vt apostolus ait: quicunque spiritu dei aguntur hii filij sunt dei [Rom. 8, 14] et ideo aliquando placare, aliquando feruore, aliquando canore implent oraciones suas voluntarie per graciam assumptas, vocaliter id est voce corporali vel saltem tantum in mentali siue lingua mota siue non mota, impleant eas vt communiter loquar. Sed diligentissime notet lector, quod dixi, vt communiter loquar. Nam intencio autoris est quod in hoc opere, non comuniter, sed specialiter, ymmo vt pre raritate talium loquar quasi singulariter, practicus contemplatiuus sic furiose quodammodo affectus, nescit proferre vnum verbum corporali, sed nec spirituali voce. Assumptus et absorptus est vino defecato, vnde et fere moritur; ymmo et moreretur pro certo, nisi deus vel modum temperaret, vel eum viuum continere[.] O excellencia huius operis; gloria, laus et honor deo.[51]

On the passage:

For I may not trowe þat a soule contynowyng in þis werk niȝt & day wiþ-outyn discrecion schuld mowe erre in any of þees outward doinges; & elles me þink þat he schuld alweis erre.[52]

Methley has two glosses:

Quoniam credere non possum et cetera. A. Nocte et die, vigilans non semper, sed opportune; orans, meditans, non semper, sed frequenter; omnino semper in voluntate et in habitu, et tandem cum placueritante vel post predicta; hoc opus exerce. Vide eciam si placet proximum predictum capitulum. *Alioquin et cetera.* B. Qui spiritum sanctum habent in se, pro tempore errare non possunt. Alioquin ad vnguem, sed notanter dico ad vnguem discreccionem seruare maxime semper, aut impossibile aut vix possibile est. Quod ait de nulla discrecione in hoc exercicio tenenda, vide proximum predictum capitulum. Ibi Non dico quod semper poteris eodem feruore et cetera. Eundem sensum posui in presenti, scilicet: Nocte et die, vigilans non semper, et cetera. Quod si non solum de indiscrecione temporis secundum habitum et voluntatem, sed eciam de ipso exercicio intelligere volueris, scito quod discrecionem supergreditur, et hoc virtuose; qui quasi semper consurgit ignote in deum pure propter seipsum.[53]

Though Methley shows himself fully capable of handling scholastic concepts in his glosses, his reading in the scholastics seems not to have been wide, for on occasion he clearly fails to recognise well-known texts. He also displays no knowledge of the other writings of the *Cloud*-author, which somewhat diminishes the value of his testimony that *The Cloud* was written by a Carthusian. He may well not have read Denis even in the Latin versions current in his time, nor is it certain that he knew the commentaries of Thomas Gallus. Such knowledge as he displays in this field may well have come from such a compilation as the Bodleian Library Douce MS. 262, which contained not only an extract of Hugh of Balma's *Viae Syon Lugent*, but also an *Exposicio super quaedam verba libri beati dionisii de mistica theologia*. To judge from the evidence of his phrasing it is tempting to think that he had read Guigo du Pont's *De contemplatione*, but we cannot be certain of this. No manuscript from an English Charterhouse is extant, – the Stonyhurst MS. LXVIII came from the Charterhouse of Ruremond in Holland. Colledge and Walsh do point out, however, that Guigo du Pont had 'distinguished between a perfect and an imperfect "excessus mentis", the imperfect being "ubi pia mens ad aspectum divine claritatis raptim in deum subvehitur", whereas in the perfect "excessus" "deus videtur per essentiam" '.[54] Methley declared in a gloss to chapter 71 of *The Cloud*:

Intellige quod rapi pure in deum propter seipsum gratis, solius diuine largitatis est. Ad caliginem autem ignorancie, quinymmo et ad quemdam statum glorie, non abstractis omnino, quamuis ex parte sensibus pertingere, eciam industrie humane cooperante gracia cum diuturno labore contingit, et hoc quasi sine vllo labore in fine, quia tanquam naturalis suo modo efficitur.[55]

However, even this and other possible affinities[56] may be attributable to the common tradition which Guigo du Pont and Methley shared.

Considering his lack of a university training, one may admire not only Methley's fluency but also his general soundness as a traditional theologian, obviously well-equipped to be just such a director of souls as the *Cloud*-author undoubtedly was; but neither the Methley version nor that contained in the Bodleian MS. 856 shed decisive light on the vexed question of authorship or lead to a more profound understanding of the text, though both, in their differing approaches, serve to demonstrate how *The Cloud* was utilised by those seeking perfection in the late fifteenth and early sixteenth centuries, and the Pembroke manuscript is an eloquent witness to the esteem in which the Carthusians held the treatise. Furthermore, Walsh maintains that Methley had at his disposal a manuscript or manuscripts superior to any of the Middle-English manuscripts that have survived,[57] though I venture to suggest that a revision of the Middle-English text in the light of Methley's Latin version would not necessitate any radical revision of Hodgson's life work.

NOTES

1. *Early English Text Society*, London, 218, 1944. Phyllis Hodgson's latest thoughts on *The Cloud* are contained in her edition *The Cloud of Unknowing and Related Treatises*,

Analecta Cartusiana 3, Salzburg, 1982. It is unfortunate that this study contains some errors of fact regarding the Carthusians. Thus, for instance, on p. xvii she repeats the assertion that Andrew Boorde, a monastic misfit from the London Charterhouse, became 'Suffragan Bishop of Chichester', when in fact he was merely licensed to act as chaplain in that diocese. On the same page she asserts that the Cambridge Pembroke College MS. 221 came from Mount Grace Charterhouse. As far as I can see, there is no evidence to support this claim, and the difficulty in interpreting Maurice Chauncy's inscription on the Parkminster Charterhouse MS. D. 176 was finally resolved by Michael G. Sargent, 'William Exmewe, Maurice Chauncy, and *The Cloud of Unknowing*', *Spiritualität Heute und Gestern*, Analecta Cartusiana 35:4, 1984, 17–20.

2. Cf. the numerous bibliographical entries in the *14th Century English Mystics Newsletter* and in V. M. Lagorio & R. Bradley, *The 14th Century English Mystics: A Comprehensive Annotated Bibliography*, New York & London, 1981. The first printed edition of *The Cloud* appeared as late as 1871. On the transmission of texts, cf. Placid Spearitt, 'The Survival of Mediaeval Spirituality among the Exiled English Black Monks', *The American Benedictine Review*, 25 (1974), 287–316. Two full-length studies of *The Cloud* were published in the Analecta Cartusiana in 1983: Robert William Englert, *Scattering and Oneing: A Study of Conflict in the Works of the Author of The Cloud of Unknowing*, Analecta Cartusiana 105, and Rosemary Ann Lees, *The Negative Language of the Dionysian School of Mystical Theology: An Approach to The Cloud of Unknowing*, Analecta Cartusiana 107, 2 vols.

3. James Walsh and Edmund Colledge, '*The Cloud of Unknowing* and *The Mirror of Simple Souls* in the Latin glossed translations of Richard Methley of Mount Grace Charterhouse, edited from MS. Pembroke College Cambridge 221,' prepared a critical edition of the Pembroke MS. with copious notes and a full introduction in 1967 for the *Archivio italiano per la storia della pietà*. Unfortunately, this luxurious series ran into financial difficulties, and, though the proofs were prepared, the edition was never issued. Much of the introduction now needs revision in the light of the publication of most of Methley's works and the fact that Michael Sargent maintained in his dissertation, *James Grenehalgh as Textual Critic*, University of Toronto 1979, that virtually none of the annotations are in Grenehalgh's hand, as Walsh and Colledge had supposed, and Sargent had accepted on their authority in his article, 'The Transmission by the English Carthusians of some Late Medieval Spiritual Writings', *Journal of Ecclesiastical History*, 27 (1976), 225–240, p. 238. Sargent holds that it is possible that a monogram on f. 31^r, col. 2, may be by Grenehalgh, and a very small monogram on the top of f. 47^r col. 1 could be in his hand. As A. I. Doyle, *A survey of the origins and circulation of theological writings in English in the 14th, 15th and early 16th centuries with special consideration of the part of the clergy therein*, Cambridge University dissertation 1953, Vol. 1, p. 279, had also attributed the annotations to Grenehalgh, I had followed his authority in my previous writings. Cf. Michael G. Sargent, 'James Grenehalgh: The Biographical Record', *Kartäusermystik und -mystiker*, Analecta Cartusiana 55:4, 1982, 20–54. Michael Sargent stresses that the 'd' of the annotator in the Pembroke MS. is totally different in its form to that in any manuscript known to be annotated by Grenehalgh. Richard Methley's works have appeared as follows: James Hogg, 'Carthusian Materials in the London Public Record Office Collection SP I/239', *Analecta Cartusiana*, 37 (1977), 142–43 (indication of a fragment of Methley's *Experimentum veritatis* and 'A pystyl of solytary lyfe now a dayes'); James Hogg, 'Richard Methley: To Hew Heremyte: A Pystyl of Solytary Lyfe Nowadayes', *Analecta Cartusiana*, 31 (1977), 91–119—a transcription by W. E. Campbell was printed in *The Thought & Culture of the English Renaissance: An Anthology of Tudor Prose 1481–1555*, ed. Elizabeth M. Nugent, Cambridge, 1956, pp. 387–93 (this edition unfortunately left a good deal to be desired); a facsimile edition of Methley's *Scola amoris languidi, Dormitorium dilecti dilecti*, and *Refectorium salutis* appeared in James Hogg, *Mount Grace Charterhouse and Late Medieval English Spirituality*, Vol. 2: *The Trinity College Cambridge* MS. 0.2.56, Analecta Cartusiana, 64, 1978: the texts were transcribed and printed in James Hogg, 'A Mystical Diary: The *Refectorium Salutis* of Richard Methley of Mount Grace Charterhouse', *Kartäusermystik und -mystiker*, Vol. 1, Analecta Cartusiana, 55, 1981, 208–38; James Hogg, 'The *Scola Amoris Languidi* of Richard Methley of Mount Grace Charterhouse

transcribed from the Trinity College Cambridge MS. 0.2.56', *Kartäusermystik und -mystiker*, Vol. 2, Analecta Cartusiana 55, 1981, 138–65; and James Hogg, 'The *Dormitorium Dilecti Dilecti* of Richard Methley of Mount Grace Charterhouse transcribed from the Trinity College MS. 0.2.56', *Kartäusermystik und -mystiker*, Vol. 5, Analecta Cartusiana 55, 1982, 79–103. In Vol. 2 of *Kartäusermystik und -mystiker* Michael G. Sargent presented 'The Self-Verification of Visionary Phenomena: Richard Methley's *Experimentum Veritatis*', 121–37. An account of Methley's life and works is to be found in the introduction to my edition of 'Richard Methley: To Hew Heremyte: . . .', (*op. cit.*), and in James Hogg, 'Mount Grace Charterhouse and Late Medieval English Spirituality', in *Collectanea Cartusiensia* 3, Analecta Cartusiana 82, 1980, 1–53, particularly pp. 25–39, and in my article 'Richard Methley' in *Dictionnaire de Spiritualité*, 10, Paris, 1979, 1100–1103.

4. *The Cloud of Unknowing*, The Classics of Western Spirituality, New York, Ramsey, Toronto, 1981.

5. *Ibid.*, pp. 14–19.

6. The text of Methley's Latin version of *The Cloud* including his glosses will be printed in Analecta Cartusiana 120, the concluding volume of the series. The Bodleian MS. 856 and Pembroke MS. 221 will be produced on facing pages to facilitate the comparison.

7. Dr. Vincent Gillespie examined the MS. for me, but was unable to throw any light on the question.

8. F. Madan & H. H. E. Craster (eds.), *The Summary Catalogue of Western MSS. in the Bodleian Library*, II, 456, in describing this manuscript under the no. 2625, declare that *The Cloud of Unknowing* is attributed to Walter Hilton! The MS. has currently the shelf-mark R 6.15/2. On two fly leaves the indication 'Bod. 856' appears, on one of which 'Olim MS Super D. 26 (2625) Arch. F. 26' is inscribed.

9. F. Madan & H. H. E. Craster, *op. cit.*, 456, maintain 'the first half of the 15th cent'.

10. The folios measure 9¾ × 7 inches.

11. It is composed of gatherings of 10.

12. Cf. E. M. Thompson, *The Carthusian Order in England*, London 1930, pp. 313–334, and James Hogg, 'Mount Grace Charterhouse and Late Medieval English Spirituality, *op. cit.*, pp. 14–17.

13. *Op. cit.*, I, p. 280.

14. Cf. the description of the MS. on p. xi of her Early English Text Society edition *op. cit.*, and her comments on its relationship to Bodleian 856 on pp. xxvi–xxvii.

15. *Ibid.*, p. xxvi.

16. *Op. cit.*, 1, p. 280.

17. *The Cloud of Unknowing*, ed. Phyllis Hodgson, Early English Text Society, O.S, 218, London, 1944, p. 45, l. 19. All references to the text of *The Cloud* are to this edition which is more readily available in libraries than the Analecta Cartusiana edition.

18. This passage is quoted by Hodgson in a footnote on p. xxvi.

19. *Idem.*

20. *Ibid.*, p. 173.

21. *Ibid.*, pp. 173–76.

22. Michael Sargent recently suggested to me that perhaps Methley thought the *Speculum Animarum Simplicium* was in some way connected with the Order or, at least, that he found both the texts contained in Pembroke MS. 221 in a manuscript that has not come down to us. On f. 41ʳ, over the left hand column before the prayer preceding *The Mirror*, Dom Darker wrote: 'Iste liber aliter intitulatur Ruushbroke qui fuit prior de ordine cartusiensi et hunc libellum primo composuit'. It seems that Groenendael near Brussels was mistaken for the Charterhouse of Vauvert near Paris, Vallis viridis, of which house Ruusbroec was assumed to have been the prior! I abstain from any discussion of the Latin version of *The Mirror*, as Michael Sargent is treating this topic at the congress at the Benedictine Abbey of Engelberg in Switzerland in September 1984.

23. His obit is recorded in the Parkminster Charterhouse MS. B. 62, f. 171ᵛ.

24. The description of the manuscript in M. R. James, *A Descriptive Catalogue of the Manuscripts in the Library of Pembroke College, Cambridge*, Cambridge, 1905, pp. 197–99, is inadequate in the light of more recent research.

25. I follow the actual numbering on the MS. Walsh & Colledge, *op. cit.*, p. 55, report one folio as missing. Their numbering for their projected edition, to judge by the proofs, must be based on a different system.

26. The squares appear to contain an interlaced 'b' and 't'.

27. Walsh and Colledge, *op. cit.*, p. 56.

28. Unfortunately, the MS. cannot be located at the moment, so the folio cannot be indicated.

29. Walsh and Colledge, *op. cit.*, p. 58, report: 'The same hand has written, in the margin of f. 5c, opposite "Et si tui ipsius oblitus fueris, ergo nullam cognicionem in actu pro tunc de deo habebis" [this is in chapter 3 of *The Cloud*], another "cave". . .'. The ink must have faded badly at this point, as the word is not visible on the microfilm supplied by the Cambridge University Library.

30. Neither the date nor the source of its acquisition is known.

31. F. 39^v, col. 2.

32. *Testamenta Eboracensia* IV, ed. James Raine, Surtees Society 53, 1868, 189.

33. Parkminster Charterhouse MS. B. 62, f. 17^v. This manuscript contains the original *cartae* of the General Chapter.

34. The possibility that *The Cloud* was translated to facilitate its circulation on the continent through Carthusian channels, as was the case with some of the works of Rolle and Hilton is extremely doubtful, as not only has no Latin copy of *The Cloud* been located on the continent to date, but no catalogue entries can be found referring to it. Also the presence of *The Mirror* in the Pembroke MS. suggests a more local and specific purpose. On the circulation of such Latin versions abroad, cf. Michael Sargent, 'The Transmission by the English Carthusians of some Late Medieval Spiritual Writings', *op. cit.*, 234–36. A further copy of the Latin *Scala perfectionis* is to be found in the Biblioteca Nazionale di Napoli MS. VII G 31: cf. *Cenci, Manoscritti francescani della Biblioteca Nazionale di Napoli*, Quaracchi, Florentiae 1971, p. 595.

35. *Op. cit.*, p. 65.

36. This in spite of the testimony of *The Book of Margery Kempe* concerning the 'enthusiasm' of Methley and his colleague, John Norton. These references are collected in James Hogg, Richard Methley: To Hew Heremyte: A Pystyl of Solytary Lyfe Nowadayes', *op. cit.*, p. 91, fn. 2.

37. *Op. cit.*, p. 65.

38. Ff. 1^v, col. 1–2^r, col. 1. My transcription differs on a number of points from that offered by the Walsh and Colledge proofs.

39. Some of his preface seems to echo Hugh of Balma's *Viae Syon Lugent*, from whom Methley may have borrowed quotes from Denis the Areopagite.

40. *Op. cit.*, p. 13, ll. 9–10.

41. F. 4^v, col. 1.

42. *Op. cit.*, p. 15, ll. 10–12.

43. F. 5^r, col. 1.

44. *Op. cit.*, p. 32, ll. 17–21.

45. F. 9^v, col. 1.

46. *Op. cit.*, p. 33, ll. 11–14.

47. F. 9^v, col. 1.

48. *Op. cit.*, p. 48, ll. 14–16.

49. F. 15^r, col. 1.

50. *Op. cit.*, p. 74, ll. 5–7.

51. F. 22^v, col. 2.

52. *Op. cit.*, p. 81, ll. 5–8.

53. F. 24^v, col. 2.

54. Walsh and Colledge, *op. cit.*, pp. 67–68. Walsh, *The Cloud of Unknowing*, *op. cit.*, pp. 23–26, repeats the hypothesis of Methley's possible dependence on Guigo du Pont. The quotation from Guigo du Pont was taken from the article by J. P. Grausem, 'Le "De Contemplatione" de Guigues du Pont', *Revue d'Ascetique et de Mystique*, 10 (1929), 259–289, p. 282ff. To date, apart from the Italian translation by Emilio Piovesan, 'Guigo du Pont: *Della Contemplazione*', *Analecta Cartusiana* 45, (1979), 5–111, Grausem's article and short lexical entries have remained the only source for even extracts of the text of

Guigo du Pont's *De Contemplatione*. A full critical edition by Dom Philippe Dupont will appear in May 1984 as Analecta Cartusiana 72. Cf. in the meanwhile, Dom Philippe Dupont, 'L'Ascension mystique chez Guigues du Pont', *Kartäusermystik und -mystiker*, Analecta Cartusiana 55:1, 1981, p. 47–80.
55. F. 38ʳ, col. 1, Gloss A.
56. Walsh and Colledge, *op. cit.*, p. 68, gives a list of them.
57. *The Cloud of Unknowing, op. cit.*, p. 15.

AN APPROACH TO THE MYSTOGRAPHICAL TREATISES OF THE *CLOUD*-AUTHOR THROUGH CARL ALBRECHT'S PSYCHOLOGY OF MYSTICAL CONSCIOUSNESS

FRANZ WÖHRER

1

The most profound and sublime experience of which man is capable is the awareness of the mystical. In it lie the seeds of true science.

Albert Einstein

WHEN THE GERMAN psychologist Carl Albrecht (1902–1965) began in the late 1930s to apply meditational techniques for therapeutic purposes he could not presume that the therapeutic protocols so gained would provide him with valid psychological insights into a realm of human consciousness that had hitherto been considered entirely inaccessible to empirical psychology. More than twenty years of meticulous research eventually resulted in what can now be considered the first and, as yet, only systematic 'psychology of mystical consciousness' verified by empirical data. Unlike its 'classical' antecedents,[1] Albrecht's psychology of mysticism is substantiated not merely by the spiritual autobiographies of the great mystics of the eastern and western traditions, but also upheld by the mystographical records of Albrecht's patients and by personal experience.[2] Endowed with the deep humility of a true mystic, Albrecht never revealed his charisma in his publications. We would presumably have never known that he was gratified with intimations of the mystical at various stages of his life, had not some of his private mystographical recordings been discovered by coincidence after his death. These spiritual 'protocols' seem to have escaped Albrecht when, shortly before his death, he destroyed his spiritual diaries and much of the original stock of his research materials. Initially a sceptical scientist with a keen medical interest in the structure of the human mind, Albrecht later in life, illuminated by genuine mystical experience, became a scientist-mystic, converting to Roman Catholicism and devoting his life to the exploration of the psychological dimension of religious experience. The results of his research were first published in two book-length studies in the 1950s—the first entitled *Psychologie des Mystischen Bewußtseins*, and the second *Das Mystische Erkennen*.[3] The fact that the former publication was re-issued in 1976 and the latter in 1982 illustrates topical scholarly interest. A third volume, entitled Das *Mystische Wort*, was published in 1974 from Albrecht's manuscripts, edited by H. A. Fischer-Barnicol.[4] In German-speaking countries these studies have won wide acclaim and are equally valued among theologians, psychologists and scholars in mysticism from other fields. Karl Rahner, for instance, has acknowledged Albrecht's achievement as an 'important contribution to a new theology of mysticism'.[5] Regrettably, none of these studies has been translated to date, a fact which might explain why Albrecht's psychology has so far gone virtually unnoticed outside Germany, Austria and Switzerland.[6]

Before the attempt is made to illustrate the relevance of Albrecht's psychology to the elucidation of the mystical treatises of the *Cloud*-author, it seems necessary to offer a concise resumé of the major results of his empirical research. This, however, is a task not easily accomplished. First, because a summary of what has been systematically expounded in two book-length studies is not easily achieved within the limited scope available in this paper, and, secondly, because many of Albrecht's intricate and highly specialised concepts, though all lucid and meticulously precise in their definitions, elude adequate translation into English.

Albrecht's 'psychology of mystical consciousness' is based on the scientific analysis of several hundred records of mystical and pseudo-mystical experiences, collected over a period of twenty-four years from persons he had introduced to the practice of meditation and, in addition, on his own recordings of personal mystical experiences. By critically separating 'authentic' from pseudo-mystical phenomena (e.g. phenomena of the paranormal, pathological or hypnagogic phenomena, phenomena induced by drugs, or evoked by hallucination etc.), he was able to disclose a wide range of phenomena constituting the structure of 'mystical consciousness'—or, more precisely, the limited realm of 'mystical consciousness' accessible to empirical research. Albrecht, never presumed that he achieved the impossible—a *full* phenomenology of what is ultimately ineffable and inexplicable. He emphasises that empirical psychology can grasp only a few specific modes of mystical awareness and describe—within the limits imposed by language and scientific method—the phenomenological structure of only one mental state in which mystical phenomena may become manifest. Albrecht likewise stresses that a scientific concept of mysticism must not operate with terms charged with philosophical or religious meanings. He therefore dispenses with the traditional terminology of mystical psychology and introduces a series of new technical terms, which are all carefully and clearly defined. A few conventional terms, however, which are semantically not charged with oblique or speculative connotations, are retained by him, but all are psychologically re-defined so as to meet the demands of modern science. Epitomized in a single sentence, Albrecht's definition rests on three complex psychological key-concepts:

> mysticism, is the 'in-coming' of an 'all-encompassing' in the state of 'sunkenness'. (Mystik ist das Ankommen eines Umfassenden im Versunkenheitsbewußtsein.[7]).

The following exposition of these key-concepts will provide a short introduction to Albrecht's mystical psychology.

A The state of 'sunkenness'

Albrecht's definition, while asserting that the mystical is experienced in a specifically structured mental condition, which he calls 'sunkenness', does not imply that genuine mystical experience cannot occur in mental states other than 'sunkenness', (e.g. in the normal waking state, in dreams etc.). The implication is only that with the methodological means currently available empirical psychology can only hypothetically sustain, but not verify any such claim. Due to the limitations imposed by the scientific method, the psychological concept of mysticism must be strictly confined to a mental condition against the background of which the apprehension of genuine mystical phenomena can be distinguished from pseudo-mystical apparitions (e.g. illusions, hallucinations, dreams, visions induced by drugs, etc.). Psychological criteria of authenticity, in other words, can be provided only if the spiritual experience occurs in a

> . . . coherently structured hyper-lucid, unified mental state, which is entirely voided of (conceptual) content and permeated by a mood of calm

> (. . . ein durchgängig geordneter, überklarer, vereinheitlichter Bewußtseinszustand, dessen Bewußtseinsraum entleert ist und dessen Grundbefindlichkeit die Ruhe ist[8]

as 'sunkenness' is defined. Its psycho-phenomenological structure thus differs fundamentally from that of the heterogeneous 'waking-state'; unlike it, the state of 'sunkenness' is voided of all conceptual activities, of sense impressions conveyed through the physical senses; the mind is entirely screened off from stimuli from the outside world; it is emptied of pictures evoked by the subconscious or by the imagination; of the diversity of feelings and desires related to objects of the material world; and it is undisturbed by acts of the will, inner tensions, urges, afflictions, sorrows etc. of the every-day world. The state of 'sunkenness' is furthermore clearly distinguished from all other mental states by virtue of its exceptionally high degree of lucidity and homogeneity. In fact, 'it is the clearest and most lucid state we know'[9]. Though voided of all the disturbing elements of the 'waking state', 'sunkenness' does not constitute a 'mental blank'. Anyone experiencing this mental condition retains, as Albrecht emphasises, a clear awareness of self, of the basic mood of calm permeating his mind and of the spontaneous activity of the 'inner eye' ('Innenschau', subsequently translated as 'intro-spection'), operating entirely independent of the intellect and acts of the will. Anyone in the state of 'sunkenness', says Albrecht,

> . . . who becomes aware of this state . . . experiences consciousness as an organically structured space in which something happens which he can observe with perfect clarity and in a mood of calm.

> (Jeder Versunkene, welcher sich des Zustandes der Versunkenheit bewußt wird, erlebt sein Bewußtsein als einen einheitlich gefügten Raum, in dem etwas abrollt, dem er klar bewußt, in der Ruhe stehend, zuschaut.[10]

The perceptions of the 'inner eye' are cognitively experienced as either emerging from within 'the sphere of the self' ('Selbstsphäre'), or as penetrating ('incoming', 'arriving') from 'beyond the individual consciousness' ('von außerhalb des Bewußtseinsraumes ankommend'). The former are ruled out by Albrecht as instances of genuine mystical experience. On the other hand, 'in-coming phenomena', intuitively perceived as penetrating from 'beyond the sphere of the self' only qualify as genuinely mystical if they are experienced as 'all-encompassing' in substance. What Albrecht means by this will be detailed under *C* below. Albrecht distinguishes eleven different 'forms' in which 'in-coming' phenomena can become manifest in 'intro-spection'. These eleven 'forms' are, however, only a small selection of the vast number of 'forms' that can actually be encountered in empirical reality. In psychological reality the individual forms only rarely occur in isolation. More often than not the inner apprehensions are composed of 'composite forms' ('Gesamtform') or a dynamic series of 'composite forms'. The specific nature of these 'composite forms' is to some extent shaped by the individuality of the experiencing self and may change in the course of a successive series of 'in-coming' experiences during lifetime. Within the limited scope of this paper it may suffice to refer briefly to six of these 'forms'.

B The 'in-coming' phenomenon—'forms' of manifestation

'In-coming' phenomena may manifest themselves in 'intro-spection' ('Innenschau'):

i visually, in the shape of a mental picture (e.g. images emerging spon-taneously in consciousness; visual memories, visions, with or without symbolic import, etc.). These mental pictures 'arrive' spontaneously in the vista of the 'inner eye'. They may but need not necessarily have mystical quality. According to Albrecht, a visionary experience in the state of 'sunkenness' can be called genuinely mystical only if it is concomitant with the non-visual awareness of the presence of the 'all-encompassing' and/or with the cognition of the spiritual vision or 'showing' as being something bestowed or 'in-wrought' ('eingewirkt') by the 'all-encompassing'. For the experiencing self this cognitive awareness is a fundamental truth which is beyond all doubt.

ii emotionally, in the shape of a 'responsive feeling' ('antwortendes Fühlen'). Here feelings are perceived as 'in-coming' phenomena or the 'objects' of inner apprehension, which permeate consciousness, e.g. profound feelings of love, awe, 'angst', peace, or a deep sense of yearning for something unknown and unknowable; rapture, bliss, etc.

iii cognitively, in the shape of 'intuition'. By this Albrecht understands the instantaneous 'in-coming' of cognitive insights, not derived from syllogisms but perfectly true. The instantaneous insight of the scientist, the inspiration dawning upon the artist and the mystic's cognitive awareness of the non-visual presence of the divine are all instances of this form of 'in-coming'.

iv verbally, 'in the shape of language'. Here single words or sets of words become manifest visually as the objects of the 'inner perception'.

v non-visually—in the shape of an 'awareness of the presence of the all-encompassing experienced as a persona' ('die Form der unanschaulichen Bewußtheit von der Anwesenheit des personalen Umfassenden').[11] One of the most frequently recorded phenomena of genuine mystical experience, this is the intuitive awareness of a presence, numinous and all-encompassing and often experienced as a guiding or protecting persona or as loving thou.

vi auditively—in the shape of 'audition' ('das in auditiver Form Ankom-mende').[12] The 'in-coming' phenomenon is here perceived as an inner hearing of individual words, sentences, spoken snippets, or sound sequences etc. Auditions can be rated among the genuine modes of mystical experience if apprehended and verified as 'messages' originating from the 'all-encompassing'—for instance, if subjectively experienced with absolute certainty as words spoken by the all-encompassing loving thou and verified, at least tentatively as not intruded from within the sphere of subjective consciousness. Syntactically, auditions often take the form of a command, order or a summons.[13]

The pivotal concept in Albrecht's definition is that of

C The 'all-encompassing' ('das Umfassende').

The cognitive awareness of the 'all-encompassing' nature of the 'spiritual object' apprehended in 'intro-spection' is a distinctive feature and 'conditio sine qua non' of genuine mystical experience. The unique psycho-phenomenological characteristics adhering to it are the qualities of:

i 'alienness and finality' ('Fremdheit und Letztheit'). The 'all-encompassing' is perceived as something absolute and primordeal, originating from an unknown and unknowable sphere to whose 'wholeness' ('ganzheitliche Einheit') all past, present and future experiences relate in a way incomprehensible to reason.[14]

ii the ultimate incomprehensibility of the 'all-encompassing'. The 'all-encompassing' can be perceived with the spiritual senses, but it cannot be known. The 'mystical object' is experienced as something ultimately unknowable, incomprehensible and ineffable. However, this sense of the unknowable nature of the 'all-encompassing' is reduced in the more ecstatic stages of mystical awareness and must be assumed to be entirely removed in the highest state of mystical ecstasy, which Albrecht, adopting the conventional term, calls 'union' ('Einigung'). This latter statement is rendered by him in hypothetical terms, since the inner structure of the unitive experience eludes psychological description. Some features of the 'ecstatic consciousness', however, can be grasped psychologically. They can be inferred hypothetically from the 'phenomenological antecedents' of ecstasy experienced in the state of 'sunkenness'.

iii the personal, a-personal or 'crypto-personal' nature of the 'all-encompassing'. The 'all-encompassing' can either be perceived as a persona, dwelling in, loving, acting in or upon the perceiving self, or as something entirely a-personal, for example, when apprehended as the infinite, the all, the void, endless space etc. It may finally be intuitively recognized as something originating from and sent or 'wrought by' the all-encompassing persona. Thus, intuitions, auditions or visions can be experienced as being 'harbingers' or tokens of the 'all-encompassing'.

iv 'revelation' ('Offenbarung').[15] The manifestation of the 'all-encompassing' is experienced as a spiritual revelation.

v 'numinosity'. The apprehension of the 'all-encompassing' is a numinous experience in that it evokes an intense emotional response composed either of a deep sense of joy, peace, bliss, love, rapture, ecstasy etc., elicited when the 'all-encompassing' is perceived as a 'mysterium fascinosum', or of intense feelings of 'angst', awe, anguish, despair etc., released when the 'all-encompassing' is perceived as a 'mysterium tremendum'.

Apart from the 'narrow', i.e. strictly empirical concept of mysticism, Albrecht proposes a supplementary one, which is less stringently empirical in that it is hypothetically inferred rather than analytically deduced from empirical research. It is based on the proposition that the most intense forms of mystical awareness are not perceived in the serene state of 'sunkenness', but in the exalted state of 'ecstatic consciousness'. According to this 'extended' ('erweiterter') concept, mysticism

> . . . is both the 'in-coming' of an 'all-encompassing' in the state of 'sunkenness' and the ecstatic experience of an 'all-encompassing'.
>
> (Mystik ist sowohl das Ankommen eines Umfassenden im Versunkenheits-bewußtsein als auch das ekstatische Erleben eines Umfassenden).[16]

The central phenomenological characteristic of the 'ecstatic consciousness' is the reduced sense of self-awareness. In the highest state of mystical ecstasy any awareness of an ontological distinction between the contemplating self and the 'mystical object' contemplated is allegedly entirely suspended. However, despite the sincere and impassioned reassurances of all the great mystics of east and west that mystical union involves the 'total loss', 'extinction', 'dissolution', 'annihilation' and the complete merging or 'onyng' of the self with the divine, Albrecht argues persuasively that the claim of the total suspension of self-awareness is psychologically not tenable. Even if transported into the state of highest ecstasy the mystic must necessarily retain some sense of self-awareness, however dim, otherwise any memory of such a unitive experience would be impossible. However 'real', the spiritual union with the transcendental power is perceived by the mystic subjectively, in empirical reality the complete extinction of any conscious-ness of self is an objective psychological fact only—the moment of cerebral death aside—in the state of unconsciousness. Described in strictly psycho-logical terms, the 'unio mystica' is the most intense mode of awareness of the mystical involving the maximal reduction of self-awareness. Albrecht agrees with most scholars in mysticism that the unitive experience is only a rare or even a unique event in the life of a mystic, but unlike many other scholars he categorically denies that the experience of union is the ultimate criterion for a spiritual apprehension to be accepted as genuinely mystical. For him the difference between unitive and non-unitive mystical experience is merely one of intensity, but not substance. All forms of spiritual apprehension of the 'all-encompassing' in the states of 'sunkenness' and 'ecstasy' are thus equally genuine instances of mystical experience.

Albrecht's psychology, though acclaimed in Germany as a unique achievement in the study of the spiritual nature of man, is certainly not uncontroversial and will undoubtedly be met with objections, particularly on the part of theology and modern behaviourist psychology. Since Christian mysticism is theologically conceived as a 'cognitio Dei experimentalis' bestowed on man by an act of grace, theology might object that Albrecht's strictly psychological definition is incompatible with the orthodox theological concept. Albrecht would refute such criticism. As a scientist he has to dispense with any theological concept, but this does not imply that his psychology of mysticism cannot be reconciled with the theology of grace. There is not the slightest indication in his studies that he denies the necessity of grace for the divine vision to be bestowed. Incidentally, Albrecht remains emphatically insistent throughout that meditational techniques alone, though instrumental to the integration of higher states of consciousness, can neither evoke mystical experience nor are they a necessary precondition for it. Moreover, he makes it unmistakably clear that any conscious endeavour to evoke or induce mystical apprehensions by artificial means (e.g. by drugs, hypnosis, suggestion etc.) will be abortive, since mysticism is 'per definitionem' the self-revelation of the 'all-encompassing' and thus expressly an experience bestowed rather than attained. And this in fact is a way of saying in psychological terms that grace is indispensable. Albrecht's concept, finally, is only apparently at variance with Biblical accounts of visionary mystical experiences which were obviously perceived in mental conditions other than 'sunkenness' or 'ecstasy', in particular in dreams (e.g. Samuel) and in the waking state (e.g. Aaron).[17] As has been briefly mentioned above, Albrecht's definition does not imply that manifestations of the mystical cannot occur during sleep, in the normal waking state or in any other mental condition. He merely insists that empirical psychology has neither the criteria nor scientific methods available to verify such experiences as authentic. The phenomenological method, invaluable as it is for the identification and verification of mystical experiences perceived in the state of 'sunkenness', reaches its limits if applied as a method of distinguishing genuine from pseudo-mystical phenomena manifested in dreams or in the waking consciousness.

With these considerations in mind it will be attempted in the following section to relate Albrecht's insights to the psychological data underlying the *Cloud*-author's spiritual guidance. That is to say that the interdisciplinary approach to the treatises starts from the proposition that the psychological phenomena germane to the treatises, though largely couched and interpreted in religious terms, and regardless of whether they reflect personal experience or to what extent non-experiential data are incorporated, are open to psycho-phenomenological analysis. The results of this analysis should permit insights not only into the psychological dynamics pertaining to the meditative process described and into the nature of the emotional responses evoked at various stages of the 'mystic ascent', but also into the structure of mystical consciousness, including specific 'forms' of 'in-coming' phenomena, and into the structure of non-mystical states of consciousness and the specific 'in-coming' phenomena relating to them.

2

Before actually turning to this analysis, however, a few words must be said on the issue of the originality of the *Cloud*-author's Christian psychology of mysticism. Recent scholarship has persuasively demonstrated that the mystical theology germane to the treatises is highly eclectic, incorporating and assimilating a wide range of fundamental concepts derived from major and minor authorities of the Christian mystical tradition. Among the sources and influences identified to date are Augustine, the Pseudo-Dionysius, Gregory the Great, Bernard of Clairvaux, Thomas Gallus, Hugh of Balma and Richard of St Victor, to name only a few.[18] On the other hand, it has also been noted that, despite the author's manifold debts to Christian mystical psychology—which is, for instance, reflected in his terminology, imagery, the adoption of the traditional pattern of the mystic ascent (purgation-illumination—union/perfection),[19] and, to some extent in the pheno-menological descriptions of specific mental states and spiritual experiences pertaining to different stages of 'meditation' and 'contemplation'—his practical spiritual guidance is also 'profoundly original in the sense that no other either before or after, sets out exactly the same points of emphasis'.[20] Apart from being an erudite theologian, the anonymous spiritual, mentor was undoubtedly an advanced contemplative himself, 'who had known his method to work'[21]—and this is where his originality ultimately seems to derive from. Endowed with a rare gift of acute psychological observation, the *Cloud*-author evidently incorporated personal experience into his practical exposition of traditional mystical doctrine. His rare psychological acumen is particularly manifest in his perceptive spiritual counsel, which is carefully adapted to the individual needs of the young aspirant to the contemplative life to whom *The Cloud* and *Privy Counselling* are addressed, and in which he displays a most sensitive understanding of the difficulties, pitfalls and dangers inherent in the spiritual struggle for self-transcendence. But it is also evident in his discerning phenomenological insight into the structure of mystical consciousness and its dynamics within the meditational process. His rare gifts of keen psychological observation and penetrating self-analysis—particularly reflected in the perceptive and ramified psycho-logical descriptions of those mental states and spiritual phenomena, which we may assume to be transcriptions from personal experience rather than expositions of mystical doctrine or the author's anagogic exegesis of

Scripture—will presumably be more fully acknowledged if collated with Albrecht's empirical phenomenology of mystical consciousness.

The process of meditation, to begin with, as conceived by the *Cloud*-author, corresponds functionally and, to some extent phenomenologically (though not formally), to the structure of the 'meditative process' ('Versenkungsablauf') as described by Albrecht. While assuming the traditional pattern of the mystic ascent, with the successive stages of *purgation, illumination* and *perfection* or *union*, the spiritual guide devotes most of his psychological exposition to the purgative stage. Motivated by the 'nakid entent' stretched 'out vnto God' the contemplative's progress to 'perfeccion' develops from the troubled state of 'waking consciousness' to the untroubled, lucid and unified state of 'contemplation'.[22] Like Albrecht, the *Cloud*-author characterizes 'meditation' psychologically in terms of a mental process effecting the 'voiding' of consciousness of diversity and multiplicity, thereby incidentally using a term which perfectly matches the Albrechtian concept of 'Entleerung'. The medieval mystagogue takes considerable pains to expound to his disciple the purpose and essence of the meditative purification of consciousness. The 'ful acordyng abilnes to resseyue [the gift of] grace',[23] he says, cannot be attained unless the contemplative has radically emptied his mind of any object that might stand 'betwix' him 'and his God'. And:

. . . ʒif euer schal þis grace be getin, it behoueþ to be lerned of God fro wiþinne, vnto whom þou hast listeli lenid many day before wiþ alle þe loue of þin herte, vtterly voiding fro þi goostly beholding alle maner of siʒt of any þing bineþe him, þof al þat som of þoo þinges, þat I bid þee þus voide, schuld seme in þe siʒt of som man a ful worþi mene to gete God bi.[24]

The spiritual advisor stresses in particular (and again in striking agreement with Albrecht) that the process of the 'voiding' of normal waking consciousness involves, first of all, the complete screening off from the stimuli and objects of the physical world ('Abblendung').[25] Harking back to the Dionysian image of the 'cloud' the spiritual guide exhorts his friend to put 'a cloud of forʒeting bitwix þee & alle þe creatures þat euer ben maad'.[26] It involves, secondly, the complete divestment of the mind of any conceptual activities: the state of 'sunkenness', and thus the state of pure receptivity to 'in-coming' phenomena is, according to Albrecht, incompatible with discursive thought or any mental process governed by the will. The *Cloud*-author likewise instructs his pupil that conceptual thought must be blotted out, otherwise any further progress towards more integrated states of consciousness would be disrupted. Aware of the difficulties involved in the struggle against conceptual operations persistently assailing the mind he emphatically warns his disciple never to submit to a train of thought intruding upon him:

. . . þe scharp steryng of þin vnderstanding, þat wile alweis prees apon þee when þou settest þee to þis blynd werk, behoueþ alweys be born doun; & bot þou bere him doun, he wile bere þee doun; insomochel þat whan þou wenest best to abide in þis derknes, & þat nou3t is in þi mynde bot only God, & þou loke witterly þou schalt fynde þi mynde not ocupied in þis derknes bot in a cleer beholdyng of som þing beneeþ God. . . .[27]

The *Cloud*-author's demand for the removal of conceptual content is—like Albrecht's—absolute and includes expressly any form of conceptual religious worship. Devotion, vocal prayer or meditation on the Passion, though indispensable to the initial stage of the contemplative life, would interfere with the mental development towards homogeneity and must therefore be temporarily suspended:

. . . in þis werk it profiteþ litil or nou3t to þink of þe kyndenes or þe worþines of God, ne on oure Lady, ne on þe seintes or aungelles in heuen, ne 3it on þe ioies in heuen: þat is to say, wiþ a special beholding to hem, as þou woldest bi þat beholding fede & encrees þi purpos. I trowe þat on no wise it schuld be so in þis caas & in þis werk. For þof al it be good to þink apon þe kindenes of God, & to loue hym & preis him for hem: 3it it is fer betyr to þink apon þe nakid beying of him, ...[28]

The third category of disturbing 'mental objects' to be removed are pictures of the imagination. The divestment of the mind of

. . . dyuerse vnordeynd ymages of bodely creatures; or elles sum fantasye, þe whiche is nou3t elles bot a bodely conseyte of a goostly þing, or elles a goostly conseyte of a bodely þing . . .[29]

impetuously intruding upon the 'meditating self' and lingering in the mind with unflagging perseverance is seen by the *Cloud*-author as the most arduous and frustrating part of 'meditation'. In fact he asserts that even long-term practice and persistent endeavour will be of no avail unless the contemplative is assisted in his struggle by God's special grace. Theologically this postulate is consonant with orthodox mystical teaching, in particular with that of Richard of St Victor (died 1173),[30] which propounds that the corrupting power of the imagination is a consequence of original sin. Once vitiated by the Fall the imaginative faculties of man will never cease to elicit 'sum fantasye' or 'vnordeynd image' unless 'refreyned by . . . grace'. Read in strictly psychological terms, the above passage would imply that mental images are more resistant to being banished by meditative techniques than other conceptual content of 'waking consciousness'. Incidentally, several of Albrecht's subjects reported to have had similar difficulties in their struggle against persevering images or fantasies haunting their minds. These data were, however, statistically not significant. The overall results of Albrecht's research do not allow the inference that the activities of the imaginative faculty are more persevering in the meditative process than other conceptual faculties.

When the contemplative has succeeded in 'vtterly voiding fro . . . [his] goostly beholding alle maner of si3t of any þing bineþe him [i.e. God]',[31] he will be left with a 'blynde feling' of his 'own nakid beying' and with a clear awareness that his 'inner eye' is confronted with a 'nou3t' or mental 'derknes'; that is to say in Albrecht's terminology, that the contemplative has reached the initial stage of 'sunkenness', in which he becomes passively aware of his own consciousness as a mental blank, for the time being devoided of all content. At that incipient stage the contemplating self is perceptive to (but as yet unaware of) 'in-coming' phenomena. Such 'in-coming' phenomena will gradually 'arrive' in the vista of 'introspection' and are, at that stage of 'lower contemplation', usually non-mystical in nature. Both Albrecht and the *Cloud*-author are equally unanimous in their insistence that the novice will first meet with phenomena emerging from 'within the sphere of the self'. In particular he will be confronted with a spontaneous awareness of his own true self—an 'in-coming' phenomenon called by Albrecht 'spontaneous self-recognition' ('schauendes Selbstverstehen')[32] and characterised as a passive confrontation with one's own wretchedness, faults, weaknesses or moral transgressions committed in life. The *Cloud*-author describes such a purgative 'in-coming' experience in chapter 69 of *The Cloud*:

> . . . at þe first tyme þat a soule lokiþ þerapon, [i.e. þe nou3t] it schal fynde alle þe specyal dedes of sinne þat euer he did siþen he was borne, bodely or goostly, priuely or derkly, peyntid þerapon. & howsoeuer þat he torniþ it aboute, euermore þei wil apere before his i3en, vnto þe tyme be þat wiþ moche harde trauayle, many sore si3inges, & many bitter wepynges he haue in grete party rubbid hem away.[33]

Albrecht's research fully corroborates the *Cloud*-author's propositon that such a cognitive awareness of one's own sinful self will effect either a temporary or a lasting renewal of the individual personality. There is also perfect agreement that the passive confrontation with one's own true self is a pivotal experience in the life of a contemplative and of vital significance for his further spiritual development. The *Cloud*-author's promise that his disciple, once he has gained 'a trewe knowyng & feling of' himself as he is, will 'sone after . . . haue a trewe knowyng & felyng of God as he is'[34] is strikingly consonant with the records of those subjects of Albrecht who were gratified with intimations of the 'all-encompassing', all of which confirm that the purgative experience precedes and prepares for the 'in-coming' experience of the 'all-encompassing'. The spiritual director's instruction

> . . . þat he schal be maad so vertuous & so charitable by þe vertewe of þis werke þat his wille schal be afterwardes, whan he condescendiþ to comoun or to pray for his euen-Cristen— . . . fro þe hei3t of þis werk [i.e. contemplation] . . . —as specialy þan directe to his foo as to his freende, his fremmyd as his sib. 3e! somtyme more to his fo þen to his freende . . .[35]

is thus perfectly in line with reports by Albrecht's subjects affirming that the moral change effected by the meditative confrontation with one's own self becomes particularly manifest in a deep sense of charity and humility.

Among the other forms of non-mystical 'in-coming' phenomena reported by Albrecht's subjects and the *Cloud*-author in strikingly similar terms are a wide range of specifically religious moods, feelings and desires. The advanced contemplative 'abiding' in the state of 'sunkenness' may, for instance, be instantaneously overwhelmed, or gradually become aware in 'intro-spection' of deep feelings and desires directed at or related to God, which are, however, definitely not perceived as penetrating from beyond the individual consciousness. The *Cloud*-author instructs his spiritual friend that he may, for example, be transported by 'diuerse wonderful swetnes & counfortes', afflicted by a 'holy sorow', or moved by 'a reuerent stering of lasting loue' and by a 'holy desire' to offer up his own 'nakid beyng'. Phenomenologically, the 'stronge & deep goostly sorow' afflicting the advanced contemplative when absorbed in a mental condition which the *Cloud*-author appropriately likens to 'a slepe' corresponds to what Albrecht calls the deep sense of 'yearning for something unknown and unknowable' emerging in 'sunkenness'. Especially important is the instruction that the contemplating self must passively surrender to the mood emerging in consciousness:

> . . . þou schalt beware in þe tyme of þis sorow þat þou neiþer to rudely streyne þi body ne þi spirit, bot sit ful stylle, as it were in slepying slei3t, al forsobbid & forsonken in sorow.[36]

The caution that the contemplative should 'beware' lest he should strain his 'body' or his 'spirit' when absorbed in this holy 'sorow' is in keeping with Albrecht's insight that the structure of 'sunkenness', and with it, the sensitivity to 'in-coming' or 'in-dwelling' phenomena, is inevitably destroyed by a single act of the will.

The apprehension of deep religious feelings, however delightful, reassuring or comforting, is, however, only a corollary of the mystic way, but not the ultimate goal of the contemplative life. The 'goostly sorow', the 'nakid felyng of loue strecht out vnto God' and the 'holy desire to [offer] up' one's 'nakid beyng' are, as the mystagogue stresses, merely 'tokens' confirming that the contemplative has reached the 'ful acordyng abilnes to resseyue' the gift of special grace. The final progression to the 'hi3er partye of contemplacion', and thus to 'perfeccion', entirely depends on grace, which is 'bestowed' or 'wiþheld' 'whan it likiþ vnto God'.[37] In this 'higher part of contemplation' the contemplative is gratified with various modes of 'vnknowing' awareness of God's presence, which can be unitive—in the contemplative having reached 'perfeccion'—or non-unitive—in the contemplative having reached the stage of 'illumination'.

In the *Cloud*-author's canon there are several instances in which he discloses with penetrating insight specific aspects of the psychological nature of individual modes of non-unitive mystical experiences. Although his mystographical descriptions are, on the whole, rather short (the most comprehensive ones scarcely exceed three sentences) they nevertheless recapture all the crucial phenomenological characteristics of mystical consciousness as defined by Albrecht. This is perhaps best illustrated by a passage from *Privy Counselling*:

> . . . wel is þis werk licnyd to a slepe. For as in þe slepe þe vse of þe bodely wittys is cesid, þat þe body may take his ful rest in fedyng & in strengþing of þe bodely kynde: riȝt so in þis goostly sleep þe wantoun questyons of þe wilde goostly wittys, ymaginatyue resons, ben fast bounden & vtterly voided, so þat þe sely soule may softely sleep & rest in þe louely beholdyng of God as he is, in ful fedyng & strengþing of þe goostly kynde.[38]

The non-unitive mystical experience described here corresponds phenomenologically to what Albrecht calls 'the non-visual awareness of the presence of a personal all-enccompassing' ('unanschauliche Bewußtheit von der Anwesenheit des personalen Umfassenden'),[39] apprehended in 'sunkenness'. The experience definitely occurs against the background of a peaceful, untroubled mental state which is 'vtterly voided' of all intellectual activities ('þe vse of þe bodely wittys' and of 'þe wantoun questyons of þe wilde goostly wittys . . . is cesid') as well as of all activities of the imagination ('ymaginatyue resons' are 'fast bounden'). The state is again aptly and significantly 'licnyd to a slepe'—the simile illustrating suggestively that the mind is entirely screened off from disturbing external and internal stimuli. The contemplating self, in a state of solemn repose, is absorbed in the apprehension of the non-visual presence of God ('þe louely beholdyng of God as he is') and responds to the numinous essence of the 'non-visual mystical object' 'beheld' in 'intro-spection' with feelings of heavenly bliss ('sely soule') and reverent love ('louvely beholdyng').

Another non-unitive mode of mystical awareness is briefly touched upon in chapter 34 of *The Cloud*. It is the dynamic experience of the divine penetrating into and acting within the contemplative. In this case, 'a þing', is taking hold of the experiencing self 'þat steriþ þee to wilne & desire þou wost neuer what'. The mystagogue succinctly recaptures the experiental essence of this 'in-coming phenomenon' in his important instruction:

> . . . lat þat þing do wiþ þee & lede þee wher so it list. Lat it be þe worcher, & þou bot þe suffrer; do bot loke apon it, & lat it alone. Medel þee not þerwip as þou woldest help it, for drede lest þou spille al. . . . It suffisiþ inowȝ vnto þee þat þou fele þee steryd likyngly wiþ a þing þou wost neuer what, . . .
> . . . ȝif it be þus, trist þan stedfastly þat it is only God þat steriþ þi wyl & þi desyre, pleynly by hymself, wiþouten mene ouþer on his party or on þin.[40]

In *Privy Counselling* the spiritual guide describes an analogous experience, though with a more pronounced emphasis on the distinctly personal nature of the 'incoming' phenomenon:

> I fele verely, wiþoutyn errour or doute, þat Almiȝty God wiþ his grace behoueþ algates be þe cheef sterer & worcher, ouþer wiþ mene or wiþoutyn; & þou only, or eny oþer liche vnto þee, bot þe consenter & suffrer: sauying þat þis consent & þis suffring schal be, in þe tyme of þis werk, actuely disposid & ablid to þis werk in purete of spirit, & semely borne up to þi Souereyn. . . .[41]

Incidentally, several of Albrecht's subjects, agnostics and non-Christians among them, recorded in strikingly similar terms such an experience of being guided or acted upon by a transcendental persona or loving thou. Albrecht, after collating and phenomenologically analysing these reports, classified this experience as one specific mode of genuine mystical awareness, psychologically characterised as:

> . . . an encounter with a Thou, who is not only a Being affecting the experiencing self in the state of 'sunkenness', but also an agent acting within and working upon it. The experiencing self is not just affected, but also addressed, summoned, laden with responsibility, assessed, loved.
> (Das Ankommen eines personalen Umfassenden ist eine Begegnung mit einem Du, das nicht nur eine sich auswirkende, sondern eine von sich aus handelnde Wesenheit ist, die als Person mit dem versunkenen Ich umgeht. Das Ich wird nicht nur betroffen, sondern es wird angeredet, aufgerufen, mit Verantwortung belastet, bewertet, geliebt.[42]

This mode of mystical awareness as well as all the other 'forms' of divine manifestation described by the *Cloud*-author as part of his spiritual guidance are exclusively non-visual, non-auditive and deeply emotional. His critical attitude to all visual and auditory modes of mystical apprehension, reflected throughout, and an important feature of his mystagogic strategy, is evidently a heritage of tradition, though the specific point of emphasis of his critical attitude seems original. His profound distrust of visions, auditions and revelations has its ultimate origin (apart from the teaching of Richard of St Victor) in Augustine, who, in *De Genesi ad Litteram* (Book twelve), distinguishes three kinds of hierarchically ordered mystical visions: the '*visio intellectualis*' (i.e. non-visual modes of divine awareness), ranking highest, followed by the '*visio spiritualis*' or '*imaginaria*' (i.e. visions, auditions or illuminations apprehended by the spiritual senses) and the '*visio corporalis*' (revelations i.e. apparitions perceived by the physical senses).[43] But despite the *Cloud*-author's obvious strictures on the spiritual significance of visions and revelations within the context of the mystic ascent, he does not go as far as to deny that visual manifestations of God, whether spiritual or corporeal, can be potential instances of mystical experience in the life of a contemplative. He merely repudiates abortive attempts of pseudo-contemplatives to aspire to visionary experiences rather than to a 'blind and nakid' awareness of God. Visions and revelations, although rare charismata miraculously bestowed on a few of God's elect, are rated by him as inferior to non-visual, affective apprehensions of the divine, because they are 'mediated' forms of divine manifestation. The 'blynde felyng' of God's loving presence, on the other hand, is 'wrouȝt of þe hande of Almiȝty God wiþouten mene'[44] and is therefore the ultimate goal of a true contemplative's aspirations.

In the few and sparse descriptions of mystical experience the *Cloud*-author refers only briefly and, so it appears, reluctantly, to the specific nature of the emotional response released in the contemplative during the fleeting moment of God's loving touch. However short and ephemeral, and whatever the 'form' of divine manifestation—whether it is a 'goostly felyng' of God's 'sensible presence', or the 'louely beholding of God as he is' or a flash of 'goostly liȝt'—the experience is always described in terms of a 'fascinosum', albeit different in quality and intensity. Intimations of the divine may thus 'enflame' the contemplative 'wiþ þe fiire of his [i.e. God's] loue',[45] or elicit in him feelings of 'pees & rest', or 'ravish' him 'abouen hymself by . . . a great multytude of loue'.[46] On the whole, however, the *Cloud*-author declines to disclose more specific aspects of the inner essence of mystical experience. But this is not merely because of the ultimate ineffability of this experience. Even if language could achieve the impossible, he tells his spiritual friend he would never 'dar' to take it upon himself 'to speke wiþ [his] blabryng fleschely tongue' about 'þat werke þat falliþ to only God'.[47] Any endeavour to reveal more would, in his view, amount to a gross desecration of a sacred mystery. What he dares to reveal is merely what he feels licensed to by orthodox mystical doctrine. His strict reliance on traditional idiom and received doctrine is particularly manifest in the very few passages in which he touches upon the unitive experience. There is in fact only one passage in his canon which amounts to a phenomenological circumscription of 'goostly onyng'. Almost exclusively couched in terms derived from pseudo-Dionysian and Augustinian mystology, and focussing in particular on the phenomenon of the mystic's loss of self-awareness, the description suggestively recaptures the essence of a non-ecstatic experience of 'goostly onyng':

In þis tyme [i.e. the moment of mystical experience] it is þat þou boþe seest þi God & þi loue, & nakidly felist hym also bi goostly onyng to his loue in þe souereyn poynte of þi spirit, as he is in hymself, bot blyndely, as it may be here [i.e. on earth], vtterly spoylid of þiself & nakidly cloþed in hymself as he is, vncloþed & not lappid in any of þees sensible felynges [i.e. feelings evoked by formal prayer or religious devotion] . . . þat mowen falle in þis liif. Bot in purete of spirit propirly & parfitly he is parceyuid & felt in himself as he is, fer lengþid fro any fantasye or fals opinion þat may falle in þis liif.[48]

3

Despite the many arresting analogies in their conception of mystical experience, there seems to be a fundamental difference between Albrecht and the *Cloud*-author as regards the conception of the 'meditative process'. Whereas the *Cloud*-author remains emphatic throughout that 'meditation' is essentially a technique of *concentration* involving a long-term training of the will, Albrecht claims that concentration, though important as a preliminary technique and preparation for 'meditation' is incompatible with the 'meditative process' itself. Once initiated by an act of the will in 'waking consciousness' and motivated by the desire for the untroubled state of 'sunkenness', the 'meditative process' will, as Albrecht insists, continue to develop spontaneously towards the desired goal. Distractions and unwanted stimuli are shielded off from awareness not by conscious effort, but by a 'sub-mental inhibition', i.e. a 'habit' or conditioned reaction acquired in long-term practice. Once established as a function of higher states of consciousness, 'sub-mental inhibition' is an effective temporary barrier against mental distractions and disturbing external stimuli. Thus it is the development of this 'habit', that depends on persistent conscious effort and the intense long-term practice of concentration, but not the 'meditative process' as such. Albrecht would undoubtedly approve of the *Cloud*-author's instruction that his disciple should begin the 'hard werk' by concentrating on a 'litil worde' as a means of preventing his thoughts and emotions from scattering, and he would acknowledge that it could be a most effective technique for developing 'sub-mental inhibition'. That is to say that the difference in their conception of 'meditation' is a formal rather than a functional one. In both Albrecht and the *Cloud*-author the psychological function of meditation is basically the same: both conceive of 'meditation' as a process of re-structuring consciousness, originating in the troubled 'waking state' and developing by degrees to the untroubled state of 'sunkenness' ('goostly slepe') and both emphasize that 'meditation' or, as Albrecht would put it, 'concentration' as a preliminary to sub-mentally governed 'meditation', involves a progressive surrender of the will. Most important, however, is that both are equally emphatic that a single act or 'stirring' of the will would immediately destroy the unified structure of 'sunkenness' and is therefore incompatible with mystical awareness. In this context the passage from *The Cloud* should once more be referred to in which the spiritual guide exhorts his pupil never to interfere with the 'þing' (i.e. the 'in-coming' mystical phenomenon) 'working upon' him when absorbed in 'contemplation'. The passive surrender to God 'þat steriþ' him becomes imperative, otherwise he would 'spille al':

. . . lat þat þing do wiþ þee & lede þee wherso it list. Lat it be þe worcher, & þou

bot þe suffrer; do bot loke apon it, & lat it alone. Medel þee not þerwiþ as þou
woldest help it, for drede lest þou spille al.
. . . It suffisiþ inowȝ vnto þee þat þou fele þee steryd likyngly wiþ a þing þou wost
neuer what . . . ȝif it be þus, trist þan stedfastly þat it is only God þat steriþ þi wyl &
þi desyre, pleynly by hymself, wiþouten mene ouþer on his party or on þin.[49]

The psychological insight that acts of the will and genuine mystical
experience are mutually exclusive is most categorically articulated in
chapters 52 to 57 of *The Cloud*, in which the spiritual advisor takes
considerable pains to alert his pupil to the potential dangers inherent in
'meditation' if misapplied. He entreats the novice never to employ concentration as a technique for evoking mystical apprehensions. Once he has
reached higher states of consciousness any attempt to strain his mind
forcefully, particularly when frustrated by the mental 'blank' ('nouȝt') to
which his 'inner eye' is exposed in the initial state of 'contemplation', could
have disastrous effects. The medieval mystagogue was keenly aware of the
dangers involved in such an undertaking. 'Unnatural straining' would not
merely disrupt the 'ful acordyng abilnes to resseyue' God's grace and entail
the stagnation of further spiritual progress, but could also generate delusive
fantasies or bogus visions of the Divine and, ultimately, lead to distraction
and insanity. To obviate mental harm in his disciple the *Cloud*-author
drastically warns him not to follow the abortive examples of pseudo-
contemplatives and their futile endeavours to evoke spiritual apprehensions
by conscious effort:

. . . þei turne þeire bodily wittes inwardes to þeire body aȝens þe cours of kynde; &
streynyn hem, as þei wolde see inwardes wiþ þeire bodily iȝen, and heren inwardes
wiþ þeire eren, & so forþe of alle þeire wittes, smellen, taasten, & felyn inwardes.
& þus þei reuerse hem a ȝens þe cours of kynde, & wiþ þis coriouste trauayle þeire
ymaginacion so vndiscreetly, þat at þe laste þei turne here brayne in here
hedes. . . .[50]

Incidentally, the necessity of being guided by an experienced spiritual
advisor is emphatically postulated not only by all spiritual teachers in the
mystical traditions of east and west, but also by modern physicians and
psychiatrists applying meditation for therapy. Albrecht, for instance, was so
keenly aware of and concerned about the dangers inherent in the techniques
of concentration and meditation if practised by novices without expert
guidance, or under the care of untrained or inept would-be-mentors that, in
order to forestall potential misuse, he declined to disclose details of his
technique in his publications.

4

The foregoing exemplary considerations, cursory and rudimentary as they
are, can of course not presume to offer more than a tentative suggestion of

the research potential residing in an approach to mystical literature through Albrecht's psychology of mystical consciousness. If one accepts the proposition that mystical texts, whether *mystographical* (i.e. the transcription from personal spiritual experience as filtered through the categories of thought and language), *mystological* (i.e. descriptions, interpretations or analyses of non-mystics of the spiritual experience reported by mystics)[51] or a synthesis of both, are data of spiritual experience which contain within their religious idiom and theological framework a psychological substratum, or 'deep structure', not necessarily connected with religious or theological issues, one will have to concede that the understanding of such texts will be greatly advanced if approached through the psychology of consciousness. Albrecht's empirical psychology of mysticism, as yet the first and only one of this kind which is non-reductionist and non-speculative, has opened up a new dimension to the multi-disciplinary study of mystical literature and, ultimately, to a new understanding of the spiritual nature of man.

NOTES

1. For example, W. James, *Varieties of Religious Experience*, London, 1902, J. N. Leuba, *The Psychological Study of Religion*, New York, 1912, and E. Underhill, *Mysticism*, London, 1911.
2. W. James, by comparison, admits that in his study of 'religious experience', he cannot call on 'the direct authority' of personal experience. (See W. James, 'A Suggestion About Mysticism', in *Understanding Mysticism*, ed. R. Woods, London, 1981, p. 215).
3. C. Albrecht, *Psychologie des Mystischen Bewußtseins*, Bremen, 1951. (reprinted Mainz, 1976); (in the following abbreviated: *P.M.B.*) and C. Albrecht, *Das Mystische Erkennen*, Bremen, 1958 (reprinted Mainz, 1982).
4. C. Albrecht, *Das Mystische Wort*, ed. H. A. Fischer-Banicol, Mainz, 1974.
5. See K. Rahner's preface to C. Albrecht, *Das Mystische Wort*, ed. H. A. Fischer-Barnicol, Mainz, 1974, p. xiv.
6. There is no reference to Albrecht in any of the more recent English and American studies in the field of mysticism. Albrecht's publications are, for instance, not included in the otherwise fairly complete and representative bibliographies appended to important studies such as W. Johnston's *The Inner Eye of Love*, London, 1978, Sir Alister Hardy, *The Spiritual Nature of Man*, Oxford, 1979, or *Understanding Mysticism, op. cit.*
7. *P.M.B.*, p. 254.
8. *P.M.B.*, p. 204.
9. *P.M.B.*, p. 73.
10. *P.M.B.*, pp. 132–3.
11. *P.M.B.*, p. 245.
12. *P.M.B.*, p. 246.
13. *P.M.B.*, p. 246.
14. *P.M.B.*, p. 218.
15. *P.M.B.*, p. 219.
16. *P.M.B.*, p. 254.
17. In the traditional anagogic exegesis of Scripture Aaron is interpreted as a 'type' of the perfect contemplative who was gratified with apprehensions of the divine 'as ofte as him likid' (*The Cloud of Unknowing*, ed. P. Hodgson, Analecta Cartusiana 3, Salzburg, 1982, p. 71, 14–15; in the following abbreviated *The Cloud*. All references to this edition are

followed by page and line numbers. References to the other treatises ascribed to the *Cloud*-author are likewise to this edition).

18. For a comprehensive study of the sources and influences on the mystical theology and psychology of the *Cloud*-author see: *The Cloud*, introduction, especially pp. xxix–lvi, and A. Minnis, 'The Sources of *The Cloud of Unknowing*', in *The Medieval Mystical Tradition in England*, ed. M. Glasscoe, Exeter, 1982, pp. 63–75.
19. Cf. *The Cloud*, Introduction, p. xxxii.
20. D. Knowles, *The English Mystical Tradition*, London, 1961, pp. 72–3.
21. *The Cloud*, Introduction, p. 1.
22. The *Cloud*-author's clear distinction between 'meditation', denoting the meditational process ('hard werk' and 'ful grete trauayle') leading up to the higher reaches of consciousness, and 'contemplation', signifying the state of spiritual communion with God, is traditional and upheld throughout his work. Original, however, is his subdivision of 'contemplation' into a higher and a lower 'partye'. (Cf. P. Hodgson's Introduction to *The Cloud*, pp. xxxi–ii.).
23. *The Cloud*, p. 46, 14–15.
24. *Epistle of Discretion of Stirrings*, (in the following abbreviated *Stirrings*) p. 117, 11–16.
25. Cf. *P.M.B.*, pp. 52 ff., 105 ff.
26. *The Cloud*, p. 13, 27.
27. *The Cloud*, p. 18, 25–31.
28. *The Cloud*, p. 14, 4–11.
29. *The Cloud*, p. 65, 27–30.
30. Cf. *The Cloud*, Introduction, p. xxxii.
31. *Stirrings*, p. 117, 13 f.
32. *P.M.B.*, p. 172.
33. *The Cloud*, p. 68, 23–30.
34. *The Cloud*, p. 23, 14–16.
35. *The Cloud*, p. 33, 10–16.
36. *The Cloud*, p. 46, 18–22.
37. *The Cloud*, p. 71, 27.
38. *The Book of Privy Counselling*, (in the following abbreviated *Privy Counselling*), p. 86, 17–23.
39. *P.M.B.*, p. 246.
40. *The Cloud*, p. 39, 1–4, 7–13.
41. *Privy Counselling*, p. 88, 20–26.
42. *P.M.B.*, p. 241.
43. See A. Augustinus, *Psychologie und Mystik (De Genesi ad Litteram 12)*, transl. and introd. by M. E. Karger and H. U. von Balthasar, Einsiedeln, 1960, pp. 5–23.
44. *The Cloud*, p. 50, 35–36.
45. *The Cloud*, p. 34, 34–35.
46. *Benjamin Minor*, p. 144, 18–19.
47. *The Cloud*, p. 34, 36–37.
48. *Privy Counselling*, p. 97, 11–22.
49. *The Cloud*, p. 39, 1–13.
50. *The Cloud*, p. 53, 32–38.
51. The terms 'mystography' and 'mystology' have been coined by I. Behn in her penetrating study on the Spanish mystics, entitled *Spanische Mystik. Darstellung und Deutung*, Düsseldorf, 1957.

THE TRIPARTITE REFORMATION OF THE SOUL IN *THE SCALE OF PERFECTION*, *PEARL* AND *PIERS PLOWMAN*

A. P. BALDWIN

THE IDEA THAT God left traces of his own tripartite being in man probably derives from Plato. In the *Timaeus* (the only work of his to be well known in the medieval west[1]) God is described as a kind of trinity of the Form of the Good, the Demiurge, and the World Soul. The Demiurge had man made as a tripartite being, dividing the soul between the head, the heart, and the liver. The rational soul in the head most resembles the World Soul, and though now relegated to the material world and impaired in its functioning, it can recover its original form by contemplating what is immortal and divine:

> As we have said . . . there reside in us three distinct forms of soul. . . . As regards the supreme form of soul in us, we must conceive that the god has conferred it upon each man as a guiding genius—that . . . which lifts us from earth towards our celestial affinity. . . . The motions akin to the divine part in us [D] are the thoughts and revolutions of the universe; these therefore every man should follow, and correcting those circuits in the head which were deranged at birth, by learning to recognize the harmonies and revolutions of the world, he should bring the intelligent part, according to its pristine nature, unto the likeness of that which intelligence discerns. . . .[2]

The Neoplatonists developed both the idea of a divine trinity (according to Plotinus, the three 'Hypostates' of 'the One' . . . , the Intellectual-Principle, and . . . the All-Soul'), and the possibility of man being restored to the image of God. 'Strive to bring back the god in yourselves to the Divine in the universe' were supposedly Plotinus' last words.[3]

Within the Christian tradition, St Paul introduced the Hebrew concept of the Fall through sin (rather than simply through material creation) into this Classical tension between man's actual and potential natures. He taught that it was through Christ that human souls could 'walk not after the flesh' in Adam, but, through grace, 'after the spirit'.[4] The Father, the Son, and the Holy Spirit are said at different places to participate in restoring man to the image of God he has lost through sin. St Augustine came to Christianity through reading Neoplatonists like Porphyry, Plotinus' disciple, and in *De Trinitate* he embodies the Platonic principle that as man learns to know God he becomes more like him. 'For St Augustine the image of God in man is a dynamic principle; it is something to be achieved, not something that is simply given.'[5] This process of reformation goes some way towards reversing the evil effects of the Fall on man's memory, understanding and will, and so restoring them, through the Redemption and through grace, to the image of the Father, Son, and Holy Spirit respectively. As St Augustine sums it up at the end of his book, men should use their reason to behold:

> that God who is Trinity in our memory, understanding and will. . . . Man ought to direct all that lives in him to remember, to see, and to love this highest Trinity, in order that he may recall it, contemplate it, and find his delight in it.[6]

J. P. Clark has abundantly demonstrated the sources, particularly in St Augustine, for Walter Hilton's discussion of the soul's reformation to the image of God.[7] I have no intention of enlarging upon his researches, but rather of using them to highlight how three important Middle English texts (*The Scale*, *Pearl*, and *Piers Plowman*) use the Platonic and Augustinian concept of the tripartite reformation of the soul, as a structural principle.

The Scale of Perfection

On a first reading of *The Scale* it seems that Hilton structures Books I and II on two different systems for perfecting the soul. Book I, chapters 4–9, describes three methods of 'contemplation' which seem to derive from Hugh of St Victor's three modes of cognition used by the rational soul: cognition, meditation and contemplation.[8] In Hilton we read of knowledge of God 'gotten bi reson, bi techyng of man, and bi studie in holy writ' (proper to sinful as well as sinless souls); contemplation 'in affection', acquired largely through meditation on Christ, and differing according to whether the soul is sinful or sinless; and contemplation 'in cognition and in affection . . . so perfectly þat bi rauishynge of lufe, þe soule is oned for þe time and confourmed to þe ymage of þe trinite' (ch. 8). Book II is based not on three ways of seeing God, but on two levels of reformation in the soul: reformation in faith, and reformation in faith and feeling. My purpose is to demonstrate that both these systems are related to the Trinity, in whose image Hilton believed the soul to be made.

The three methods of contemplation in Book I echo 'Augustine's balance between knowledge and love'.[9] Even sinful man can think, and so cognition by reason and study is available to 'yche man þat haþ vs of reson' (ch. 4). To love, however, is in itself a virtue, and so the 'a ffection' of God, which is the second part of contemplation (ch. 5), and the 'burnyng luf in contemplacion' (ch. 9), which is 'visited' and 'illumined' by grace, and is the third part (ch. 8), are only possible for souls which are in charity, albeit fitfully. Now if, as Hilton repeatedly claims, man is made in God's image, there will be a corresponding distinction in God between his powers of thinking and loving. In chapter 43, Hilton attempts such a classification, and says that the thinking capacity in man was modelled on the Father and the Son, and the loving capacity on the Holy Spirit 'þe whych is blessed lufe'. But for almost all the rest of Book I it is Jesus who represents God's love, and in searching for Jesus man becomes more like Him (ch. 44–50, 91–2). As Clark puts it, man's reason represents the image of God, and his love represents a similitude to Christ.[10] So, at the end of Book I, Hilton asserts that:

> no man mai comen to þe contemplacion of þe godhede bute he be first refourmed bi fulhede of mekenes and charite to þe liknes of Jhesu in his manhede. (ch. 92).

In spite of its introduction on the three levels of contemplation, Book I deals only with the first two levels, that is, cognition and affection, in the practice of which the soul becomes more like the Father and the Son. The third level, in which the soul is 'visited' by the Holy Ghost, is reserved for the end of Book II. However, during the course of Book I, Hilton demonstrates how the soul has not at first got the power to practise even the first two levels, because it is an image of the devil, rather than an image of Jesus or the Trinity. Reversing the Platonic idea that man becomes more like God as he learns to know Him, Hilton insists—from experience—that until man has become more like God he cannot begin to approach Him.[11] He must begin by beating down the image of sin with humility (i.e. self-disgust) before he can recover the true charity which is God's image as well as his gift. Consequently Book II is not structured on the misleading model of a direct ascent to God, but on the more realistic idea of a reformation which is in itself an ascent.

This reformation is in faith and in faith and feeling, which can also be related to man's capacity to think and to love. Reformation in faith, like the earlier cognition of God, involves a belief in the Church's teaching, to which Hilton adds a new stress on the sacraments which undertake to cleanse him of sin, and so restore him to the image of God. Realistically, however, (and unlike the *Pearl*-author, as we shall see), Hilton does not find this enough; the inclination to sin cannot be magically removed but must be gradually replaced by a love of what is good. The sacraments by themselves can save, but cannot perfect a soul. So reformation in feeling must be added to reformation in faith in order that love may enter the purged soul and give it a new understanding of God. Reformation in faith and feeling 'implies both knowledge and love, not only understanding but affection'.[12] So it includes both the higher levels of contemplation described in Book I.

This whole process is related more than once to the Trinity. In Book II Hilton looks into his own soul to find a mirror of the Trinity which controls his reformation:

For þu shalt vnderstanden þat þe luf of god is on þre maner wise. Alle are gode bot vchon beter þen oþer. Þe first comeþ oonly þruȝ faiþ withouten gracious ymaginacion or gostly knowynge of god. Þis luf is in þe lest soule þat is reformed in faiþ, in þe lowest degree of charitee, and it is good, for it sufficeþ to saluacion (ch. 30).

This capacity corresponds, though Hilton does not actually say so, to the power of the Father, whose first act of love was 'whan he made vs to his liknes' (ch. 34), and to the reasoning power in man described in Book I. The second and better way in which a soul loves God:

is þat a soule feleþ þruȝ faiþ and ymaginacion of Jhesu in his manhode. Þis luf is better þan þe first, whan þe ymaginacion is stirid bi grace . . . (ch. 30).

This corresponds to the wisdom (or the love) of the Son, for it is the Son who is loved, and it is related in chapter 34 to the greater love which God showed when he redeemed mankind.[13] It also recalls the 'meditation' or 'affection' of Book I, which was principally directed towards Jesus. The third kind of love:

þe soul feliþ þruȝ gostly siȝt of þe godhod in þe manhode as it may be seen here. . . . Þis luf a soule feliþ not vntil he be reformed in felynge (ch. 30).

This higher awareness of the Godhead is only given by grace, which Hilton identifies with the Holy Ghost and with love.[14] It is:

principally felt in vnderstandynge, when it is conforted and illumined by þe holy gost, and litel in ymaginacion (ch. 31).

It shows us that God loves us most:

whan he gifiþ vs þe holy gost þat is luf, bi þe which we knowen him and louen him and are made siker þat we are his sones chosen to saluacion (ch. 34).

To sum up: as man becomes reformed to the image of God, he becomes aware of the illumination of the Holy Spirit in his contemplation of God. Although Hilton freely calls all aspects of God's love 'Jesus' for 'Jhesu is lufe, Jhesu is grace, Jhesu is god' (ch. 42), it clarifies a reading of *The Scale* to distinguish between God as Hilton approaches and conforms to him (the Father and the Son), and God approaching Hilton (the Holy Spirit or grace). This is essentially the distinction that Augustine made between the Father and the Son considered together as Giver, and the love which derives from both—the Gift which for Augustine was essential for salvation.

Unless the Holy Spirit, therefore, imparts to everyone so much as to make him a lover of God and of his neighbour, then he is not transferred from the left to the right side. . . . Love, then, which is from God and is God, is properly the Holy Spirit, through whom the charity of God is poured forth in our hearts, through which the whole Trinity dwells in us. For this reason the Holy Spirit, since He is God, is also most rightly called the Gift of God.[15]

For Hilton, who believed men could be saved by their faith as well as their love, the Holy Spirit not only saves but actually perfects a man. It is the 'spirit of adoption' which restores a man finally to God's image and makes him 'his son'.[16]

> Ask þou þan of god no þinge bot þe gifte of lufe þat is þe holy goste. . . . For þer is no gifte of god þat is boþ þe gifer and þe gifte bot þis gift of luf, and þerfore is it þe best and þe worþiest. . . . Þe gift of luf is þe holy gost god himself and him may no soule haf and be damned withalle, for þat gifte only safeþ it fro damnacion, and makeþ it godis sone, perceuer of heuenly heritage. (II, ch. 36).

The reformation of man to God's image by a process which reflects the Trinity, can be found at a structural level in other medieval literature.[17] Perhaps it appealed to writers because it suggests both an ideal and the process whereby that ideal may be attained. The author of *Pearl*, constantly striving for both moral and artistic perfection, concentrates more on the ideal than the process by which it is reached. Langland the realist on the other hand, defines and redefines the process of reformation, and the ideal—Piers Plowman—is only discovered in glimpses. In both cases an awareness of how the Trinity corresponds to man's soul can help to expose the structure of the poems.

Pearl

L. Bleckner has developed an interpretation of *Pearl* as:

> an adventure into the realm of the spirit. . . . The three stages of that adventure correspond to the Augustinian division of the rational soul into three faculties— memory, understanding, and will—which furnish the basis for the theologians' traditional threefold division of the soul's ascent to God. . . .[18]

He draws on Hugh of St Victor's *De Sacramentis* to define man's faculties and position, and in particular his reliance on the sacrament of the Eucharist to recover the presence of Christ (cf. *Pearl*, 1209–12). He uses the more mystical *Itinerum Mentis ad Deum* of St Bonaventura as his principal analogue for the dreamer's spiritual journey, which begins in the 'erber' where God's traces are left in 'what is corporeal and temporal and outside us' and where his memory tortures him with thoughts of his loss. The dreamer then proceeds, in the dream garden, to 'enter into [his] mind, which [is] the eternal image of God', and where the Pearl-maiden instructs his understanding. Finally, he attempts, albeit unsuccessfully, 'to pass over into that which is eternal, most spiritual, and above us', and there his will and 'luf-longyng' are directed to the highest good.[19] Under this analysis the dreamer's journey corresponds to Hilton's three stages of contemplation, or his double reformation of the soul.[20]

Like Hilton, in fact, the *Pearl*-poet uses the Trinity as a structural principle, and this can be demonstrated more fully than Bleckner does, although he does explain that each of the three faculties of the soul was associated with one of the three persons of God. Thus in the 'erbere' which suggests the Garden of Eden, we are reminded of God the Father who 'clad' the pearl 'in clot' (22) as he made Adam out of clay, but also allowed her to die, as he punished Adam when he corrupted the divine image in himself.[21] In the dream garden the dreamer is taught chiefly about God the Son, who is the bridegroom of the maidens (431–480) and the keeper of the vineyard (497–588) and whose healing blood can restore all men to bliss (649–660). By his grace he clad the pearl in the 'kyste' (271: the chest which is the coffin but also Heaven) which transforms her into a 'perle of prys' (272).[22] As in the *Scale* both God the Son and God the Holy Spirit are associated with grace and love, and the final vision of Jerusalem focuses on the Lamb, rather than for example, the Dove. But inasmuch as it is a true vision rather than a personal dream, it is a gift of the Holy Spirit imparting 'luf-longyng in gret delyt' (1152). Here the pearls which symbolize the souls of each maiden are now visible 'in vchonez breste' (1103) as the Holy Spirit animates each reformed Christian.

Reading *The Scale* alongside *Pearl* not only highlights how closely the dreamer's development in the poem corresponds to the tripartite reformation of the mystic, but it also shows how the Pearl maiden herself might fit into that process of reformation. Bleckner interprets the Pearl chiefly as an image of the dreamer's own reformed soul. But she is also another individual, a baptized child, and her own personal ascent to God corresponds to that of the Christians discussed in the first part of Hilton's Book II, who have experienced only 'reformyng in faiþ'. Such souls are reformed not at first hand, through 'felyng', but through the Church and her sacraments.[23] Hilton distinguishes here between 'great and small souls':

> Be smale are vnderstandyn soules vnperfecte of worldly men and wymen and oþer, þat haþ bot a childes knowyng of god and ful litel felyng of hym, bot aren broȝt forþ in þe bosum of holy kirke and norisched wiþ þe sacraments as children are fed wiþ milk (II, ch. 10).

Hilton goes on to explain that the sacraments only remit previous sins (original sin at baptism; actual sin at penance). To borrow Augustine's definition of baptism, they 'remove the cause of the disease' but do not 'heal the disease itself, which is done gradually by making progress in the renewal of this image'.[24] Only in one case is the sacrament sufficient for permanent restoration of God's image in man, and that is when a child

> þru vertue of faiþ of holy kirk sodanly is turned fro þe likness of a fende, and made like to an aungel of heven. . . . if þei myȝt as swiþ after baptem passe out of þis world, þei suld streyt flye to heuen withouten any more lettyng (II, ch. 6).

This simple but uncompromising expression of an orthodox idea[25] indicates how easily the image of the pearl in *Pearl* can be interpreted both as the soul of the dreamer, reformed back to the image of God it had lost through Adam, and as the baptized soul of the child.[26] The sacraments were accorded more power by Aquinas than by Augustine; for him they not only cleansed but also perfected the soul. This is because the grace received through them 'is nothing else than a certain shared similitude in the divine nature'.[27] So it is that:

> sacramental grace seems to be designed chiefly to produce two effects, first to remove the defect of past sins . . . ; second to perfect the soul in all that pertains to the worship of God in the Christian life.

This power is effected by virtue of the Passion, through which Christ:

> inaugurated the rites of the Christian religion. . . . This is signified by the fact that from the side of Christ hanging on the Cross there flowed water and blood [John 19: 34] the first of which pertains to baptism and the second to the Eucharist. . . .[28]

The *Pearl*-author followed this more emphatic treatment of the sacraments when the Pearl-maiden concludes her section on grace:

> 'Innoghe þer wax out of þat welle,
> Blod and water of brode wounde.
> Þe blod vus boȝt fro bale of helle,
> And delyuered vus of þe deth secounde;
> þe water is baptem, þe soþe to telle,
> þat folȝed þe glavue so grymly grounde,
> þat waschez away þe gyltez felle
> þat Adam wyth inne deth vus drounde.' (649–656)

Baptism washes away the 'gyltez felle' which the maiden had inherited, and restores her to the image of God, which is the pearl that is the shape of heaven and the colour of the Lamb of God:

> 'For hit is wemlez, clene, and clere,
> And endelez rounde, and blyþe of mode,
> And commune to alle þat ryȝtwys were.
> Lo, euen immyddez my breste hit stode:
> My Lorde þe Lombe, þat schede Hys blode,
> He pyȝt hit þere in token of pes.' (737–742)

Consequently if the dreamer cleanses himself by means of the sacraments available to an adult, particularly the Eucharist, he too will resemble the pearl and hold the kingdom of heaven within himself. She advises him to so:

> 'I rede þe forsake the worlde wode
> And porchace þy perle maskelles' (743–744)

and at the end of the poem, the dreamer advises the reader to do so specifically by participating in the Eucharist:

þat in þe forme of bred and wyn
þe preste vus shewez vch a daye
He get vus to be His homly hyne
And precious perlez vnto His pay. (1209–1212)

Neither she nor the dreamer will of course become identical to God, and the distance between the perfection available to created man, and the perfection of the Creator, is expressed in the poem by the difference between the pearl and the Lamb.[29] The pearl, despite its beauty and mathematical purity (suggesting perhaps the circular Divine model in the *Timaeus*) is cold and dead. The Pearl-maiden's whiteness suggests the corpse as well as the pearl; we as much as the dreamer miss her lost colour and warmth. The Lamb on the other hand, is an active being, pouring out both light to illumine heaven (1047) and blood to redeem mankind (1135–1137) with equal joy:

The Lombe delyt non lyste to wene;
þa3 He were hurt and wounde hade,
In His sembelaunt watz neuer sene,
So wern His glentez gloryous glade. (1141–4).

The pouring out of light and blood suggests the pouring out of love and grace, such as Hilton describes at the culmination of *The Scale*:

Ðis luf is not elles bot Jhesu himself, þat for lufe wirkiþ al þis in a mannessoule and reformiþ it in felynge to his liknes. . . . Ðis luf draweþ þe soule fro fleschhod in to gostlynes, fro erþly felynge in to heuenly savour, and fro vayn biholdynge of earthly þinges in to contemplacioun of gostly creatures and of goddis pryvites (II, ch. 34).

But the dreamer is unable to sustain this vision and wakes up to the 'fleshly sleep' of ordinary life.

Piers Plowman

Just as there is a distinction in *Pearl* between the reformed or baptised soul (pearl) and God whom it resembles (the Lamb), so in *Piers Plowman* there is a distinction between perfected human nature (Piers) and Christ whom he resembles. This point is made by B. Raw, who in a seminal article on 'Piers and the image of God in man'[30] suggested that the relationship between Piers and Christ echoes the distinction drawn by Aquinas between God and his image in created man and in Christ:

God's image is in his first-born Son as a king's image is in his son, who shares his nature; whereas it is in man as in an alien nature, like the king's image on a silver coin.[31]

She goes on to demonstrate how the restoration of the divine image in history and the individual soul is the unifying theme in *Piers Plowman*. She relates the process of restoration to the Trinitarian division of the poem into three stages: the *Visio* and Dowel (under God the Father), Dobet (under God the Son), and Dobest (under God the Holy Spirit).[32] For Raw, Piers' three appearances in the B-text represent man's potential restoration to the image of God through human history, and in particular the Incarnation, when God became like Piers. It will be completed only in heaven, which is why Piers disappears before the end of the poem. Will's transformation to God's image is an individual and more partial one, related more directly to Augustine's division of the soul into memory, understanding and will. The turning-point for Will is when in *Passus* IX he abandons lust, curiosity and vanity, and listens instead to 'Reason and Ymaginatif', that is, the memory and the understanding, until, with Conscience as his guide, 'he learns to direct his will', to love others, and finally to follow Piers. Her analogue for this process is Ailred of Rievaulx's development of *De Trinitate* in *Speculum Charitatis*:

> The memory is restored by the teaching of Holy Scripture, the understanding by the sacrament of faith, and love by the daily increase of charity[33]

—a passage which could be applied equally well to *Pearl* or *The Scale*. If the last two *Passus* of *Piers Plowman* are not the final happy visions of my other two texts, it is because Langland is describing actual society in history, as well as the personal development of an individual. *Unitas* fails, but Will is at last on a true path in his search for grace and the Holy Spirit.

I have described Raw's argument in some detail because it fits so well with my approach here to *The Scale*[34] and *Pearl*, and because she is the first of three recent critics to demonstrate how successfully *Piers Plowman* can be interpreted as the image of God in man: D. M. Murtaugh, *Piers Plowman and the Image of God* followed in 1978, and M. E. Galbraith, *The Figure of Piers*, which uses as its subtitle *The Image on the Coin*, in 1981.[35] Since all three studies concentrate on the B-text, I propose to round off my observations on the reformation of the soul in Middle English texts by a brief consideration on the *Dobet* section of the C-text, not in order to repeat other scholars' analyses of Piers, but in order to show how Langland uses the Trinity as Hilton and the *Pearl*-author do, to illumine the process by which a man may be reformed, as well as the goal of that reformation.

It seems likely that Langland intended the *Dobet* section in the C-text to concern the reformation of man's soul to the Trinity. It opens with an account of the tree which grows allegorically in man's heart, a tree which is not called 'Charity' as it is in the B-text, but '*Ymago-Dei*'. (C, XVIII, 7). Its fruit is Charity, which is also 'Cristes oune fode' (14), and supported by 'the trinite of heuene' (26). It is tended by *Liberum Arbitrium*, who as Donaldson suggested in *The C-text and its Poet*, probably corresponds to St Bernard's account of 'that part of man which bears the impress of the image of God to which man was created'.[36] Bernard said that man most fully resembled God when he directed his will to charity[37], but as Langland dramatically shows, after the Fall the fruit of man's charity is constantly stolen by the devil. In other words, man has lost the power to resemble God by his own efforts, and needs God's help expressed through God's Holy Spirit or Free Will[38], to reverse the effect of the Fall:

> Thenne moued hym moed *in magestate dei,*
> That *Libera-Voluntas-Dei* lauhte þe mydel shoriare, . . .
> *Filius,* by þe fadres wille, fley with *Spiritus Sanctus*
> To go ransake þat ragman and reue hym of his apples,
> That thorw fals biheste and fruyt furst man disseyued (C, XVIII, 118–123).[39]

The rest of *Dobet* (C, XVIII, 124–XX. 478) can be read as a discussion of how the Holy Trinity enables man to recover the lost 'Ymago-Dei'. Langland's emphasis is apparently entirely upon Christ; it is he whom Abraham expects (C, XVIII, 282), whom Moses searches for (XIX, 7–8), and whom the Samaritan represents as the only possible healer and restorer of fallen man (C, XIX, 81–86). At the culmination of *Dobet*, is, afterall, the great *Passus* on the Crucifixion and Harrowing of Hell (C, XX), in which Christ takes man's likeness and so restores to him the possibility of recovering God's likeness (see C, XXI, 12–14, 63–65). But the dialogues between Will and Abraham, Moses and the Samaritan are much occupied with the Trinity, and in particular the doctrine of its indivisibility. Abraham explains this scholastically (C, XVIII, 188–239), the Samaritan uses the more intelligible metaphors of the three interdependent parts of the hand (C, XIX, 111–166) and the taper (C, XIX, 167–273). These arguments counterbalance the effect of dividing the poem (or human history) into three parts, and associating the age of the Father with loss and corruption, and the age of the Son with restoration and healing. Both Father and Son are 'fol god' (130) and desire to love and help mankind.

Moreover the third part of the poem will be devoted to the present age, that of the Holy Spirit, and the Samaritan here introduces the idea that it is the Holy Spirit who completes the work of man's restoration. He himself claims only to begin this work by baptizing fallen men with 'þe blood of a barn' (C, XIX, 84), and in the words of Augustine, baptism only 'removes the cause of the disease'. The gradual 'renewal of this image'[40] was finally accomplished for Augustine by the power of the Holy Spirit, the love that emanates from the Father and the Son and kindles a corresponding love in men's souls. So, in the Samaritan's graphic image of the taper, the Holy Ghost (the flame) that springs from the Father (the wax) and the Son (the wick) has the power both to melt God's justice into mercy, and to light a candle within men's souls and so transform them into his image:

> 'For to a torche or to a taper þer trinite is likned,
> As wexe and a weke were twyned togyderes

And thenne flaumymge fuyr forth of hem bothe. . . .
So doth þe sire and þe sone and seynt spirit togyderes
Fostren forth amonges folke fyn loue and bileue
That alle kyne cristene clanseth of synne (C, XIX, 167–9, 173–5).

'So þat the holy gost gloweth but as a glede
Til þat loue and bileue leliche to hym blowe,
And thenne flaumeth he as fuyr on fader and on *filius*
And melteth myhte into mercy, . . .
So grace of þe holi gost the grete myhte of þe trinite
Melteth al to mercy to merciable and to non oþere' (C, XIX, 188–191, 194–5).

The alliterated f of God's fire (169, 190) reappears on earth in 1.174; and key words like 'mercy' apply equally well to God (191, 195) and to man (195), for man resembles God in particular in his charity. The point is reinforced when Langland calls man a taper as well:

For euery manere goed man may be likned to a torche
Or elles to a taper to reuerense with the trinite. (C, XIX, 257–8).

If this corresponds to Hilton's conception of man restored to the image of God, then Hilton's opposite—a soul in the image of the devil— corresponds to Langland's description of an unkind soul, which destroys mercy and charity in itself and in God's response to it. Langland claims that such men commit the sin against the Holy Ghost (Mark 3:29), which perhaps derives from Augustine's assertion that souls without charity are damned:[41]

Thus is vnkyndenesse þe contrarie þat quencheth, as hit were,
The grace of the holy goest, godes owene kynde; (C, XIX, 250–1).

Instead of a flame, unkindness and covetousness produce only a foul smoke which drive God away from man's soul. (C, XIX, 302 ff. this proverb is used in a similar way by Hilton in *Scale* I. ch. 53):

Ac þe smoke and þe smolder that smyt in oure yes,
That is coueytise and vnkyndenesse whiche quencheth godes mercy.
(C, XIX, 323–3).

But where Hilton had looked for a contemplative charity in the soul, stirring it to love God above all, Langland is describing a practical charity, which makes men resemble Christ by behaving like him. Such men offer:

Alle manere men mercy and forȝeueness,
And louye hym yliche hymsulue. . . . (C, XIX, 328–9).

Hence the last two *Passus* of the poem, which describe the Holy Ghost at work on earth, focus upon the failure of practical love, belief, and pen- itence—simple but profound faculties of the soul which the Samaritan had taught in *Passus* XIX were fostered by the Holy Ghost, and were the means whereby God restored man to His own image.

In this article I have done little more than draw together and enlarge upon the work of different critics working on three different texts. I hope however that I have demonstrated how well-known was the doctrine of the restoration of man's soul to the image of God to Middle English writers, and how three of them used it to provide both theme and structure in their work. Two tentative conclusions may be drawn from this coincidence. Firstly it suggests that all three authors were fundamentally optimistic about man's destiny, and felt he had the capacity for perfection as well as the gift of salvation. Secondly, it indicates something we tend to overlook: that medieval Christians associated the Holy Spirit as much as the Son with the love of God, and relied on its power to perfect and save them.

NOTES

1. C. S. Lewis, *The Discarded Image*, Cambridge, 1964, p. 43.
2. *Timaeus*, 89D–90D, tr. J. Warrington, (Everyman Edition), London, 1965, pp. 131–2; see also 27C–30C, 69D–72D.
3. Plotinus, *Enneads*, tr. S. MacKenna, London, 1919, pp. xxv–xxviii; C. Elsee, *Neoplatonism in relation to Christianity*, Cambridge, 1908, p. 55.
4. Romans 8:1, see also 2:30, 12:2; 1 Corinthians 15:45–49; Galatians 5; Ephesians 4:24; Colossians 1:11–23; Titus 1:2, 3:5–7; etc.
5. Thomas Aquinas, *Summa Theologica*, Vol. 13, ed. E. Hill, Blackfriars, 1964, p. 212. (Abbreviation *S. T.*)
6. *De Trinitate* XV. 20, tr. S. McKenna, Washington, 1963, p. 506; (Patrologiae Latina, 42, 1088: 'per quod velut speculum, quantum possent, si possent, cernerent Trinitatem Deum, in nostra memoria, intelligentia, voluntate. . . . Ad quam summam Trinitatem reminiscendam, videndam, diligendam, ut eam recordetur, eam contempletur, ea delectetur, totum debet referre quod vivit.'); see also *S. T.* 1a q. 93 a. 6–8; Anselm, *Monologion*, ch. 48; Bonaventura, *Itinerarium Mens ad Deum*, ch.3; etc.
7. J. P. H. Clark, 'Image and Likeness in Walter Hilton', *Downside Review*, 97 (1979), 207–220; see also his 'The Lightsome Darkness—Aspects of Walter Hilton's Theological Background', *Downside Review*, 95, (1977), 95–109, esp. pp. 101ff; 'The *Cloud of Unknowing*, Walter Hilton, and St John of the Cross: a Comparison', *Downside Review*, 96 (1978), 281–298, esp. pp. 290–292; 'Image and Likeness in Walter Hilton', *Downside Review*, 97 (1979), 207–220; 'Augustine, Anselm and Walter Hilton', *The Medieval Mystical Tradition in England*, ed. M. Glasscoe, Exeter, 1982, pp. 102–126. See also H. Gardner, 'Walter Hilton and the Mystical Tradition in England', *Essays and Studies*, 22 (1937), 103–127, esp. pp. 118–9.
8. See H. O. Taylor, *The Medieval Mind*, London, 1965, II, 388–9. Quotations from *The Scale* are taken from MS. British Library Harley 6579. Abbreviations are silently expanded.
9. J. P. H. Clark, 'Action and Contemplation in Walter Hilton', *Downside Review*, 97 (1977), 258–274, p. 263; see also '*Cloud*, Hilton and St John', *op. cit.*, pp. 288–9. Discussed also in *S. T.* 1a q. 93 a. 7.
10. J. P. H. Clark, 'Image and likeness' *op. cit.*, p. 207; G. Ladner, *The Idea of Reform*, New York, 1976, pp. 83–107; cf. *S. T.* 1a q. 93 a. 9.
11. See Clark's distinction between *fides* and *intellectus* in 'Augustine, Anselm and Hilton', *op. cit.*, pp. 103–6.
12. J. P. H. Clark, 'Augustine, Anselm and Hilton', *op. cit.*, p. 115; see also 'Image and likeness', *op. cit.*, pp. 217–8; 'Action and contemplation', *op. cit.*, pp. 272–4.
13. Clark refers this to *S. T.* 1–2 q. 113 a. 9 ('Image and likeness', *op. cit.*, p. 220).
14. *Ibid.*, p. 216.

15. *De Trinitate* XV. 18, Patrologiae Latina, 42.1082–3: 'Nisi ergo tantum impertiatur cuique Spiritus sanctus, ut eum Dei et proximi faciat amatorem, a sinistra non transfertur ad dexteram. . . . Dilectio igitur quae ex Deo est et Deus est, proprie Spiritus sanctus est, per quem diffunditur in cordibus nostris Dei charitas, per quem nos tota inhabitat Trinitas'. see also Anselm, *Monologion*, ch. 70; J. P. H. Clark, 'Image and likeness', *op. cit.*, 219–220. The expression 'the Gift' refers to Acts 8:20.
16. Romans 8:14–15.
17. See also C. Morse, *The Pattern of Judgement in the 'Queste' and 'Cleanness'*, Missouri, 1978, p. 176, for a discussion of the theme of image and likeness in *Cleanness*; tripartite reformation is also a theme in Julian's *Showings* (e.g. Long Text ch. 44).
18. L. Bleckner, 'The Theological Structure of Pearl', *Traditio*, 24 (1968), 43–75, p. 48.
19. St Bonaventura, *The Mind's Road to God*, tr. G. Boas, New York, p. 8 (I.2: 'quod perveniamus ad primum principium considerandum . . . oportet nos transire per vestigium, quod est corporale et temporale et extra nos . . . ; oportet, nos intrare ad mentem nostram, quae est imago Dei aeviterna . . . ; oportet, nos transcendere ad aeternum, spiritualissimum, et supra nos, aspiciendo ad primum principium . . .'), cited L. Bleckner, *op. cit.*, pp. 51–2.
20. M. Mandeleva, *Pearl: a Study in Spiritual Dryness*, New York, 1975, and M. P. Hamilton, 'The Meaning of the Middle English *Pearl*', (Proceedings of the Modern Language Association, 1953), repr. pp. 37–59 in '*Sir Gawaine' and 'Pearl': Critical Essays*, ed. R. J. Blanch, Indiana, 1966, pp. 52–55, also offer a mystical interpretation of the poem.
21. On the pearl as man's lost eternal life, see M. P. Hamilton, *op. cit.*, pp. 44–6.
22. For a similarly ambiguous use of 'kyst' in *Cleanness*, see C. Morse *op. cit.*, pp. 155, 174; on transformation of rose into pearl, see A. C. Spearing, 'Symbolic and Dramatic Development in *Pearl*', *Modern Philology*, 60 (1962), 98–119, in R. J. Blanch *op. cit.*, p. 109.
23. On Hilton's sacramental doctrine, see J. P. H. Clark, 'Intention in Walter Hilton', *Downside Review*, 97 (1979), 69–80, pp. 77–80.
24. *De Trinitate.*, XIV. 17, Patrologiae Latina, 42, 1054: 'ita prima curatio est causam removere languoris . . . ; secunda ipsum sanare languorem, quod fit paulatim proficiendo in renovatione hujus imaginis'.
25. For its orthodoxy, see R. Wellek, '*The Pearl*': An Interpretation of the Middle English Poem', (Charles University, 1933), pp. 3–36 in R. J. Blanch. *op. cit.*, pp. 25–7; on baptism and eucharist in *Pearl*, see M. P. Hamilton, *op. cit.*, pp. 56–9.
26. For the use of the pearl in scriptural exegesis to suggest the 'undefiled human soul, or the soul redeemed by baptism', see M. P. Hamilton, *op. cit.*, pp. 41–3; R. Wellek, *op. cit.*, pp. 34–5.
27. *S.T.* 3a q. 62 a. 1, ref. to 2 Peter 1:4: 'gratia nihil est aliud quam quaedam participata similitudo divinae naturae', tr. D. Burke, Blackfriars ed., 1975.
28. *S.T.*, 3a q. 62 a. 5: 'per suam passionem initiavit ritum Christiaanae religionis . . . In cujus signum, de latere Christi pendentis in cruce fluxerunt aqua et sanguis, quorum unum pertinet ad baptismum, aliud ad Eucharistiam'; see also q. 69 a, 4.
29. A. C. Spearing, *op. cit.*, p. 117, puts this difference down to the dreamer's inadequacy as a mystic.
30. '*Piers Plowman: Critical Approaches*', ed. S. S. Hussey, London, 1969, pp. 143–179.
31. *S.T.* 1a q.93 a.1, 'imago Dei est in Filio suo primogenito sicut imago regis in filio sibi connaturali; in homine autem sicut in aliena natura, sicut imago regis in nummo argenteo . . .', quoted B. Raw, *op. cit.*, p. 151. Other sources of the coin image are given in M. Goldsmith, *The Figure of Piers Plowman*, Suffolk, 1981, pp. 20–26.
32. The Trinity is said to provide '*the* organizing principle in the second part' by R. W. Frank, '*Piers Plowman' and the Scheme of Salvation*, New Haven, 1957, pp. 16–17.
33. I, 4, Patrologiae Latina 195, 509: 'reparatur tandem memoria per sacrae Scripturae documentum, intellectus per fidei sacramentum, amor per charitatis quotidianum incrementum.' quoted B. Raw, *op. cit.* p. 173.
34. E. Zeeman in '*Piers Plowman* and the Pilgrimage to 'Truth', *Essays and Studies*, N.S, 11 (1958), 1–16 also compares Piers ('a symbol of the operation of the divine upon the human') with the reformed soul in *The Scale*, see pp. 10–16.
35. D. M. Murtaugh, *Piers Plowman and the Image of God*, Florida, 1978; M. E. Galbraith, The Figure of Piers: the Image on the Coin, Suffolk, 1981.

36. E. T. Donaldson, '*Piers Plowman': the C-text and its Poet*, New Haven, 1949, p. 189, see pp. 188–192.
37. E. Gilson, *La Theologie Mystique de Saint Bernard*, Paris, 1947, pp. 68–77; see also J. P. H. Clark, 'Image and likeness', *op. cit.*, p. 209.
38. According to Augustine's classification; see, e.g. *De Trinitate*, 11, ch. 4–5, see also E. Gilson, *op. cit.*, p. 64–5.
39. *Piers Plowman: an edition of the C-Text*, ed. D. Pearsall, London, 1978, p. 298.
40. See n. 22 above.
41. see n. 14 above.

MARGERY KEMPE AND THE CONTINENTAL TRADITION OF THE PIOUS WOMAN

SUSAN DICKMAN

1

EVER SINCE ITS discovery and publication in 1940, *The Book of Margery Kempe* has puzzled modern scholars. Neither a mystical treatise nor an autobiography in the modern sense, *The Book* is Margery Kempe's own account of her mystical 'feelings' and her eventful outer life, which she dictated in the third person to a priestly scribe when she was over sixty. Born in 1373, daughter of John Burnham, one of the most prominent merchants of what was then Bishop's Lynn, Margery was married before she was twenty to John Kempe, a brewer and scion of a family only slightly less successful than her own. With the important exception of a vision of Christ which cured her of a prolonged attack of 'madness' following the birth of her first child,[1] Margery Kempe seems to have lived a fairly conventional life until she was forty. As far as one can tell from *The Book's* vague chronology, it was in 1409 or perhaps 1410 that she was graced with a second vision, the sound of heavenly music, which led her to avoid sex and to begin a number of penitential practices, including wearing a hair shirt, keeping vigils, and fasting. In 1413 or 1414, Margery left on a pilgrimage to the Holy Land where she acquired the tears which became the hall-mark of her piety. In the Church of the Holy Sepulchre, on the rocky ledge medieval pilgrims believed to be Mount Calvary, Margery was completely overwhelmed by a wave of tenderness and compassion for Christ's suffering. Unable to stand, she fell to the ground, weeping and sobbing, arms spread abroad in a watery *imitatio Christi*. Although these tears were subsequently to cause her much suffering in the form of public humiliation, it was the white clothing she wore as a token of her dedication to God as well as her habit of instructing anyone who would listen which first proved problematic. She was arrested and tried twice as a Lollard in 1417 in Leicester and York as she travelled home from a second pilgrimage to the shrine of St James of Compostella in Spain. Although she acquitted herself brilliantly on both these occasions, she was not so successful when the question of her tears arose a few years later. Despite the fact that she apparently led an exemplary life in Lynn, dedicating herself to prayer and contemplation, Margery's loud sobbing at every verbal and symbolic reminder of the Passion interrupted social as well as religious rituals and made her extremely unpopular with her neighbours. In 1420, a preaching friar, probably William Melton, came to Lynn and, irritated when Margery's crying interrupted his sermons, he galvanized public opinion against her, insisting that her tears were a sign of cardiac illness rather than a gift of grace as she claimed. Drummed out of the friar's church and effectively ostracized, Margery suffered a yet deeper humiliation when her controversial tears subsequently disappeared. The last years of her life, one gathers, Margery spent in public disrepute and it is not hard to understand why she wanted to set the record straight by explaining herself in the most authoritative form she knew—the written word.

When *The Book of Margery Kempe* was published in 1940 scholars first tried to understand Margery by comparing her to her contemporary and acquaintance, the enclosed anchoress Julian of Norwich. Dom David Knowles effectively closed that avenue of approach, however, when he observed in his influential 1961 study, *The English Mystical Tradition*, that Margery was 'a figure of a different kind' from Julian; 'more homely, perhaps, and even more comprehensible, but of an altogether coarser mould.'[2] Unfortunately, Knowles did not suggest what kind of figure Margery represented, and over the past twenty years, she has been variously understood as an apprentice saint,[3] a devout lay woman[4], an instance of the success of the English programme of pastoral education[5], a neurotic housewife whose spirituality, though derived from conventional sources, was designed to solve her personal problems,[6] and an out-and-out hysteric.[7]

Recently, with the growth of interest in medieval women, scholars have begun to attend to the detailed but disorganized notes which Hope Emily Allen contributed to the Early English Text Society edition of *The Book*. Allen believed that Margery Kempe was best understood in the context of the 'remarkable contemporary feminist movement to which [she] seems to belong'[8] and her notes document some of the specific parallels betweem Margery's spirituality and that of other female mystics, particularly St Bridget of Sweden and the Blessed Dorothea of Prussia, canonized in 1976. Following Allen's lead, Wolfgang Riehle has discovered a number of other points at which Margery's piety, particularly her imagery, coincides with that of the Continental mystics.[9] Clarissa Atkinson has gone further. In her fine study of Margery Kempe, *Mystic and Pilgrim*, she juxtaposes Margery's life with that of St Bridget on the one hand and that of St Dorothea on the other, showing the systematic parallels which exist in each case.[10] Ute Stargardt's 1981 dissertation, 'The Influence of Dorothea von Montau on the Mysticism of Margery Kempe,' establishes the probability of Dorothea's having served as a model and inspiration for Margery and reaches the conclusion that Margery must have been familiar with the vernacular version of Dorothea's *vita* as well as some account of her miracles which circulated throughout Prussia after her death.[11]

While the possibility of identifying specific sources for and influences on Margery's spirituality remains tantalizing, it is somewhat remote. Except for the sources which Margery herself acknowledges, we can only speculate what a merchant's wife from Lynn would have heard from travellers and traders who passed that port or what she might have learned on her several pilgrimages. But in so far as female models are concerned, the question of specific sources is largely irrelevant. Everything we know about women in the later Middle Ages indicates that there were hundreds, if not thousands, of women like Margery, who attempted to lead quasi-religious lives while remaining in the world. The critical question which needs answering is not who inspired Margery Kempe, for her inspiration must have been in the air much as feminism is in the air today, but where does Margery fit into the complex mosaic of late medieval pious women. In this paper I want to follow Allen's lead in a different, more general direction than Riehle, Atkinson and Stargardt have done. First, I will marshall the evidence which suggests that Margery Kempe aspired to the role of a pious woman, already in being two-hundred years before her time. Second, I hope to show that Margery's life represents an identifiably late medieval, bourgeois, English adaptation of that role.

2

What Allen refers to vaguely as a 'feminist movement' in piety is a well-documented, if diffuse phenomenon. Beginning in the early twelfth century not only were a growing number of women attracted to religion but the number of female saints began to increase. Whereas women constituted 10% of those sainted before 1100, in the next three centuries roughly 30% of those canonised were women.[12] Moreover, as Caroline Bynum has shown, a recognizably female type of piety emerged in the thirteenth century.[13] Commonly associated with ecstacy and a broad range of mystical and paramystical phenomena, female piety was concentrated on three particularly 'human' moments in the Christian story: the infant Jesus, Christ the bridgroom, and the dying Christ.[14] Connected with this interest in the humanity of Christ was an intense Eucharistic devotion, now considered one of the most characteristic and important spiritual creations of the late Middle Ages, but first developed and given form by women. Juliana of Cornillon campaigned for the addition of the feast of Corpus Christi to the liturgical calendar and devotion to the Sacred Heart was, to a great extent, a creation of the nuns of the Saxon monastery at Helfta.[15]

Women were also responsible for some of the most significant late medieval innovations in the form of religious life itself. Moved by the same spirit of Christian enthusiasm and desire to follow the *vita apostolica* which led an increasing number of men into religious life beginning in the early twelfth century, more and more women sought to live 'religiously'. But they generated very different opportunities for themselves from those the men did. As is well known, a number of new male orders, including the mendicants, were created in the twelfth and thirteenth centuries. But there was no corresponding establishment of new orders for women. What we find instead is a growth in the number and population of nunneries, some of them only nominally supervised and protected by a male order, and the proliferation of even less 'regular' and less regulated religious associations like the beguines, which brought women together in a self-supporting community, dedicated to prayer and works of charity without requiring formal vows.

The traditional explanation offered for the growth of these quasi-religious association has been the existence of a 'surplus' of women interested in religion but without the money necessary to enter a nunnery, and the reluctance of the male orders to assume the *cura monalium*, or the pastoral care of nuns.[16] Recent research, however, has raised questions about the adequacy of these intertwined theories of deprivation. Although it seems to be the case that established nunneries continued to attract noble and aristocratic women throughout the medieval period,[17] there is no indication that thirteenth century beguines, either in the Low Countries or in the Rhineland area, were forced into quasi-religious communities by financial incapacity.[18] Many women seem to have preferred and cultivated structureless, non-hierarchical communities[19] and in the thirteenth century, loosely organized groups of quasi-religious women appear all over Europe. Not only are there beguines in the Low Countries and the Rhineland, but *beatae* in Spain, tertiaries in Italy, and groups of recluses such as those for whom the *Ancrene Wisse* was written in England.

What were these new quasi-religious women like? Jacques de Vitry, confessor of Mary of Oignies, witnessed the growth of one of the earliest circles of beguines in Liège. Not distracted by superficial differences in organizational forms, Jacques de Vitry understood that Mary and the women she collected around her in Liège, the Franciscan women he observed in the hospitals in Umbria, as well as the women among the Humiliati he visited in Milan were all part of the same phenomenon, and he was content to refer to them all by the same simple title, *mulieres sanctae*. All of these women impressed him with their zeal and, even more, with their dedication to the apostolic life. Of the Humiliata, he wrote:

> Vix autem invenitur in tota civitate qui resitat hereticis, ex(c)eptis quisbusdam sanctis hominibus et re(li)giosis mulieribus, qui a maliciosis et secularibus hominibus *Patareni* nuncupantur, a summo autem pontifice, a quo habent auctoritatem predicandi et resistendi hereticis qui etiam religionem confirmavit, *Humiliati* vocantur; *hii sunt, qui* omnia pro Christo relinquentes in locis diversis congregantur, *de labore manuum suarum vivunt*, verbum dei frequenter predicant et libenter audiunt, *in fide perfecti et stabiles, in operibus efficaces.*[20]

And of Franciscan women in Umbria:

> multi enim utriusque sexus divites et seculares omnibus pro Christo relictis seculum
> fugiebant, qui *Fratres Minores* et *Sorores Minores* vocabantur. . . . Ipsi autem
> secundum formam primitive ecclesie vivunt, de quibus scriptum est: *multitudinis
> credentium erat cor unum et anima una.* De die intrant civitates et villas, ut aliquos
> lucrifaciant operam dantes actione; nocte vero revertuntur ad heremum vel loca
> solitaria vacantes contemplationi. Mulieres vero iuxta civitates in diversis hospitiis
> simul commorantur; nichil ster accipiunt, sed *de labore manuums* suarum *vivunt,*
> valde autem dolent et turbantur, quia a clericis et laicis plus quam vellent
> honorantur.[21]

But it was the *mulieres sanctae* of Liège who came in for Jacques de Vitry's
most fulsome and commendatory description. Addressing the Bishop of
Toulouse in the prologue to his life of Mary of Oignies, Jacques identified a
combination of penance, renunciation and hand-work which he found
characteristic of these *mulieres sanctae* and which he saw as a bulwark
against heresy and decay within the Church:

> Vidisti enim (& gavisus es) in hortis lilorum Domini multas sanctarum Virginum in
> diversis locis catervas, quae spretis pro Christo carnalibus illecebris, contemptis
> etiam amore regni caelestis huius mundi divitiis, in paupertate & humilitate Sponso
> caelesti adhaerentes, labore manuum tenuem victum quaerebant, licet parentes
> earum multis divitiis abundarent. Ipsae tamen obliviscentes populum suum &
> domum patris sui, malebant angustias & paupertatem sustinere, quam male
> acquisitis divitiis abundare, vel inter pomposos seculares cum periculo remanere.
> Vidisti (& gravisus es) sanctas & Deo servientes matronas, quanto zelo
> juvencularum pudicitiam conservarent, & eas in honesto proposito, ut solum
> caelestem Sponsum defiderarent, salutaribus monitis instruerent. Ipsae etiam
> viduae in jejuniis & orationibus, in vigiliis & labore manuum, in lacrymis &
> oblecrationibus, Domino servientes, sicut maritis suis prius placere nitebantur in
> carne, imo ita amplius Sponso caelesti placere studebant in spiritu; frequenter ad
> memoriam revocantes illud Apostoli: Vidua, quae in deliciis vivit, mortua est: &
> quod sanctae viduae, quae Sanctorum necessitatibus communicant, quae pedes
> papuerum lavant, quae hospitalitatem sectantur, quae operibus misericordiae
> insistunt, fructum sexagesiumum promerentur.[22]

Modern scholarship has confirmed the accuracy of Jacques de Vitry's
perceptions of thirteenth-century pious women, while giving us a more
comprehensive view of the facts.[23] Springing from the same urban soil as the
mendicants, pious women represent yet a broader phenomenon. Living the
common life half-way in between the rules of a religious order and the
freedom of lay people, chaste though not excluded from marriage, often
remaining in their own houses and supporting themselves with women's
traditional work, Jacques de Vitry's *mulieres sanctae* extended the
possibility of serious religious commitment to new social classes and showed
that it might be pursued without formal religious vows, without completely
severing secular ties or abandoning the world's work.

Unfortunately, there was no observer of pious women in the fourteenth century comparable to Jacques de Vitry nor, to date, have there been any modern studies of female piety which describe the evolution of the role of the pious woman beyond the thirteenth century. The work of gathering the data necessary to an accurate description of pious women in the latter Middle Ages is enormous, for evidence lies scattered in nönnenbücher, saints' lives and mystical treatises. Until it has been sifted, all conclusions should be regarded as tentative. But, bearing that in mind, there is reason to believe that the role of the pious women did not change much after the thirteenth century. A recent study of sanctity, *Saints and Society: The Two Worlds of Western Christendom 1000–1700*, indicates that, although there were dramatic changes in the perception of sanctity in the twelfth century, the patterns of holiness established then tend to endure through to the end of the medieval period.[24] Thus, despite the fact that women are sainted in growing numbers after the twelfth century, the types of such women do not change. Since the pious woman corresponds closely to one of the sainted types,[25] it seems likely that the role was conceived in essentially the same terms in Margery Kempe's time as in Jacques de Vitry's.

Yet, when one reads the lives of those individual women who were most outstanding fourteenth-century examples of the type, one is aware that they are subtly but significantly different from the lives of their thirteenth-century sisters. While the new characteristics of pious women in the fourteenth century are less innovations than developments of thirteenth-century trends, they also reflect dynamic changes within the church, including the deepening crisis of the Schism, the growing interest in mysticism and a new emphasis on the religious value of secular life.

In the thirteenth century a number of pious women including Mary of Oignies had aligned themselves with Rome against her enemies and received revelations concerning crusades against the infidel in the Holy Land and the heretic at home. In the fourteenth century this bond between pious women and the Papacy remained unbroken, but the two most influential and widely-known women of the century, St Bridget of Sweden and St Catherine of Siena, received revelations concerning the crisis of *their* day, the Great Schism. That their advice was welcome and influential is some measure of the enhanced status of prophecy and mysticism in the later Middle Ages. But it is also a measure of the power women achieved because to religious men they represented an alternative to and criticism of male power.[26] Arising, perhaps, from Christianity's paradoxical combination of world-affirmation and world-denial, doubts about their wealth and power plagued many religious men throughout the medieval period. Some including Jacque de Vitry found an escape and the promise of repose in pious women whose lack of worldly power made them seem both an indictment and a correction of male failings. Nor were women slow to use the advantage this male perception gave them. Catherine of Siena, Bridget of Sweden, even Joan of Arc are only continuing an old female tradition in advising males and attempting to shape politics.

But it is important to notice how much more forceful, independent, and generally mobile these women were than their earlier counterparts. The lives of many fourteenth-century pious women were filled with an extraordinary amount of political activity and external movement. Women not only felt competent to solve the crises of the time they actively exerted themselves to do so. St Catherine pushed herself to the point of collapse, perhaps hastening her early death, by travelling between Siena and Rome where she advised the Pope. St Bridget travelled over much of Europe. While her husband, Ulf, was alive, she was an advisor to the King of Sweden and after Ulf's death, she made the long journey from Sweden to Rome to instruct the Pope. At the age of nearly seventy she undertook a pilgrimage to the Holy Land. In this connection one thinks as well of the more nationalistic endeavours of Joan of Arc or the movements of St Katherine, Bridget's daughter, who accompanied her mother to Rome, then to the Holy Land, and finally headed the funeral entourage which carried Bridget's body back to Sweden for burial, stopping at all the major urban centres of eastern Europe on route. Even a saint as contemplative in temperament as Dorothea of Montau forced herself to go on pilgrimage, although her body rebelled. Having travelled from Danzig to Rome with her husband, she was overcome by a kind of hysterical paralysis and had to be carried home before she recovered. While all this activity was clearly enabled by the commercial economy of the fourteenth century, which allowed more people to travel longer distances in greater safety and comfort, it also represents an important extension of the sphere of female religious life so that it became practically conterminous with the world. The early beguines brought religious life out of the cloister into the world, but beyond that they, literally, did not move. Like nuns they remained in one place and to a certain degree their physical stability was regarded as a guarantee of their spiritual legitimacy by church officials.[27] It remained for innovative women like Catherine of Siena, Bridget of Sweden and later Margery Kempe to take the next step and to legitimate pilgrimage and other 'active' versions of the quasi-religious life.

Most importantly, a growing number of pious women in the fourteenth century were wives and mothers. A new view of marriage was worked out by canonists and scholastic theologians in the twelfth and thirteenth centuries which reduced the taint of sinfulness which had been associated with the marriage relationship since the apostolic period and allowed the Church to give a fuller blessing to the institution.[28] The impact of this revision is already evident in the thirteenth century when married saints begin to appear with new frequency.[29] As mentioned above, the earliest tertiaries as well as the original circle of beguines around Mary of Oignies included not only virgins and widows but wives, whom Jacques de Vitry called 'holy matrons,' a title that might have sounded almost oxymoronic a century before. One wonders, however, how many of these thirteenth-century 'holy matrons' were partners in marriages like Mary's own. Having made a vow of chastity when they married, Mary and her husband afterwards worked together 'like brother and sister', according to Jacques de Vitry, ministering to the sick and the poor around Liège.[30]

Although there are some well-known exceptions like Elizabeth of Hungary who died in 1231, it is not until the fourteenth century that we find many female saints who were mothers as well as wives and who tried to realise their spiritual aspirations within the context of family life. Then a significant number of saints who bore children and ran households appear and their stories were made popular in contemporary hagiography. One of these was St Frances of Rome, a spiritual 'sister' of Margery Kempe's in her attempt to blend prayerful service of God with the care of her husband and children: 'It is most laudable in a married woman to be devout,' Frances is reported to have said, 'but she must never forget that she is a housewife. And sometimes she must leave God at the altar to find him in her house-keeping'.[31] Other fourteenth-century pious women, although they became wives and mothers, were not themselves entirely comfortable with the new type of sanctity which they in fact helped to establish. Although she became the very model of a Christian wife, Bridget only accepted marriage with difficulty and when she was a well-recognized pious woman she stated her feelings on marriage (which echo the teaching of thirteenth-century canonists, and theologians) quite emphatically: 'Virginitas meretur coronam, viduitas appropinquat Deo, conjugium non excludit a caelo'.[32] By no stretch of the imagination, however, could Dorothea of Montau be called a good wife. She was many times overwhelmed by her family respon-sibilities, which she regarded as a distraction from her prayers, and which she allowed to fall to the lot of her difficult and disatisfied husband.[33]

The lives of these married women saints are important documents in literary history because they represent the first popular attempt to explore the meaning and value of Christian conjugal love. But they are also important documents in the history of spirituality because they detail the specific doubts and difficulties which had to be overcome as the possibility of serious religious commitment was extended to lay people more generally. Like the new mobility of fourteenth-century pious women, the growing number of them who were wives and mothers represents an extension of the sphere of female religious activity into the midst of secular life. But pious *wives* posed a more radical challenge to established traditions for implicit in that title was a recognition of the diversity of individual effort, the breakdown of old institutional forms, and the establishment of personal experience in their place.

3

Although she found her vocation later than most, Margery Kempe's biography conforms in broad outline to those of earlier pious wives. In contrast to other pious women who tend as a group to experience a religious calling in childhood, to marry, if they do, with some reluctance and continue to pursue religious goals with or without the support of their husbands, Margery Kempe was not converted until she was almost forty, when she had been married for twenty years and born fourteen children.[34] Although Margery had her first mystical vision much earlier, at the age of twenty as mentioned above, it rather encouraged than discouraged her from secular pursuits. With the second vision, however, Margery begins to sound and act like other pious wives. As she tells the story, one night as she lay in bed with her husband, 'sche heard a sownd of melodye so swet & delectable, hir þowt, as sche had ben in Paradyse. And þerwyth sche styrt owt of hir bedde & seyd, "Alas þat euyr I dede synne, it is ful mery in Hevyn" '.[35] From that time on, she reports, she never again desired to have sex with her husband and she began to live a life of penance: fasting, keeping vigils, wearing a hair shirt, etc. Two years later, after she was humiliated by having consented to the solicitations of a male 'friend' who asked her to sleep with him in order to test her virtue, she experienced a second conversion. As she prayed in St Margaret's church, mourning her sinfulness and frailty, Christ ravished her spirit and spoke to her in the first of the long colloquies which became the characteristic form of her revelations. Assuring her that her sins were forgiven 'to þe vtterest poynt,' he commanded her to follow a programme of piety which is recognizably female in its penitential and Eucharistic emphasis:

> And, dowtyr, þu hast an hayr vp-on þi bakke. I wyl þu do it a-way, & I schal ʒiue þe an hayr in þin hert þat schal lyke me mych bettyr, þan alle þe hayres in þe world. Also, my derworthy dowtyr, þu must forsake þat þow louyst best in þis world, & þat is etyng of flesch. And in-stede of þat flesche þow schalt etyn my flesche & my blod, þat is þe very body of Crist in þe Sacrament of þe Awter. Thys is my wyl, dowtyr þat þow receyue my body euery Sonday, and I schal flowe so mych grace in þe þat alle þe world xal meruelyn þerof.[36].

If Margery began her religious life somewhat later than other pious wives, she began it with a vengeance. In an extraordinarily unself-conscious and literal fashion (which, it is worth remarking, is also characteristic of her realization of meditative traditions), she put all the motifs commonly associated with the tradition of pious women into action. Like Bridget she began travelling to local shrines with her husband and like the Swedish saint, she was informed by Christ that she would subsequently fulfill her desire to go on pilgrimage to the Holy Land; like Dorothea of Montau she acquired the gift of holy tears and began weeping for hours on end while she prayed; and like every other pious wife of note, Margery began a campaign to 'live chaste'. Chastity was a central concern of Margery's throughout her long life, and precisely on account of her unself-consciousness she allows us to understand its particular function in the lives of pious women. Not just a physical austerity or a token of the conquest of the flesh, chastity was absolutely necessary to women who aspired to a spiritual life, since the only identity open to them throughout the medieval period was to be the brides of Christ. Thus, Margery once mourned the loss of her virginity to Christ, 'me thynkyth I wolde I had ben slayn whan I was takyn fro þe funtston þat I xuld neuyr a dysplesyd þe, & þan xuldyst þu, blyssed Lorde, an had my maydenhed wyth-owtyn ende. A der God, I haue not lovyd þe all þe days of my lyue, & þat sor rewyth me'. [37] And, on another occasion, when she had learned by revelation that she was pregnant, she complained, 'Lord, I am not worthy to heryn þe spekyn & þus to comown wyth myn husbond. Ner-þe-lesse it is to me gret peyn & gret dysese'. [38]

Some modern readers find that Margery's concern for her lost virginity and her desire to dress in the white clothes of a virgin dedicated to God once she and John made a sacramental vow of chastity morbid and neurotic. But that is to ignore the advance implicit in Margery's insistence that she be recognized as the bride of Christ, although a wife and mother. Like other pious wives of her time, Margery was engaged in fashioning a spiritual identity for herself out of traditions elaborated for and by women in very different circumstances. Ironically, because of the unself-conscious and literal way she construed the traditional requirement of chastity, her position on the issue eventually became the most liberal and individualistic of all pious women. For example, Christ had told Bridget: 'Ordinary, honourable matrimony [communis laudbilis status] is pleasing to Me. Moses, who led My people out of the thraldom of Egypt, was married, Peter was called to be an apostle while his wife was still living. Judith found grace in My eyes by her widowhood. But John, who was a virgin, pleased Me most, and I gave My mother into his care. For because he lived like the angels he deserved to be the guardian of chastity'. [39] But to Margery Kempe he promised much more. On one occasion he said:

3a, dowtyr, trow þow rygth wel þat I lofe wyfes also, and specyal þo wyfys whech woldyn levyn chaste, 3yf þei mygtyn haue her wyl, & don her besynes to plesyn me as þow dost, for þow, þe state of maydenhode be more parfyte & more holy þan þe state of wedewhode, and þe state of wedewhode mor parfyte þan þe state [of] wedlake, 3et dowtyr I lofe þe as wel as anymoyden in þe world. [40]

On another occasion, when Margery worried she would be excluded from the group of one hundred and forty-four thousand virgins dancing around God's throne at the end of time, Christ assured her that:

&, for-as-mech as þu art a mayden in þi sowle, I xal take þe be þe on hand in Hevyn
& my Modyr be þe oþer hand, & so xalt þu dansyn in Hevyn wyth oþer holy
maydens & virgynes, for I may clepyn þe dere a-bowte & myn owyn derworthy
derlyng. I xal sey to þe, myn own blysed spowse, 'Welcome to me wyth al maner of
joye & gladnes, her to dwellyn wyth me & neuyr to departen from me wyth-owtyn
ende. . . .[41]

Compared to those of many other pious wives, Margery's campaign for
chastity was neither particularly long nor particularly bitter. Within four
years, John Kempe agreed to Margery's desire for a sacramental vow of
chastity, asking in return that she continue to sleep in his bed, give up her
Friday fasts and eat and drink with him again, and pay his debts.[42] The
accomplishment of that vow, which the Kempes made before Philip
Repington, Bishop of Lincoln, probably in 1413, ushered in a new phase in
Margery's life as a pious woman. Almost immediately she left on the first
and most extensive of her pilgrimages, a journey to the Holy Land and
Rome. Separated from her family and her normal obligations as a housewife
for over two years, she lived the quasi-religious life of a pilgrim which helped
her to further consolidate her identity as a pious women. Like St Bridget,
she experienced a deepening of her devotion to the dying Christ in
Jerusalem[43] and it was in Jerusalem that her gift of tears took on a new, more
'boistrous' character. Like Angela of Foligno, Mary of Oignies, and
Dorothea of Montau, Margery began to cry loudly at every verbal or
symbolic reminder of Christ's Passion.

In many ways, however, it was Rome rather than Jerusalem which
proved central to Margery's development as a pious woman. There she
sought out the house in which St Bridget had lived and spoke with the saint's
serving woman. There she gave away all she had and, briefly, lived a life of
apostolic poverty like the early beguines and tertiaries, caring for a poor old
woman and begging for food. And it was in Rome, just before she was to
begin the final leg of her long pilgrimage and depart for England and home
again, that she was married to the Godhead in one of the most intriguing of
all such ceremonies reported in devotional literature.

As Margery reports the event, she was praying one day in the Church of
the Holy Apostles when she learned by revelation that she was to be wed to
'þe Godhed'. Stunned and confused since all her love and affection was
directed toward 'þe manhode of Crist', she silently took part in a wedding in
which God the Father spoke the groom's words from the contemporary
English ceremony:

And þan þe Fadyr toke hir be þe hand in hir sowle be-for þe Sone & þe Holy Gost
& þe Modyr of Ihesu and all þe xij apostelys Seynt Kateryn & Seynt Margarete &
many oþer seyntys & holy virgynes wyth gret multitude of awngelys, seying to hir
sowle, 'I take þe, Margery, for my weddyd wyfe, for fayrar, for fowelar, for richar,
for powerar, so þat þu be buxom & bonyr to do what I byd þe do. For, dowytr, þer
was neuyr childe so buxom to þe modyr as I xal be to þe boþe in wel & in wo,—to

help þe and comfort þe. And þerto I make þe suyrte.' And þan þe Modyr of God &
alle þe seyntys þat wer þer present in hir sowle preyde þat þei myth haue mech joy
to-gedyr.[44]

Sometimes regarded as an illustration of how an uneducated woman
misunderstood and literalized the allegorical imagery of the *Song of
Songs*,[45] it is now clear that the apparently 'crude' realism of Margery's
spiritual marriage is typically female. Medieval women as a group gravitated
toward images of continuity—they are sisters, mothers and brides of
Christ—and in their elaboration of such images, women typically insist on
their concrete, sensuous meaning.[46] Margery Kempe goes no further in this
direction than Dorothea of Montau who was mystically married to Christ,
each time with a different ring, or Catherine of Siena, whose marriage to
Christ was sealed with a ring she continued to see on her finger the rest of her
life. What makes Margery Kempe's mystical marriage distinctive is not its
naive realism but its social dimension. To a much greater degree than any
other pious woman, Margery was inclined to interpret her spiritual
experience in social terms. What we see in her mystical marriage is not a
private pledge of love between the soul and God as in Catherine and
Dorothea but a public ceremony, complete with hundreds of heavenly
guests, which clearly reflects the Englishness of Margery's experience.

Margery tells us next to nothing about what transpired between her
return from Rome and her departure in 1417 on a second pilgrimage to St
James of Compostella in Spain; and, although she has much to say about her
return from Spain, the high drama of her two trials as a Lollard does not bear
directly on the question of her career as a pious woman which concerns us
here. More pertinent is the fact that once she was safely back in Lynn
Margery found herself forced to take up residence alone to quiet the gossips
who suggested that she and John Kempe still slept together despite their vow
of chastity. For the rest of her life, she appears to have dedicated herself to
prayer and good works. Though she never tells us how she supported herself
or precisely how she spent her days, the information she does give us about
her assiduous attendance at sermons, the forms of her prayers, her visits to
the nuns at Denny, her ministrations to a 'mad woman', whom no one else
could calm, all suggest that she lived a life rather like that of a solitary
beguine from 1417 until 1425 or 1426.

In that year her life assumed a new configuration when John Kempe was
incapacitated by a fall and she was forced to assume the difficult task of
nursing him. Initially distressed by the prospect of abandoning her prayers
and contemplations to care for an invalid, she was assured by Christ: 'þu xalt
haue as meche mede for to kepyn hym & helpyn hym in hys nede at hom as
3yf þu wer in chirche to makyn þi preyers',[47] and she persevered although
her labour was increased when John

'in hys last days . . . turnyd chilisch a-3en & lakkyd reson þat he cowd not don hys owyn esement to gon to a sege, er ellys he wolde not, but as a childe voydyd his natural digestyon in hys lynyn clothys þer he sat be þe fyre er at þe tabil, whepyr it wer, he wolde sparyn no place'.[48]

In the spirit of St Frances of Rome, Margery Kempe found a way to transform her domestic labours into a prolonged act of devotion:

. . . many tymys sche xuld an yrkyd hir labowr saf sche bethowt hir how sche in hir 3ong age had ful many delectabyl thowtys, fleschly lustys, & inordinat louys to hys persone. & þerfor sche was glad to be ponischyd wyth þe same persone & toke it mech þe mor esily & seruyd hym & helpyd hym, as hir thowt, as sche wolde a don Crist hym-self.[49]

On her own level of social life, within an English and domestic sphere, Margery Kempe put the motifs commonly associated with pious women into action. But, if her life corresponds in broad outline to those of earlier pious women, in certain striking particulars it does not. For instance, while Margery gave her own distinctive development to the traditional female stress on chastity, she has relatively little interest in the kind of apostolic poverty which was one of the goals of thirteenth-century beguine life. In fact, concern for poverty became attenuated in the lives of other fourteenth-century women as well. As more married women, living at home, aspired to some kind of quasi-religious status, the question of poverty necessarily assumed new dimensions. One might very well wish to divest oneself of property and 'naked follow the naked Christ', but there were the wishes of other, perhaps less religiously inclined family-members to be honoured as well. Medieval women did not often possess the power to determine the course of their own lives, much less those of their families. For better or for worse, none could behave as autocratically as Nevelone de Faenza, Patron of Shoemakers, whose religious enthusiasm led him to give away all he had despite the objections of his wife who was forced to follow him into poverty.[50] While St Frances of Rome was fortunate in having an understanding husband who encouraged her charity and protected her from the complaints of his family, St Bridget only divested herself of property after her husband died and she abandoned conventional domestic life.

Margery Kempe's dedication to poverty, however, is so attenuated that it seems insignificant. Although she must have been familiar with the mendicant orders from an early age, voluntary poverty never presented itself to her as a personal possibility until she was a pilgrim in Rome. Only when she had been transplanted to the rather different culture of Southern Italy for six months, was she commanded by Christ to '3euyn a-wey al hir good & makyn hir bar for hys lofe'.[51] In a flamboyant Franciscan gesture, Margery not only gave away all she had, but what she had borrowed from a travelling companion named Richard as well. Assuring the unhappy man that she would repay him 'in Brystowe in þe Whitsunwoke . . . for I trust ryth wel þat he þat bad me ʒeuyn it a-wey for hys lofe wil help me to payn it a-geyn',[52] Margery lived in poverty, fed and sheltered by the good Christians of Rome, for several months until she embarked for home.

While there is nothing disingenuous in Margery's experience of poverty itself, there is something about its timing (as well as the mystery of how she afterwards paid her fare back to England) which makes one wonder if the whole experience was consciously conceived as an experiment, limited in time and space and carefully insulated from life in Lynn. In any event, it is certainly true that Margery subsequently confined the experience of poverty as much as possible to her pilgrimages. Though she ardently desired it, she never found a community in Lynn like that in Rome which was willing to support her 'for the love of God'. Although she takes great pleasure in telling the story of how she was given money for her second pilgrimage to Spain (at which time she also repaid her debt to Richard, some two years late), at that point the theme of poverty disappears from her story.

There was a marked difference, as Margery's experience suggests, between northern and southern European attitudes toward poverty;[53] and one recalls that no less a pious woman than Mary of Oignies allowed her friends to dissuade her from dressing in rags and begging from door to door.[54] But, as far as we know, the kind of hand-work which became the alternative to begging for pious women in the Low Countries and the Rhineland held no sway with Margery Kempe either. Where Jacques de Vitry reports that Mary of Oignies kept a spindle before her book when she prayed,[55] all Margery's 'huswyfries' are associated with the period before her conversion. When she became a pious woman, she seems to have separated herself as completely as she could from her former responsibilities as a housewife. Although she subsequently returned to the domestic world to care for John Kempe, as we have seen, it was not the place she chose for her *imitatio Christi*.

Unlike Mary of Oignies and other pious women from the higher levels of social life for whom hand-work and housework were *voluntary* spiritual disciplines for Margery they were the unavoidable practical burdens of everyday life. Here she stands, significantly, with Dorothea von Montau, who was also a middle-class housewife and who also experienced the demands of running a household as an unwelcome interruption of her spiritual vocation. It is from this perspective that Margery's ability to integrate nursing her husband into her spiritual life can be said to represent unusual maturity—and creativity. Like few other women of her time she managed to combine her search for God with the mundane burdens of her ordinary life.

The central role which poverty or hand-work played in the lives of other pious women was filled in Margery's life by a particular, and some would say, peculiar kind of humility. We have already heard Jacques de Vitry praising the great humility of tertiaries and the *mulieres sanctae* near Liège who were distressed when men honoured them for their piety. But Jacques mentions nothing which even begins to approach Margery's dedication to what she calls 'schame' or 'dyspite of þe werld'.[56] From the time of her conversion, when she was mocked by her neighbours who felt suspicious of her new-found virtue, Margery embraced public humiliation as a sign that she had put on 'the new woman'. She tells us that she was 'as mery whan sche was repreuyd, skornyd, or japyd for ower Lordy's lofe, & mych mor mery þan sche was be-for-tyme in þe worshepys of þe world'.[57]

Clearly descended from the Franciscan desire to be the lowliest and most despised of all (*sint minores et subditi omnibus*)[58] Margery's commitment to shame finds its closest parallel in the thirteenth-century tertiary, Angela of Foligno. Like Margery, a woman whose conversion followed marriage and motherhood, Angela was also given to graphic, public displays of her feelings. For example, she wished to go naked and to wear pieces of raw meat and fish around her neck so that everyone would know how vile a woman she was.[59]

For both these pious women, shame served an obvious penitential function. It was a way to punish (while simultaneously gratifying) a particular kind of *social* pride and desire for attention. But for Margery, shame also became a substitute for poverty and the basis of her distinctive *imitatio Christi*. As she explains it:

> . . . dyspite of þe werld was þe rygth way to-Heuyn-ward sythen Cryst hym-self ches þat way. Alle hys apostlys, martyres, confessorys, & virgynes and alle þat euyr comyn to Heuyn passed be þe wey of tribulacyon, and sche desyryd no-thyng so mech as Heuyn.[60]

As Margery's spirituality developed and her unusual devotional practices including the 'boistrous' crying she began in Jerusalem and the white clothing which she began to wear after her marriage to the Godhead in Rome, made her more and more notorious, this 'apostolic' notion of shame became even more important to her. Whenever she was particularly distressed, Christ promised her, 'þe mor schame, despite, & reprefe þat þu sufferyst for my lofe, þe bettyr I lofe þe'.[61]

But as it absorbed the traditional role of poverty and became the basis of Margery's *imitatio Christi*, shame assumed another important role in her spiritual life as well. We have already had occasion to mention that in the late medieval period pious women were what Victor and Edith Turner call 'liminal' to men.[62] They were perceived as a moment of reversal of worldly standards, as an alternative and corrective to male power. To some degree Margery regarded her own femaleness as liminal in this way and during her trials for Lollardry, particularly, she rejoiced that God 'had ȝouyn hir not lettryd witte and wisdom to answeryn so many lernyd men wyth-owtyn velani or blame'.[63] But far more than gender it was shame on which Margery depended for the experience of liminality. To *her* shame was a guarantee of purity and it became the basis of her particular critique of the male clergy. In her shame, suffering in union with the suffering Christ, Margery felt free to speak out against the worldliness of the clergy. Though her scope was admittedly quite limited and local, Margery Kempe was considerably freer and more outspoken in her criticism of the clergy than almost any earlier pious woman. And it is thus that many readers of *The Book* will remember her, scolding the members of the Archbishop of Canterbury's household for swearing, reprimanding Philip of Repington, Bishop of Lincoln for 'dread[ing] more þe schamys of þe world þan þe parfyt lofe of God',[64] daring to moralise against clerical immorality even when she was on trial for her life in the court of the Archbishop of York.

Closely connected with this open critque of the clergy is the final aspect of Margery's piety which sets her apart from other pious women: her relative aloofness from Eucharistic devotion. While Margery is certainly interested in the Eucharist, which she obtained episcopal permission to receive once a week, an extraordinary privilege for a lay woman,[65] still no one would want to argue that the Eucharist was the centre of her mysticism, as it was for most earlier pious women. Margery's one Eucharistic vision, the sight of a dove rising from the cup, is not only extremely conventional but never elaborated. Furthermore, although Margery's tears were generally prompted by the sacrament and she had to be 'howselyd' alone lest the entire congregation be disturbed, her tears and visions were just as likely to be prompted by other reminders of the Passion. She cried, Margery tells us, as often as fourteen times a day:

> sumtyme in þe cherch, sumtyme in þe strete, sumtym in þe chawmbre, sumtyme in þe felde . . . whan sche saw þe Crycyfyx, er yf sche sey a man had a wownde er a best whepyr it wer, er ȝyf a man bett a childe be-for hir er smet an hors er an-oþer best wyth a whippe, ȝyf sche myth sen it er heryn it. . . .[66]

In Margery Kempe we see female mysticism moving out of its traditional Eucharistic context and, therefore, *potentially* away from clerical control. At least one person in Margery's orbit seems to have sensed this. He was the famous preaching friar, tentatively identified as William Melton,[67] who came to Lynn in 1420. When Margery had interrupted his sermons twice with her loud sobbing he ordered her out of his church, not to return unless she was willing to admit that her tears were the symptom of 'cardiakyll ersum oþer sekenesse'.[68] While the tears she wept were a gloss on his sermons, a graphic demonstration of the compassion for Christ he recommended, they made it impossible for people to hear him and directed attention away from the pulpit into the congregation, and towards the experience of grace itself. Although there are obvious psychological explanations which might be offered for Margery's behaviour, here as at other points where she seems significantly different from continental pious women, we can see the shaping influence of some of the English anti-clerical attitudes which found less orthodox expression in the Lollard movement.

It would be surprising if the English pressure which helped to mould Margery's inner spiritual impulses had not left their mark on her outer life as well—and indeed they did. What Margery calls her 'manner of living' was substantially less institutional and more individualistic than that of any earlier pious woman. As remarked earlier, female piety in the later Middle Ages tends to be a group, even a family phenomenon. Margery, however, lived most of her life in complete isolation from other pious women. Aside from a visit to Julian in her cell at Norwich, her time with the old woman she served in Rome, and occasional visits to the nuns at Denney, Margery seems to have had no contact at all with other religious women. Neither did she gather about her a spiritual 'family' like Catherine of Siena's, nor nurture a circle of 'sons' like Angela of Foligno, nor, as any number of Italian women including Angela and Frances of Rome, find community and support in a third order.

In point of fact, Margery probably could not have become a tertiary had she wanted to. Apart from two priests nothing is known of any English tertiaries in the medieval period.[69] In striking contrast to the countries of southern and northern Europe where the evangelical awakening of the eleventh and early twelfth centuries was associated with the foundation of new communities, both lay and religious, in England it was early associated with the solitary life. Indeed the author of the *Ancrene Wisse*, a twelfth-century tract intended for a group of anchoresses which helped propagate the new piety in England, at one point feels compelled to comment on the unusual harmony which binds his particular audience together and makes them a community in contrast to other more 'singular' groups.[70] Whether it reflects an aspect of national character, or the turmoil following the Conquest, or, more probably the fact that England lacked the kind of town-life in which such movements developed on the Continent, it simply did not produce lay or semi-religious association in the twelfth or thirteenth centuries. In the fourteenth century when English women began to experience the religious fervor which had swept over the towns of Europe earlier, piety generally had become more individualistic. In her singularity, isolation and individuality, Margery Kempe represents a medieval, English middle-class version of one of the most important feminist movements in history.

NOTES

1. According to her own account, Margery 'went out of hir mende & was wondyrle vexid & labowryd wyth spyritys half 3er viij wkys & odde days'. See *The Book of Margery Kempe*, ed. Sanford Brown Meech and Hope Emily Allen, Early English Text Society, O.S. 212, 1940, p. 7, in the following notes abbreviated *The Book*.
2. D. Knowles, *The English Mystical Tradition*, London, 1961, p. 142.
3. See L. Collis, *Apprentice Saint*, London, 1964.
4. See E. Colledge, 'Margery Kempe', in *Pre-Reformation English Spirituality*, ed. J. Walsh, New York, 1969, pp. 210–233.
5. See W. Pantin, *The English Church in the Fourteenth Century*, Cambridge, 1955; Medieval Academy Reprints for Teaching, 1980, pp. 256–260.
6. See H. Weissman, 'Margery Kempe in Jerusalem: *Hysteria Compassio* in the Late Middle Ages', in *Acts of Interpretation: The Text in Its Context*, ed., M. J. Carruthers and E. D. Kirk, Norman, Oklahoma, 1982, pp. 201–217. A. Goodman, 'The Piety of John Brunham's Daughter, of Lynn', in *Studies in Church History*, I, ed., D. Baker, Oxford, 1978, pp. 347–358.
7. H. Thurston, 'Margery the Astonishing', *The Month*, 168 (1936), 446–456.
8. See H. Allen, 'Prefatory Notes', *The Book*, p. lix.
9. See W. Riehle, *The Middle English Mystics*, trans. B. Standring, London, 1981.
10. C. Atkinson, *Mystic and Pilgrim*, Ithaca, 1983, esp. pp. 157–194.
11. U. Stargardt, 'The Influence of Dorothea von Montau on the Mysticism of Margery Kempe', Ph.D. diss., University of Tennessee, 1981, pp. 129–143.
12. See M. Goodich, 'The Contours of Female Piety in Later Medieval Hagiography', *Church History*, 50 (1981), 20. R. Bell and D. Weinstein, *Saints and Society: The Two Worlds of Western Christendom, 1000–1700*, Chicago, 1981, pp. 220, 224.
13. See C. Bynum, *Jesus as Mother*, Berkeley, 1980, pp. 170–174, pp. 247–262. C. Bynum, 'Women Mystics and Eucharistic Devotion in the Thirteenth Century', *Medieval Women*, ed. H. Weissman, (forthcoming).
14. C. Bynum, 'Eucharistic Devotion', *op. cit.*
15. *Ibid.* See also E. McDonnell, *Beguines and Beghards in Medieval Culture*, New York, 1969, pp. 219–319.
16. For this theory and its principal variations, see H. Grundman, *Religiose Bewegungen im Mittelatter*, Rptd. Hildesheim, 1961. R. Southern, *Western Society and the Church in the Middle Ages*, Harmondsworth, 1970, pp. 318–331.
    B. Bolton, 'Mulieres Sanctae', *Studies in Church History*, 10, ed. D. Baker, Oxford, 1973; Rpt. *Medieval Woman*, ed. S. Stuard, Philadelphia, 1976, pp. 141–158.
17. E. Power, *Medieval English Nunneries*, Cambridge, 1922, pp. 4–6. E. McDonnell, *op. cit.*, pp. 81–90.
18. *Ibid.* pp. 96–99.
19. See C. Bynum, 'Women's Stories, Woman's Symbols', *Anthropology and the Study of Religions*, ed. F. Reynolds and R. Moore, (University of Chicago Press, forthcoming).
20. *Lettres de Jacques de Vitry*, ed. R. Huygens, Leiden, 1960, pp. 72–76.
21. *Ibid.*, pp. 75–76.
22. Jacques de Vitry, 'Vita Mary Oigniacenis', in *Acta Sanctorum*, June 4, Antwerp, pp. 636–637.
23. See especially E. McDonnell, *op. cit.*, p. 36, pp. 81–100, pp. 120–140; B. Bolton, *op. cit.*, A. Mens, 'Les beguines et beghards dans le cadre de la culture medievale', *Moyen Age*, 64 (1958), 305–315; S. Roisin 'L'efflorescence cistercienne [et le courant feminin de piete au XIII siecle,]' *Revue d'Histoire Eccliastique*, 39 (1943), 342–378.
24. R. Bell and D. Weinstein, *op. cit.*, pp. 246–248, and see also the statistical profiles of saints, pp. 123–138.
25. *Ibid.*, pp. 132–133, cf, the profile of those women 'Converted to Chastity'.
26. For an excellent discussion of women's liminality for men, see C. Bynum, 'Women's Stories, Women's Symbols', *op. cit.*
27. E. McDonnell, *op. cit.*, pp. 124 & 127.

28. For an excellent summary of the development of marriage doctrine, see. L. Godefroy and G. LeBras in *Dictionnaire de theologie catholique*, ed. A. Vacant, E. Mangenot, and E. Amann, Paris, 1927, 9, pt. 2, pp. 2044–2335. For a more specialized treatment, bearing directly on the lives of pious women, see M. Glasser, 'Marriage in Medieval Hagiography', *Studies in Medieval and Renaissance History*, 4 (1981), 3–34.

29. R. Bell and D. Weinstein, *op. cit.*, pp. 123–137. M. Glasser, *op. cit.*, p. 32, n. 58.

30. Vita Mary Oigniacensis, *op. cit.*, p. 642.

31. Alban Butler, *Lives of the Saints*, ed., rev., and supplemented H. Thurston and D. Attwater, New York, 1956, I, p. 530.

32. J. Jørgensen, *St. Bridget of Sweden*, trans. I. Lund, 2 vols., New York, 1954, 1, p. 45.

33. For Dorothea's domestic difficulties, see U. Stargardt, *op. cit.*, pp. 65–66.

34. *The Book*, p. 115.

35. *The Book*, p. 11.

36. *The Book*, p. 17.

37. *The Book*, p. 50.

38. *The Book*, p. 48.

39. Quoted in J. Jørgensen, *op. cit.*, 1, p. 145.

40. *The Book*, p. 49.

41. *The Book*, pp. 52–53.

42. *The Book*, p. 24.

43. For Bridget's experiences in Jerusalem, see J. Jørgensen, *op. cit.*, 2, pp. 232–291, esp. pp. 248–249.

44. *The Book*, p. 87.

45. For example, W. Riehle, *op. cit.*, pp. 37 and 98.

46. C. Bynum, 'Women's Stories, Women's Symbols', *op. cit.*

47. *The Book*, p. 180.

48. *The Book*, p. 181.

49. *Idem.*

50. R. Bell and D. Weinstein, *op. cit.*, p. 113.

51. *The Book*, p. 92.

52. *The Book*, p. 92.

53. R. Bell and D. Weinstein, *op. cit.*, pp. 175–193, esp. Table 8, pp. 188–191. E. McDonnell, *op. cit.*, pp. 141–153.

54. Jacques de Vitry, *op. cit.*, pp. 650–651.

55. *Ibid*, p. 648.

56. *The Book*, p. 13.

57. *Idem.*

58. Quoted in E. Auerbach, *Mimesis*, trans. W. Trask, Princeton, 1953, p. 256.

59. *The Book of Divine Consolation of the Blessed Angela of Foligno*, trans. M. Steegman, rpt. New York, 1966, pp. 18–19.

60. *The Book*, p. 13.

61. *The Book*, p. 81.

62. Victor Turner and Edith Turner, *Image and Pilgrimage in Christian Culture*, New York, 1978, esp. pp. 243–255.

63. *The Book*, p. 128.

64. *The Book*, p. 35.

65. A Benedictine of Stanbrook, 'Margery Kempe and the Holy Eucharist', *Downside Review*, 56 (1938), 468–482.

66. The Book, p. 69.

67. See *The Book*, p. 321, Allen's note on 148/28–29, for the identity of the preaching friar.

68. *The Book*, p. 151.

69. C. Moorman, *History of the Franciscan Order in England*, London, 1974, p. 45.

70. For an excellent discussion of the issue of 'singularity', see C. Kirschberger, 'Some Notes on the *Ancrene Riwle*', *Dominican Studies*, 7 (1954), 215–238.

MYSTICS AND FOLLOWERS IN SIENA AND EAST ANGLIA: A STUDY IN TAXONOMY, CLASS AND CULTURAL MEDIATION

DAVID WALLACE

1

FOR OVER FIFTY YEARS now critics have worried over Margery Kempe's standing as a religious writer.[1] How is Margery to be classified as an English mystic? Hope Emily Allen admits that Margery's *Book* cannot easily be aligned with 'the English tradition of medieval piety, which seems to run with such continuity from the early Middle English *Ancrene Riwle*, through Rolle, Hilton [and] *The Cloud of Unknowing*'.[2] Allen ascribes Margery's aberrations to contacts with 'the flotsam and jetsam of popular devotion' (which represents 'a cruder type of English piety') and to the influence of foreigners.[3] Yet having suggested that it is not easy to perceive of Margery as an authentic English mystic, Allen announces her intention to treat her as if she were: 'I have studied the mysticism of Margery Kempe on the basis of her being a true mystic'.[4]

Such confusion stems not from the writings of Margery Kempe, but rather from the concepts that are brought to bear on them. Much of the abuse that has been lavished on Margery reflects such critical frustration: her *Book* refuses to adapt itself to the critical categories that have been prepared for it. What are these categories? We assume that a writer may be either secular or religious, and that her writings may be popular or (to borrow a phrase from Dante)[5] illustrious. This generates four combinations: a writer may be religious and illustrious, religious and popular, secular and illustrious or secular and popular. Such concepts are useful as points of reference, but not as mutually-exclusive, air-tight compartments. There is, of course, a great temptation to group the English mystics within one such compartment. The mystic stands at a remove from the secular world, walled off from popular and profane influences. Her domain is religious, her style illustrious.

Another pair of opposed concepts, at once literary and social, is currently in vogue: the 'carnivalesque' and 'official' cultures of the Middle Ages. Mikhail Bakhtin proposes that 'a boundless world of humorous forms and manifestations opposed the official and serious tone of medieval ecclesiastical and fuedal culture'.[6] Medieval people lived two lives: 'one the *official*, monolithically serious and gloomy life, subject to a strict hierarchical order, filled with fear, dogmatism, reverence and piety, and the other, the *life of the carnival square*'.[7] These propositions are certainly suggestive: they invite us to consider Margery Kempe as a carnivalesque figure[8] struggling to occupy official space. Bakhtin concedes that his categories are not mutually exclusive: he speaks, for example, of the 'carnivalized Catholicism'[9] of St Francis of Assisi. But such a concession is not enough: institutional Christianity has constantly sought (with more or less success) to catch up with, to contain, to adapt itself to the core of carnival that forms the organic centre of its writings and liturgical practices. Bakhtin sees the essence of carnival as '*the pathos of vicissitudes and changes, of death and renewal*'.[10] It was just such an essence that medieval people of all backgrounds discovered and responded to in pictorial and literary representations of the life of Christ. Medieval culture sees continuous movement between secular and religious, carnival and official, popular and illustrious, parochial and international, visual and literary traditions and constantly eludes the taxonomical structures that we prepare for it.

This paper considers the cultural practices that took shape around Catherine of Siena: how popular, secular and extra-literary phenomena contributed to Catherine's mystical experience; and how some of her most educated and devout followers appropriated a popular and secular genre of narrative (known as the *cantare*) in communicating with popular audiences. Various aspects of such cultural mediation are related to the activities of English religious authors, mystics and their followers. It is hoped that this expansion of historical, geographical and taxonomical parameters will help liberate Margery's *Book* from the narrow confines of insular, illustrious mysticism within which it is habitually condemned. To achieve this we must take into account those cultural influences that Hope Emily Allen chooses to exclude: 'the flotsam and jetsam of popular devotion'; 'a cruder type of English piety'; the influence of foreigners.

2

Saint Catherine, whose apostolate was first practised 'in the streets and squares of Siena',[11] was alive to this free trafficking between diverse spheres of culture. Catherine has often been compared, as a well-educated, highly disciplined mystic, to Julian of Norwich.[12] But she has much in common with Margery Kempe, too. Catherine and Margery were public and not reclusive figures. Both travelled extensively, visiting both anchorites of exceptional piety and figures of exceptional ecclesiastical authority: Catherine sought out popes and Margery archbishops.[13] Both met with much misunderstanding and opposition, especially from clerics; both were accused of heresy.[14] Both thought themselves susceptible to worldly vanities: the young Catherine dyed her hair, and Margery delighted in 'pompows aray'.[15] Both carried self-mortification to extreme lengths: Catherine practised flagellation, and Margery bit her own hand so violently that she was scarred for life.[16] Both were profoundly influenced by visual imagery; and both were personally devoted to St Catherine of Egypt.[17] Both were ambitious to secure not only their own salvation, but that of many thousands.[18] Catherine's writings first became widely known in England through *The Orcherd of Syon*, a full and faithful paraphrase of Catherine's *Dialogo*[19] which was prepared for the first generation of Bridgettine nuns at Syon Abbey.[20] It has been suggested that Julian was acquainted with Catherine's writings,[21] and it is highly probable that Margery heard of Catherine during her travels through Italy, and especially during her winter residence at Venice in 1413–14.[22]

Catherine and her twin sister Giovanna (who died in infancy) were the twenty-third and twenty-fourth of twenty-five children in a Sienese family of the lower middle class, or *popolo minuto*.[23] Catherine's formative years, spent in the 'swarming hurly-burly'[24] of this household, evidently influenced her concept of a *famiglia* or family of disciples. And her socio-political ideal of *communitas christiana*—which seems archaic and naive when viewed in the context of late fourteenth-century Europe—also reflects her Sienese upbringing.[25] The Sienese *commune* stressed civic rather than individualistic values: between 1287 and 1355 it provided one of the most stable and complete forms of government known to the medieval world.[26] Supervision by the *commune* was pervasive: hospitals, leprosarium, *studium*, planning permission, brothels, accqueducts and fire brigade were all subject to state control.[27] Siena was, however, severely hit by the Black Death of 1348, losing half its population. Although Catherine was only an infant at this time, the whole of her brief life was spent in the aftermath of this disaster. She suffered severe personal losses in the renewed plague outbreaks of 1363 and 1374.[28] Members of her family came into political favour in 1355, but needed the protection of Catherine's religious reputation when the new regime failed in 1368.[29] This 1368 failure brought about the most broad-based government in Tuscan history: but this also collapsed in 1385, five years after Catherine's death.[30] Julian's childhood in East Anglia was similarly coloured by the 1348 disaster.[31] Margery's *Book* bears the signs of both recurrent and original disruptions to civil life.

The public circumstances of Catherine's upbringing and apostolate brought her into daily contact with popular traditions of lyric and narrative verse. She certainly knew of the popular hymns known as *laude*: but this tradition was taken up and developed most vigorously by another Sienese religious leader, Giovanni Colombini, who founded a lay congregation known as the Gesuati in 1366.[32] Catherine is, however, closely associated with the deliberate cultivation of one popular Tuscan tradition: the *cantare*. The three men who adapted the *cantare* for religious purposes at Siena—Pagliaresi, Tancredi and Cicerchia—were dedicated members of Catherine's *famiglia*; all three were at Avignon in 1376 for the most famous episode in Catherine's political career, her meeting with Pope Gregory XI. A *cantare* is a stanzaic narrative in *ottava rima* (hendecasyllables rhyming abababcc) which is publicly performed by a street-singer or *canterino*. In meeting a taste for spectacular combats and fantastic adventures, the authors of the *cantari* made much use of translations from French *lais*, *fabliaux* and romances. Before members of Catherine's Sienese *famiglia* appropriated the genre for evangelising purposes, the *cantare* was dedicated almost exclusively to secular subjects. *Canterini* beguiled the populace with tantalising visions of a distant world of aristocratic manners. In this and much else they had a good deal in common with the English tail-rhyme romancers.

The religious *canterino* who was closest to Catherine was undoubtedly Neri di Landoccio Pagliaresi. Born of a noble Sienese family in 1350, Pagliaresi held important civic offices at Siena in 1371 and 1375. He was perhaps the most esteemed of Catherine's personal secretaries, playing an important part in the drafting of her *Libro della divina dottrina*.[33] He travelled extensively in the service of Catherine and received at least eleven letters from her.[34] A number of *laude* are attributed to him, together with two *cantari*. His major work was the *Leggenda di santo Giosofà*, a fourteen-part version of the popular and widely diffused life of Buddha.[35] His other *cantare* was the *Istoria di santa Eufrosina*, a saint's legend which had been one of Catherine's childhood favourites.[36] When Catherine died in 1380, Pagliaresi composed a *lauda* celebrating her return to heaven.[37] This and other works suggest that he was a sensitive and dependable mediator of Catherine's mysticism. In later years he dedicated himself to collecting and transcribing Catherine's letters, and to supervising the translation of *Legenda Maior*, Raymond of Capua's Latin life of Catherine, into Italian.[38]

Pagliaresi's fellow *canterini* in Caterina's *famiglia* were Niccolò Cicerchia, a layman, and Felice Tancredi da Massa, an Augustinian. In 1364, Cicerchia composed a *cantare* known as *La Passione*.[39] This proved hugely successful: the work survives in at least fifty-eight manuscripts.[40] Cicerchia was persuaded to write a sequel, a two-part *Risurrezione*. This was less enthusiastically received. The Augustinian Tancredi da Massa began work on his *cantare* around 1380. This is referred to, somewhat mis-leadingly, as La Fanciullezza di Gesù, 'the childhood of Jesus', and covers events from the Incarnation to the Temptation in the Desert. Tancredi died in 1385, his work incomplete. He may have intended to narrate the whole life of Christ; or, more plausibly, he may have wished to complement Cicerchia's work. At any event, we can deduce from the manuscripts that these three *cantari* were often read as a continuous life of Christ.[41] Around 1421, for example, all three were copied into a single manuscript by a tailor from Brescia.[42] I shall follow his example by considering Cicerchia and Tancredi in tandem. Following brief biographical outlines, their work will be considered under three aspects: firstly, their adaptation of a secular genre for religious purposes; secondly, their common usage of a common source text, the celebrated *Meditationes Vitae Christi*; and thirdly, their relationship to the visual arts. Each of these aspects generates comparisons with Margery Kempe and the English mystics.

3

Born into a family of the minor Sienese nobility, Cicerchia held a key position in the Biccherna, Siena's chief financial magistracy, during the turbulent year of 1355.[43] As treasurer of the General Gabella, Cicerchia inherited a disastrous financial situation. Siena had been slowly recovering from the effects of the Black Death when, in 1354, it was forced to pass the largest budget in its history in order to buy off the murderous and destructive mercenary band of Fra Moriale. In March 1355 the Emperor Charles IV marched in to Siena, sparking off the looting and burning which evolved into full-scale insurrection. Although this brought down the Noveschi regime, Cicerchia somehow remained in office throughout this violent revolutionary period.[44] Nothing more is known of him until his appearance at Avignon in 1376. The unsettling events of 1355 may have persuaded Cicerchia to turn to religion, as they persuaded Giovanni Colombini. Following his conversion in that year, Colombini undertook menial tasks in the Palazzo Communale where he (and Cicercia) had once held office. He had himself whipped outside the building, asking his followers to shout denunciations of his past business practices.[45] However Cicerchia came to follow Catherine, there is no doubting the quality and sincerity of his devotion. In the *Passione*, for example, he describes the ensemble of disciples and holy women as a 'famiglia'.[46] This group is very definitely under female control: all family members instinctively look to Mary for guidance, and it is Mary who teaches Peter (the first pope) the theological significance of the Crucifixion.[47]

Cicerchia was by far the most gifted of the Sienese *canterini* even though he committed the Layman's error of muddling the order of events at the Passion.[48] Tancredi made no such errors. Born on Sienese territory at Massa (the birthplace of San Bernadino), he joined the Augustinians at his home town before studying at Verona and Florence. He was probably resident at Lecceto when Catherine visited William Flete there in 1374 or 1375. He returned to spend the rest of his life at this hermitage some time after the Avignon mission of 1376.[49] A letter that he received from Catherine suggests that they were in close personal contact.[50] His *cantare* is painstakingly embroidered with images and themes familiar from Catherine's teachings:[51] blood, drinking, drowning, self-hatred and the Trinity.[52] Whereas Cicerchia visualises the life of Christ as human drama, Tancredi sees it as 'dottrina e amaestramento' (9,2), 'doctrine and instruction'.

The differing conceptions that Cicerchia and Tancredi have of their task as religious writers are reflected in their differing exploitation of the same secular genre. The layman Cicerchia is evidently at home with the *cantare*, employing its characteristic tags, epithets and diminutives[53] with admirable adroitness. He sometimes applies familiar *cantare* terms to his religious personages[54] and sometimes substitutes religious references: 'santa' ('holy') replaces 'cortese' ('courteous') as a constant epithet. He makes good use of terms that have both secular and religious associations: the *canterino's* favourite adjectives 'dolce' ('sweet') and 'bello' ('beautiful') are widely applied; Mary describes Jesus as both an 'olente giglio' (*Passione*, 'fragrant lily') and as 'aulente più che giglio' (*Risurrezione*, 'more sweet-smelling than the lily'), elegant variations on the common *cantare* tag 'fresco giglio', 'fresh lily'. Cicerchia puts the *cantare* fondness for a language of flowers and pearls to good use in the scenes which conclude his *Risurrezione*, a vision of heaven.[55] He follows *canterino* practice in employing present participles for narrative continuity,[56] in featuring an abundance of inexpressibility topoi[57] and in making frequent references to his source.[58] In short, Cicerchia shows an impressive mastery of his adopted medium, and is quite undaunted by the cultural compromise he is striking with it. The subtlety of this compromise is apparent in his very first stanza. *Canterini* (like English romancers) often begin their narrative by invoking the Trinity, a pious preliminary which in the antecedent oral traditions served to attract the attention of a potential audience. Cicerchia follows their example (and their characteristic use of a quadripartite stanza) but at the same time announces serious religious intentions: he addresses each person of the Trinity through the individual aspects of power (Father), wisdom (Son) and love (Holy Ghost).[59]

It is not surprising that the *Passione*—on the evidence of two fifteenth-century manuscripts—was long attributed to Boccaccio.[60] Certain moments of Cicerchia's Marian laments achieve a combination of pathos and resilient vigour that is highly reminiscent of Ovid's *Heroides* and of the passages that Chaucer (and Boccaccio) derived from them. Here Mary speaks like an Ovidian heroine in reproaching her lover (the crucified Jesus) on his breach of promise:

'O dolce figliuol mio, è questo l' "Ave"
che mi facesti dir a Gabrïello,
che mi fu tanto allor dolce e soave!'[61]

This pathetic recall of the Annunciation at the Crucifixion in the form of a dramatic complaint is taken up by the author of a fifteenth-century English lyric known as 'Fillius Regis Mortuus Est'.[62] The Sienese friar Tancredi, however, is less willing to dally with secular modes of expression: 'melodies, instruments, songs and juggling tricks do not touch that mind which has cast off the evil world and its galling ways'.[63] This determined resistance to worldly entertainments recalls the temptation of St Anthony as depicted by the Tuscan Dominican Domenico Cavalca in his *Vite dei Santi Padri*, a work much admired by Catherine.[64] Anthony is distracted from his prayers by devils who 'leap in front of me, whistling and carrying on as if they were minstrels' ('giullari').[65] Anthony steels himself to more fervent prayer, and drives them off by singing psalms. Such exteme reactions are, in a way, a tribute to the attraction of secular forms: they represent a serious challenge to the religious. Cavalca accepts this challenge of competing for the attention of a popular audience: his St Anthony battles like a popular hero with a devil who takes the shape of 'armed knights', of 'monstrous beasts' or of a 'huge giant'.[66] Cavalca is willing to move his Latin source in the direction of popular romance.[67]

Tancredi is much more nervous than Cavalca about the act of cultural compromise that he has involved himself in.[68] But even this cautious Augustinian observes the spirit of Jacques de Vitry's dictum: 'aliter clericis, aliter laicis est praedicandum'.[69] The large sermon corpus of this French cleric (who died in 1240) contains some four hundred *exempla*, many of them drawn from oral tradition.[70] Many religious writers imitated his marriage of the sermon and the folk tale. The Franciscans were, of course, most adept at this: tales such as that of the wolf of Gubbio (translated into Tuscan in the period 1370–90)[71] charmed and captivated their audiences, allowing an almost unconscious absorption of religious material.

Religious writers sought not only to compete with the content of secular narrative, but also to annex its form. This two-fold process is readily apparent in England as well as in Italy and France. At the outset of the thirteenth-century poem known as *The Passion of Our Lord*, for example, the author appeals for attention as peremptorily as any secular poet before proceeding to inform us that he speaks 'nouht of karlemeyne ne of þe Duzeper', but rather 'of cristes þruwinge'.[72] He employs the metrical form and narrative apparatus of the *chanson de geste*, attempting to wean his lay audience away from worldly adventures. The slightly later *Southern Passion* covers the same ground as *Cicerchia*'s oeuvre (Passion, Resurrection and Ascension) and shares its cross-cultural strategy.[73] Poems such as the *Northern Passion* and the *Stanzaic Life of Christ* further this strategy; and at the beginning of *Cursor Mundi* the strategy is openly discussed.[74] A similar policy was pursued in converting secular song to religious devotion: 'Bele Alis', for example, becomes 'Bele a lis', the Blessed Virgin.[75] The English religious carol has been described as 'a pious imitation of secular popular song which is itself a development from folk-song'.[76] Its history has much in common with that of the Italian *lauda*, the most vigorous expression of medieval religious popular song, which 'occupies the middle ground between folk-song and learned lyric'.[77]

Not all professional religious were sanguine about this exploitation of secular forms. Chaucer's Parson, for one, refuses to involve himself in it.[78] Tancredi da Massa remorselessly loads his *cantare* framework with dogma and moralising. He does not begin story-telling proper until his twenty-ninth stanza: by then, of course, any popular audience would (given the chance) have drifted quietly away. Wycliffe condemned the singing and dancing that went on at Christmas, but generously recognised that young women could derive honest religious benefit from their carolling.[79] The appropriation of secular forms for religious purposes was undeniably problematic. In *Sir Gawain and the Green Knight*, for example, the conquest of romance idiom by a religious author is so complete that many readers remain cheerfully impervious to the poem's religious implications.

Further problems arise when secular authors from popular quarters enter the religious domain. The author of the bulkiest collection of fourteenth-century *laude* was the reformed wool-carder Bianco da Siena. He was received into the Gesuati in 1367, having overcome the initial resistance of Colombini, who thought him too weak to withstand the rigours of religious life. Like other writers, Bianco brought the techniques of secular verse to the service of his religion: but in doing so he often gives religious themes a worldly gloss. His focussing upon the prospect of his own damnation is remarkably sensuous and self-indulgent.[80] He is espoused to Jesus, but has not yet enjoyed him in bed. The favours he has received have served only to inflame him; he is crazed with desire, and goes shouting for love. Margery Kempe, famed for her spiritual shouting, is similarly willing to embrace God in bed.[81] Margery's *Book*, like Bianco's *laude*, contains some extraordinary conflations of religious and worldly motifs. One 'Mydsomyr Evyn in rygth hot wedyr', for example, we encounter Margery 'komyng fro-ʒorke-ward beryng a botel wyth bere in hir hand & hir husbond a cake in hys bosom'.[82] This scene of cakes and ale develops into a histrionic dispute over conjugal rights that might have been plotted by Chaucer.

Catherine of Siena, through her own experience and that of her *famiglia*, had an especial sympathy for those who wished to practise religious self-mortification in domestic circumstances.[83] She herself confessed to having an inordinate affection for the infants who swarmed in her mother's kitchen.[84] Catherine's prose style blends learned disquisition with popular, idiomatic, dialectal and familiar forms of expression.[85] In writing to Queen Giovanna of Naples, for example, she is able to link the love of God with doing the washing up, and this in the course of constructing a grandiose vision that climaxes in a call for a new Crusade against the infidel.[86] Cicerchia writes in the same spirit in proclaiming that the risen Jesus was among his disciples 'like the yolk in the midst of an egg'.[87] In fashioning a hair-shirt from a malt-sack,[88] Margery Kempe acts out this principle of discovering the devotional in the domestic.

The distinction between images and actions that are intrinsically religious, and those which are not, is highly problematic. St Bernadino of Siena built upon the lively example of his Sienese predecessors by interspersing his preachings with the telling of tales, the singing of songs, and even the impersonation of animals; and all this was perceived as authentically religious.[89] It is, of course, the perception of material that is crucial here, rather than the material itself: religion is in the eye of the beholder. Popular audiences willingly lent credence to professional religious who borrowed from popular culture. Some Veronese housewives, Boccaccio tells us, willingly believed that Dante, a learned layman, could descend to the Inferno whenever he felt like it.[90] But the faithful were sceptical and intolerant of a travelling housewife from Lynn who proclaimed the joys of heaven from within their own culture:

'Why speke ʒe so of þe myrth þat is in Heuyn; ʒe know it not & ʒe haue not be þer no mor þan we.'[91]

4

Jacques de Vitry recognised that popular audiences could not be satisfied with hearsay in matters of revelation, but rather wished to witness and experience it for themselves: 'oportet quasi ad oculum et sensibiliter omnia demonstrare'.[92] Walter Hilton makes a similar concession to the need for religious images, by which 'slow and carnal minds' ('mentes pigre et carnales') may be stirred to compunction and devotion.[93] No medieval text stirred such devotion, on a European scale, more effectively than did the *Meditationes Vitae Christi*.

The *Meditationes* has been variously considered as 'a life of Christ, a biography of the Blessed Virgin, the fifth gospel, the last of the apocrypha, one of the masterpieces of Franciscan literature, a summary of medieval spirituality, a religious handbook of contemplation, a manual of Christian iconography, one of the chief sources of mystery plays',[94] and as 'the most popular gospel harmony of the Middle Ages'.[95] Essentially, however, it balances story-telling against homily: a life of Christ (containing many arresting and original details) is intercalated with pious meditations (many of them derived from St Bernard). The work is addressed to a nun (a Poor Clare), which accounts for the emphasis that is placed upon family relationships and domestic details. The Latin original was (it is generally agreed) composed on Sienese territory towards the end of the thirteenth century.[96]

It was then diffused through Europe via Franciscan channels. The *Meditationes* was exceptionally popular in England: forty-three of the 113 Latin manuscripts enumerated by P. C. Fischer are of English origin.[97]

Many vernacular versions were made of the *Meditationes*.[98] Nicholas Love's *Myrrour of the Blessed Lyf of Jesu Christ*, the first complete English translation, was licensed for the reading of the devout in 1410 by Thomas Arundel, the Archbishop of Canterbury visited by Margery Kempe in 1413.[99] A Tuscan translation of the *Meditationes* provided a source for Cicerchia's *Passione*, for a section of the second part of his *Risurrezione* and for the whole of Tancredi's *Fanciullezza*.[100] The Augustinian follows *canterino* practice in working closely with his prose source; the more gifted Cicerchia elaborates upon the *Meditationes* in a more creative and independent manner. Whereas Tancredi accentuates the homiletic aspects of the *Meditationes*, Cicerchia (like Nicholas Love, but to a much greater extent) chooses to concentrate upon its scenes of intimacy and drama. His protagonist is Mary: the drama of the Passion is realised chiefly through her reactions. Even where Mary is not physically present, her putative reactions play a part.[101] Despite his poetic independence, Cicerchia is fully in accord with the spirit and intentions of the *Meditationes*. He prefaces his storytelling with an appeal that each man should share in Jesus' pain, torments and crucifixion: 'di quel ch'esso sentì ciascun uom senta!'[102] Julian of Norwich opens her *Showings* by making a similar plea for herself; and Richard Rolle makes a similar petition to Mary in his *Meditations on the Passion*.[103] Both of these English writers are indebted to the *Meditationes Vitae Christi*.

The Passion section of the *Meditationes* was influential in England long before it was taken up by Cicerchia. In fact, it had not long been written before it helped to shape the *Southern Passion*.[104] The *Meditationes* is referred to by the author of the *Fasciculus Morum* in 1320, and at around the same date the first English translation of its Passion section was made, the so-called *Meditacyuns on the Soper of our Lorde*.[105] In the course of the fourteenth century, no fewer than seven independent translations of this section of the *Meditationes* were made.[106] In England as elsewhere, the *Meditationes* was commonly ascribed to St Bonaventure.[107] Not surprisingly, it was also ascribed to the most influential writer of the century, Richard Rolle, who has been described as 'the English Bonaventura'.[108] The *Meditationes* encouraged 'the cult of the Holy Name of Jesus, which became the centre of Rolle's devotion and propaganda', a cult which gave a name to the movement led by Rolle's Sienese contemporary Colombini, the Gesuati. The *Meditationes* also urged the faithful to feel their way into scenes from the gospel, to actually play a part in the divine drama. Rolle's own *Meditations on the Passion* (Text 1) see him acting out this injunction to the full: he will cling to the foot of the cross and be drenched with Jesus' blood; unworthy to stand at the cross with Mary and John, he would hang 'os þe thef hangyd'.[109]

The famous Thornton manuscript, which contains many of Rolle's works, also contains the partial translation of the *Meditationes* known as *Privity of the Passion*.[110] This immensely popular prose treatise, which does not seem much out of place among Rolle's writings, may well have exerted a direct influence on Julian of Norwich.[111] The conclusion that Julian knew some version of the Passion section of the *Meditationes* is, in the opinion of Elizabeth Salter, 'irresistible'.[112] Meditation on the Passion (considered particularly apt for lay people by Hilton and the author of *The Cloud of Unknowing*)[113] formed the heart of Margery Kempe's spirituality. As we shall see, Margery's devotional mentality owed much to the *Meditationes*.

The birth and childhood of Jesus inspired some of the *Meditationes'* most memorable details. Many of these, such as the Magi kissing the toes of the infant Jesus, have become standard motifs of European iconography.[114] Although Tancredi's *Fanciullezza di Gesù* reports such details, it generally fails to realise their affective potential. Details are often obscured: where, for example, the *Meditationes* pictures Mary spinning, Tancredi reports her performing 'alcuna operazione', 'some task'.[115] And where in the *Meditationes* God refers to Jesus as 'my son', in Tancredi's account this becomes 'la Sapïenza', 'Wisdom', the Son considered in his Trinitarian aspect. Tancredi places a marked emphasis on the Trinity: when his Mary loses the infant Jesus in the temple, for example, she spends nine stanzas appealing, in turn, to the Father, Son and Holy Ghost.[116] In this and much else, Tancredi goes against the grain of his source, which delights in emphasising the humanity of Jesus. He develops the didactic, rather than story-telling, aspects of the *Meditationes*, often replacing the meditations of Bernard with the sharper strictures of Augustine.[117] He repeatedly condemns 'perfidious heresy' and dwells upon damnation and torment.[118] He introduces anxiety where, in his source, none exists. The *Meditationes* states that Mary was not afraid of Gabriel at the Annunciation because she had seen him many times before: Tancredi's Mary trembles at the angel's effulgence. Tancredi then introduces the terrifying possibility that Mary might not 'consent to the infinite word', and then the 'exalted Trinity' would not move from its 'supreme dominion', and we would all be damned. At the scene which produces the *Meditationes'* most joyful and intimate moments, the Nativity, Tancredi introduces a twenty-two stanza excursus on sodomy: at this moment, all sodomites are struck down, buried and eternally tormented[119]. The sustained ferocity of this condemnation finds a parallel only in the Middle English *Cleanness*. In his transformation of the *Meditationes*, Tancredi seems to share the rhetorical strategy of his English contemporary: each attempts to unsettle and galvanise his audience by alternating tenderness with terror.

Nicholas Love's adaptation of the *Meditationes* adopts a less strenuous strategy. The *Myrrour* is sympathetic to the needs of 'symple creatures. the whiche as children hauen nede to be fedde with mylke of ly3te doctrine/and not with sadde mete of grete clergie and of hi3e contemplacioun'.[120] This approach proved successful and the *Myrrour* exerted an extremely wide influence.[121] Love appears to have made use of several of the partial fourteenth-century translations of the *Meditationes*,[122] and his work in turn was taken up by the author of several of the *Ludus Coventriae* plays (which probably originated at Norwich).[123] More importantly, it helped spread the influence of the *Meditationes* through all sections of fifteenth-century society. The extent of this influence, readily discernible in the visual art and the drama, is perhaps best suggested by the lyric known as 'Brother, Abide'. In the short space of twenty-eight rhyme royal stanzas, this fine lyric presents a concise digest of the entire *Meditationes*. The poem begins with an appeal for attention spoken, presumably, by an *imago pietatis*. Then (as in the *Meditationes*) we see Christ 'a-bove the sterrys, in hevyne emperiall'[124] before he descends to humble himself in the Incarnation. The *Meditationes* then supplies the poet with details of Christ's childhood:[125]

> I lede my yought with children in the strette,
> Poorly a-rayed in clothes bare and thyne,
> Such as my mother for me dyde make and spyne.

In considering the Passion scenes of 'Brother, Abide', Rosemary Woolf oberves that 'the author proceeds with the timing and control of a master poet'.[126] This poet is, of course, indebted to Chaucer's pioneering of the rhyme royal stanza. Chaucer's mastery of stanzaic form owes much to Boccaccio, who is himself indebted to the eight-line stanzas of the *canterini*.[127] This complex genealogy links writers of all backgrounds and persuasions, secular and religious, popular and cultivated.

The Christmas carol is a natural medium for the *Meditationes*' affective details: the ox and ass who warmed the infant Jesus with their breath were doubtless designed to please a popular audience.[128] Many such details find a home in *The Book of Margery Kempe*. But Margery's allegiance is more radical than this: her whole *Book* reads like an obedient response to the *Meditationes*' religious imperatives. The Latin author begins his account of the life of Christ by reminding his female reader that she 'must learn all the things said and done as though you were present'.[129] Following this, he repeatedly urges her to participate imaginatively in the divine drama:

> Now take here good hede and haue inwardly compassioun of that blessed lady and mayden/marye. how sche so 3ong and of so tendre age/that is to saye of XV 3ere and grete with childe as nyh the birthe/trauailleth that longe wey of sixty myle and ten or more in so grete pouerte. and 3it whan sche cam to the citee forseide there sche schulde reste/and with her spouse asked herborgh in dyuers places/

schamefastly as amonge vnkouthe folke/ alle they werned hem and lete hem
goo. . . .[130]

This and similar requests meet with an active response from Margery
Kempe.[131] Here she seeks to amend, single-handedly, all the shortcomings
of such 'vncouthe folke':

And þan went þe creatur forth wyth owyr Lady to Bedlem & purchasyd hir
herborwe euery nyght wyth gret reuerens, & owyr Lady was receyved wyth glad
cher. Also sche beggyd owyr Lady fayr whyte clothys & kerchys for to swathyn in
hir Sone whan he wer born, and, whan Ihesu was born, sche ordeyned beddyng for
owyr Lady to lyg in wyth hir blyssed Sone. And sythen sche beggyd mete for owyr
Lady & hir blyssyd chyld[132]

The sixth and seventh chapters of Margery's *Book* constitute a most
vivid response to the Annunciation, Nativity and Epiphany scenes of the
Meditationes. Later in chapter twenty-nine, however, Margery proves
herself even more obedient to the *Meditationes*' plea for imaginative
involvement: she actually rides on an ass to Bethlehem and worships at the
crib where Christ was born. The *Meditationes*' female dedicatee had been
recommended to visit the crib daily at Christmas:[133] but the *Meditationes*'
author can hardly have anticipated that his recommendation would be acted
out historically. Shortly before visiting Bethlehem, Margery had been at
Calvary. Here she had let out the first of her great cries, a cry which (it
has long been recognised) echoes the cry of the dying Christ in the
Meditationes.[134]

One further aspect of Margery's spirituality merits comparison with the
Meditationes: the acceptance (and even welcome) of public humiliation and
ridicule. The *Meditationes*' author puzzles over what Jesus did between the
ages of twelve and thirty. If he had done anything significant, it would surely
have been reported: therefore we must imagine that he did nothing of note.
He frequented the temple, helped out at home (laying the table and making
the beds) and tried his hand at carpentry. Because of this, he was
contemptuously regarded as a village lay-about: in Love's words, 'men
skorned hym/and helde hym as an ydiote and as an ydel man and a fole'.[135]
Jesus' endurance of neighbourly ridicule (suffered as a spiritual
discipline in preparing for a great public mission) must have proved
heartening and exemplary for the much-abused Margery.

5

Margery's intense, quotidian devotion to the humanity of Christ is, then,
remarkably faithful to the spirit of the *Meditationes Vitae Christi*: more
faithful, in fact, than is Tancredi's adaptation of the text. The Augustinian is
obviously working against the grain of his source. He does so deliberately
but not, I believe, through sheer idiosyncratic perversity. He is addressing

the generation that survived the Black Death. As Millard Meiss has shown, Tuscan artists of this period passed over the humane emphases of the *Meditationes* in favour of ritualistic, doctrinal, abstract and Trinitarian themes.[136] Eye contact between painted figures diminishes; anguish becomes more private and intense as the Godhead becomes more mysterious and remote. Such shifts are accurately recorded in the Augustinian's poem. His Madonna recalls the 'cold and indifferent Virgin'[137] depicted in the Sienese church of St Augustine in the 1370s. The European image of the Madonna of Humility (which originated at Siena) was decisively recast in this post-plague period: Mary is no longer perceived as a humble, earth-bound handmaiden, but rather as a celestial apparition, the Woman of the Apocalypse. It is in this guise that she appears (just before the Nativity) to the Emperor Octavius in the *Fanciullezza di Gesù*[138].

The artistic preferences of the *gente nuova* who assumed power in Siena after the 1355 revolution were markedly more cautious and conservative than those of their cultured Noveschi predecessors. In 1357, for example, the Sienese government ordered the destruction of the Lypsippan Venus, a pagan statue unearthed in 1325 that had been much admired by Ambrogio Lorinzetti.[139] Cultural conservatism also prevailed in post-plague England. Wall painters adopted abstract and schematic themes, often of a morbid cast.[140] Some men came to question the employment of paintings and sculpture as devotional aids, initiating a debate which climaxed in the trial of Oldcastle in 1413.[141] In translating the *Meditationes* (upholding its powerful challenge to the visual imagination) Nicholas Love wages a vigorous polemic against Lollard teaching.[142]

Some religious writers (such as John Mirk and Walter Hilton) were moved to an explicit defence of visual images; other simply assumed that their audiences were familiar with them.[143] The Sienese painters' guild upheld the Gregorian view of pictures as *libri laicorum*: this traditional justification of their craft appears in the preamble to their statutes.[144] In practice, however, they strove for the expressive ideal of St Bernard: paintings should be emotionally compelling as well as instructive. The *Meditationes* (with its wealth of visual detail and of Bernadine commentary) was uniquely qualified to serve this double purpose. Its adoption by Niccolò Cicerchia resulted in one of the most painterly poems of the fourteenth century.

Cicerchia thinks in pictures: his *Passione* unfolds a sequence of highly-organised dramatic scenes. Within each scene, Cicerchia takes great care in describing the disposition of figures around the protagonist.[145] He makes much use of the phrase 'guarda fiso' ('he or she looks intently, fixedly'). For most *canterini* this is no more than a convenient tag: but Cicerchia employs it to great effect in freezing the frame of his narrative so that we may contemplate dramatic relationships. So Jesus 'guarda fiso' at his sleeping disciples at Gethsamane.[146]

Pilate looks intently at Jesus[147] and so do the Jews.[148] Jesus looks at Peter;[149] their eyes meet[150] and (in a truly painterly moment of self-realisation) Peter perceives his betrayal.[151] Mary struggles to catch sight of Jesus across a turbulent, public scene.[152] Such eye contact, we have noted, is not common in art of this period. It is, however, a vital feature of earlier Sienese painting. Such painting formed part of Cicerchia's working environment in the Palazzo Communale,[153] and part of his worshipping environment in the Sienese churches and religious houses.

Cicerchia's *Passione* is, in fact, intimately connected with a great work of painting: Duccio di Buoninsegna's *Maestà*. The front of this altarpiece depicts the Virgin in majesty; the back contains 'one of the most continuous and richly devised pictorial narratives of the life of Christ in existence'.[154] These panels form the basis of all subsequent Sienese Gospel iconography. In June 1311, the *Maestà* was carried from Duccio's workshop to the cathedral in a huge public procession amid festivities that lasted for three days. It immediately became the most celebrated symbol of Sienese civic and religious pride.[155] Cicerchia's poem, which issues from prolonged contemplation of Duccio's narrative sequence, assumes an audience that is familiar with the altarpiece. Its most moving episodes offer detailed verbal equivalents of Duccio's memorable images.[156]

Fourteenth-century England has bequeathed nothing that survives comparison with Duccio's masterpiece. The most ambitious Crucifixion is perhaps that painted by John Siferwas for the Sherborne Missal, circa 1396–1407. Siferwas presents a crowded, dramatic scene that reveals Italian influence but exhibits 'no understanding of the relation of the figures to the ground or to each other in the group'.[157] The fantastic costumes worn by Siferwas' figures are related to those of another Italian-influenced work, the Norwich Retable. This series of five panels on the Passion and Resurrection is the closest that fourteenth-century England comes to Duccio's narrative sequence. The gulf in conception and execution that divides these two works is immense. It reminds us of the limitations within which English religious writers laboured in an age when verbal and visual imagery were so inter-dependent.

Putting questions of artistic quality aside, however, it is possible to compare the social and religious functions of *Maestà* and Retable. Like the *Maestà*, the Retable is a symbol of civic and religious pride: it was probably commissioned in the late fourteenth century by the group of powerful Norfolk families whose arms appear on the back of the glass panels in the outer frame. Both *Maestà* and Retable were originally conceived of as altarpieces.[158] And, most importantly, they performed the same function for the devout.

The importance of visual imagery for Catherine, Julian and Margery can hardly be exaggerated. The course of Catherine's brief life was determined more powerfully by images than by words. In her earliest vision, the six-year-old Catherine encountered Christ and some saints 'just as she had seen them painted in the churches'.[159] She experienced the pains of the stigmata shortly after praying before a crucifix at Rome in 1375. Five years later, again at Rome, Catherine buckled under a crushing downward weight whilst contemplating Giotto's Navicella: it was as if the weight of the ship had descended upon her shoulders.[160] The lower half of her body remained paralysed until her death. Julian of Norwich was deeply susceptible to the influence of religious art.[161] Her responses to her revelations have been likened to responses to paintings.[162] But these responses are distanced and meditated, intellectual rather than (as for Catherine and Margery) physical. Julian insists upon the space between signifier and signified;[163] she stands back from artefacts rather than being drawn into them (or crushed under them).

Margery's responses to paintings (as to much else) place her closer to Catherine than to Julian and the English mystics. Margery was illiterate. For her, as for the mass of the population, paintings assumed a special significance as the only texts that could be read without direct clerical intervention. It was appropriate, therefore, that the Gesyne (a depiction of the Nativity) at Lynn should (like the *Maestà* at Siena) be carried in procession through the streets of the city.[164] In her *Book*, Margery depicts herself before the Gesyne in its usual resting place, the church of St Margaret, Lynn.[165] The Nativity, we have noted, was a scene that Margery often entered into. Margery thinks in pictures, thinks of pictures and thinks from picture to picture. Pictures are malleable, compliant to imaginative elaboration: on seeing a crucifix, Margery wishes that it 'xuld losyn hys handys fro þe crosse & halsyn hir in tokyn of lofe'.[166] Margery reproves herself for this fantasy, which was perhaps engendered by her habit of narrating between pictures.[167] The sight of one scene often causes Margery's imagination to run forwards (or backwards) to a scene that comes later (or earlier) in the same narrative sequence. Such imaginative movement acknowledges no boundaries between present and past, actuality and fantasy, life and art. So when a woman suckling a 'manchylde' gives Margery some wine in a stone cup, Margery weeps for Mary and Jesus at the Passion.[168] One Good Friday, Margery tells us, she 'behelde preystys knelyng on hir kneys & oþer worschepful men wyth torches brennyng in her handys be-for þe Sepulcre, deuowtly representyng þe lamentabyl deth and doolful berying of owr Lord Ihesu Crist. . .'.[169] This painterly composition puts Margery in mind of a related scene, the anguish of our lady. And this leads to a more intense visualisation of another scene, the Passion, registered 'wyth hir gostly eye in þe syght of hir sowle'. Margery then encounters the crucified Jesus 'wyth hir bodily eye'. This accumulative image-making process finally erupts in a great physical outburst: Margery 'sobbyd, roryd, & cryed and, spredyng hir armys a-brood, seyd wyth lowde voys, "I dey, I dey" '.[170] Her crying increases in intensity until (inevitably) a priest carries her out of the church. 'And þis maner of crying' (Margery reports) 'enduryd þe terme of X ȝer'.[171] Margery's powerfully physical reactions to visual stimuli were (and perhaps are) regarded as excessive, outrageous, affronts to public propriety. Catherine's physical reactions were no less extreme: yet these were cited as proofs of sanctity. It would be interesting to analyse the taxonomical processes by which such discrepancies were established, and by which they are maintained.

6

Margery Kempe was persecuted more at home than abroad; and she suffered abroad chiefly at the hands of her countrymen. Her personal style of devotion would not, I believe, have seemed particularly outlandish in medieval Siena. Her cries and public outbursts match those of Colombini and his Gesuati; her mixing of sacred, secular and domestic imagery parallels that of Bianco da Siena and of Catherine herself. Within Catherine's circle there was genuine understanding of the differing forms of religious expression that were natural to differing social classes; and much of this understanding stemmed from the experience and development of Catherine herself. Three members of her *famiglia* made concerted attempts at cultural meditation by adopting the forms and conventions of popular narrative. Two of them exploited the universal popularity of the *Meditationes Vitae Christi*. And one, the most talented, designed his narrative to incorporate the experience of the illiterate in observing the detail and sequence of Duccio's *Maestà*, the focus of civic and religious pride for Sienese of all classes.

There were, however, limited attempts at such cultural mediation in England. Religious writers who referred to or explicitly defended the use of visual imagery understood the fundamental importance of this medium to the illiterate. The promotion of the *Meditationes Vitae Christi*, a text which mounts a strong challenge to the visual imagination, recognises and legitimates the popular impulse to participate in the drama of revelation. And the religious appropriation of secular forms (such as the popular song and the *chanson de geste*) indicates a willingness to accomodate cultural preferences that lie beyond the pale of religion. This mediatory project was, of course, initiated as a one-way movement from clergy to populace that would remain subject to clerical control. Margery's *Book* is a consequence of this initiative: it bears witness to the motivating force of visual imagery, responds to the *Meditationes*' urge for personal involvement and discovers materials for religious observance in the forms of domestic life. But it also seeks to invert this initiative: the *Book* records a life that was not content to remain subject to clerical regulation, but rather aspired to be self-directing, auto-biographical. This aspiration could not, of course, be fully realised: Margery requires a clerk to record her dictation and speaks not *in propria persona* but as a third-person 'creatur'. Not content to remain the object of clerical teachings, Margery did not possess the means to become the subject of her own life and writings. When her weeping and crying before a *pietà* at Norwich is interrupted by an officious cleric, Margery is not lost for words:

> 'Damsel, Ihesu is ded long sithyn.' Whan hir crying was cesyd, sche seyd to þe preste, 'Sir, hys deth is as fresch to me as he had deyd þis same day, & so me thynkyth it awt to be зow & to alle Cristen pepil'.[172]

Margery repeatedly confounds clergy's critique of her personal devotional practice: but only by mirroring back the truths that clergy has supplied her with. Margery's triumphs over clergy, however exhilarating, do not amount to a triumph over clerical discourse.

NOTES

1. For an account of the 'sympathetic bewilderment' with which Margery's writings have been received, see Susan Dickman, 'Margery Kempe and the English Devotional Tradition', in *The Medieval Mystical Tradition in England*, ed. M. Glasscoe, Exeter, 1980, pp. 156–72.
2. *The Book of Margery Kempe*, ed. S. B. Meech and H. E. Allen, Early English Text Society, O.S., 212, London, 1940, p. lviii. (Abbreviation *Book*).
3. H. E. Allen, *Book*, *op. cit.*, pp. liii–lviii.
4. H. E. Allen, *Book*, *op. cit.*, p. lx.
5. See Dante's account of the *vulgaris illustris* in *De Vulgari Eloquentia*, ed. and tr. A. Marigo, third edition updated by P. G. Ricci, Florence, 1957.
6. M. Bakhtin, *Rabelais and His World*, tr. H. Iswolsky, Cambridge, Mass., 1968, p. 4.
7. M. Bakhtin, *Problems of Dostoevsky's Poetics*, tr. R. W. Potsel, Ardis, U.S.A., 1973, pp. 106–7.
8. The self-portrait that emerges from Margery's *Book* has much in common with that of Chaucer's Wife of Bath: see Stephen Medcalf, 'Inner and outer', in *The Context of English Literature. The Later Middle Ages*, ed. Stephen Medcalf, London, 1981, p. 113.
9. *Rabelais*, *op. cit.*, p. 57.
10. *Dostoevsky's Poetics*, *op. cit.*, p. 102.
11. *I, Catherine. Selected Writings of St Catherine of Siena*, ed. and tr. Kenelm Foster and M. J. Ronayne, London, 1980, p. 17.
12. See M. A. Follmar, 'St Catherine of Siena and Julian of Norwich', in *Congresso Internazionale di Studi Cateriniani. Siena-Roma 24–29 Aprile 1980*, Rome, 1981, pp. 110–120.
13. See Robert Fawtier, *Sainte Catherine de Sienne. Essai de critique des sources*, 2 vols, Paris, 1921–30, 2, pp. 138–60; E. Dupré Theseider, 'Caterina da Siena' in *Dizionario biografico degli italiani*, 22 vols (incomplete), 22, pp. 261–79; *Book*, pp. 36–7, 122–8, 136–7.
14. See Millard Meiss, *Painting in Siena and Florence after the Black Death*, Princeton, 1951, p. 104; *Book*, p. 28.
15. See E. Dupré Theseider, *op. cit.*, p. 262; *Book*, p. 9.
16. See E. G. Gardner, *St Catherine of Siena*, London, 1907, p. 13; *Book*, p. 7.
17. See M. Meiss, *op. cit.*, p. 107; *Book*, p. 39.

18. See E. Dupré Theseider, *op. cit.*, p. 265; *Book*, p. 20.
19. See S. Caterina da Siena, *Il Dialogo*, ed. G. Cavallini, Rome, 1968.
20. See *The Orcherd of Syon*, ed. Phyllis Hodgson and Gabriel M. Liegey, Early English Text Society, O.S., 258, London, 1966. The foundation stone of Syon Abbey was laid by Henry V in 1415; first professions were made in 1420.
21. See Arrigo Levasti, tr. D. M. White, 'St Catherine of Siena and Dame Julian of Norwich', *Life of the Spirit*, 7 (1953), 334.
22. Margery spent thirteen weeks in Venice during the winter of 1413–14. During this period evidence of the sanctity of Catherine was still being collected there, forming a testimony known as 'the Venetian Process'. See H. E. Allen, *Book*, pp. 287–8.
23. See Blessed Raymond of Capua, *The Life of St Catherine of Siena*, tr. George Lamb, London, 1960, pp. 19–29; E. Dupré Theseider, *op. cit.*, p. 261.
24. Kenelm Foster and M. J. Ronayne, *op. cit.*, p. 13.
25. See Achille Tartaro, *La letteratura civile e religiosa del Trecento*, Bari, 1972, pp. 100–1.
26. See William M. Bowsky, *A Medieval Italian Commune. Siena under the Nine, 1287–1355*, Berkeley, 1981.
27. W. M. Bowsky, *op. cit.*, pp. 260–98.
28. Catherine lost a brother in 1363 and a sister in 1374. The 1374 outbreak killed eight of the eleven grandchildren residing in her mother's house; Catherine buried these herself. See Millard Meiss, *op. cit.*, p. 88.
29. *Idem.*
30. *Ibid.*, p. 62.
31. See *A Book of Showings to the Anchoress Julian of Norwich*, ed. Edmund Colledge and James Walsh, 2 vols, Toronto, 1978, p. 52.
32. See M. Baptist Stohrer, 'St Catherine and the Sienese Laudesi', in *Congresso* (1980), 121–31.
33. See Achille Tartaro, *op. cit.*, p. 132–3; *Cantari religiosi senesi del Trecento*, ed. G. Varanini, Bari, 1965, pp. 455–8.
34. See Robert Fawtier, *op. cit.*, 2, 277–80.
35. For an edition of this work, see G. Varanini, *op. cit.*, pp. 7–189.
36. *Ibid.*, p. 464; Raymond of Capua, *Life*, *op. cit.*, p. 23.
37. See Achille Tartaro, *op. cit.*, pp. 133–5.
38. See Robert Fawtier, *op. cit.*, 2, pp. 81–124; Achille Tartaro, *op. cit.*, p. 133.
39. The date is provided by an authoritative Sienese MS: see G. Varanini, *op. cit.*, p. 537. References to the *Passione* follow *Cantari del Trecento*, ed. Armando Balduino, Milan, 1970, pp. 161–235; references to the other *cantari* follow G. Varanini.
40. The list of manuscripts provided by Varanini (pp. 551–5) does not claim to be exhaustive.
41. All three manuscripts containing the *Risurrezione* also contain both of Cicerchia's *cantari*: see G. Varanini, *op. cit.*, pp. 494–8.
42. See G. Varanini, *op. cit.*, pp. 495–6.
43. See P. Stoppelli, 'Cicerchia, Niccolò', *Dizionario biografico degli italiani*, 25, pp. 380–1; W. M. Bowsky, *Commune*, *op. cit.*, pp. 299–303; W. M. Bowsky, 'The Impact of the Black Death Upon Sienese Government and Society', *Speculum*, 39 (1964), 1–34.
44. See W. M. Bowsky, *Commune*, *op. cit.*, p. 303.
45. See Achille Tartaro, *op. cit.*, pp. 95–9; Millard Meiss, *op. cit.*, pp. 86–7; W. M. Bowsky, *Commune*, *op. cit.*, p. 262.
46. *Passione*, 14,5; 145,3; 275,8.
47. *Passione*, 273–7.
48. See *Passione*, 185–7 (and Armando Balduino, p. 313).
49. See G. Varanini, *op. cit.*, pp. 483–7.
50. See Robert Fawtier, *op. cit.*, p. 214; G. Varanini, *op. cit.*, pp. 485–7.
51. For a convenient summary, see Kenelm Foster and M. J. Ronayne, *op. cit.*, pp. 28–39; E. Dupré Theseider, *op. cit.*, pp. 271–7.
52. See *Fanciullezza* 4–6, 140, 198. 376; Tancredi's Trinitarian imagery is discussed below.
53. See V. Branca, *Il cantare trecentesco e il Boccaccio del Filostrato e del Teseida*, Florence, 1936; V. Branca, 'Nostalgie tardogotiche e gusto del fiabesco nella tradizione narrativa dei cantari', in *Studi di varia umanità in onore di Francesco Flora*, ed. G. B. Pighi, Milan,

1963, pp. 88–108; Armando Balduino, 'Tradizione canterina e tonalità popolareggianti nel *Ninfale fiesolano*', *Studi sul Boccaccio*, 2, 1964, pp. 25–80; D. J. Wallace, 'Chaucer and the Early Writings of Boccaccio', unpublished Ph.D. dissertation, Cambridge University, 1983, pp. 130–87. See *Passione*, 19, 5–7 ('figliuol . . . cortese;/figliuol . . ./ Deh! . . . speranza mia); 130, 4 ('dolce 'l mio riposo'); 125, 2 ('a gran furore'); 44, 7 ('senza fallo', a tag that generates a rhyme for the cock ('gallo') announcing Peter's betrayal).

54. On losing Jesus, Mary describes herself with the same word chosen by the *cantare* Isolde on losing Tristan: 'tapina!' (*Passione* 212, 4; *Ultime imprese e morte di Tristano*—in Armando Balduino, *Cantari*, pp. 101–27—66, 6). In the same lament she refers to Jesus as 'dolce amor mie bello' (215, 6) and 'dolce figliuol mio caro' (218, 6).

55. *Passione*, 263, 6; *Risurrezione*, II, 23, 4; *Risurrezione*, 11, 165–6; Armando Balduino, *Tradizione canterina*, pp. 49–50.

56. See *Passione* 14, 1–15, 1; D. Wallace, *op. cit.*, pp. 148–9.

57. See *Risurrezione*, II, 125, 161.

58. See *Risurezzione*, II, 127, 1 and 128, 1 (with the *canterino*'s characteristic doubling of the verb). References to sources in popular works are, of course, generally spurious.

59. Dante adheres to this traditional distribution in *Inferno* III, 5–6.

60. Razzolini's edition of 1878 upholds the attribution to Boccaccio: see G. Varanini, *op. cit.*, pp. 539–42.

61. *Passione*, 149, 1–3: 'O my sweet son, is this the "Ave" that you made me speak to Gabriel, that was so sweet and pleasing to me!'

62. See *Religious Lyrics of the XVth Century*, ed. Carleton Brown, Oxford, 1939, pp. 8–13 (lines 57–8): 'Gabriel, þu dedeste calle me full of grace;/now full of sorwe þu me seyste!'

63. *Fanciullezza*, 14, 4–6, my translation.

64. See Kenelm Foster and M. J. Ronayne, *op. cit.*, p. 39; C. Delcorno, 'Cavalca, Domenico', *Dizionario biografico*, 22, pp. 577–86.

65. See 'Vita di Sant' Antonio Abate', in *Prosatori minori del Trecento. I. Scrittori di religione*, ed. D. G. De Luca, Milan-Naples, 1954, pp. 399–453, esp. pp. 421–2.

66. D. G. De Luca, *op. cit.*, pp. 421–2.

67. For a comparison with the Latin source, see Achille Tartaro, *op. cit.*, pp. 75–7.

68. Tancredi rarely makes use of *cantare* tags; and those he employs—such as 'stella matutina' (151, 5); 'rosa senza spina' (266, 3)—have religious associations.

69. See Achille Tartaro, *op. cit.*, p. 84; Paul Verhuyck, 'Jacques de Vitry', in *Dizionario critico della letteratura francese*, ed. Franco Simone, 2 vols, Turin, 1972, 552–4.

70. See *The Exempla of Jacques de Vitry*, ed. T. F. Crane, Publications of the Folk-Lore Society, 26, London, 1890.

71. See *I Fioretti di San Francesco*, in D. G. De Luca, *op. cit.*, pp. 891–1002 (esp. pp. 936–8).

72. See *The Passion of Our Lord* (from Jesus College, Oxford MS. I. Arch. I. 29), in *An Old English Miscellany*, ed. Richard Morris, Early English Text Society, O.S, 49, London, 1872, lines 1–4.

73. See *The Southern Passion*, ed. B. D. Brown, Early English Text Society, O.S, 169, London, 1927.

74. See *The Northern Passion*, ed. F. A. Foster, 2 vols, Early English Text Society, O.S, 145, 147, London, 1913–16, vol. 2 containing a French source in *chanson de geste* style; *A Stanzaic Life of Christ*, ed. F. A. Foster, Early English Text Society, O.S, 166, London, 1926; *The Cursor Mundi*, ed. R. Morris, 7 vols, Early English Text Society, O.S, 57, 59, 62, 66, 68, 99, 101, London, 1874–93; and see Elizabeth Salter, *Nicholas Love's 'Myrrour of the Blessed Lyf of Jesu Christ'*, Analecta Cartusiana, 10, Salzburg, 1974, pp. 55–102.

75. See *The Early English Carols*, ed. R. L. Greene, second edn., Oxford, 1977, pp. cxlv–cxlvii.

76. *Ibid.*, p. clix.

77. *Ibid.*, p. cl.

78. See 'The Parson's Prologue', X, 30–60 in *The Complete Works of Geoffrey Chaucer*, ed. F. N. Robinson, second edn., Oxford, 1966.

79. See *The English Works of Wyclif Hitherto Unprinted*, ed. F. D. Matthew, Early English Text Society, O.S, 74, London, 1880, p. 206.

80. See Bianco da Siena, 'Amor, Iesù, dolcissimo amore', in *Poeti minori del Trecento*, ed. N. Sapegno, Milan-Naples, 1952, pp. 1127–8.
81. See 'L'anima desiderosa', in *Poeti minori del Trecento*, pp. 1124–6 (lines 54–68, and *Book*, p. 90.
82. *Book*, p. 23.
83. See E. Dupré Theseider, *op. cit.*, p. 271.
84. See Kenelm Foster and M. J. Ronayne, *op. cit.*, p. 19.
85. See G. Petrocchi, 'S. Caterina da Siena', in *La prosa del Trecento*, Messina, 1961, pp. 105–118.
86. See D. G. De Luca, *op. cit.*, I, pp. 130–3.
87. *Risurrezione* II, 101, 3.
88. *Book*, p. 12.
89. See Philippe Monier, *Le Quattrocento*, 2 vols, Paris, 1901, 2, pp. 191–203.
90. See Giovanni Boccaccio, *Trattatello in Laude di Dante*, ed. P. G. Ricci, Milan, 1974, I, 113.
91. *Book*, p. 11.
92. 'It is necessary to explain everything in a way that is immediately intelligible to eye and sense'; see Achille Tartaro, *op. cit.*, p. 84.
93. J. Russell-Smith, 'Walter Hilton and a Tract in Defence of the Veneration of Images', *Dominican Studies*, 7 (1954), p. 194.
94. *Smaointe Beatha Chríost*, ed. Cainneach Ó Maonaigh, Dublin, 1944, pp. 325–6. Ó Maonaigh offers a useful account of the diffusion and influence of the *Meditationes* (pp. 343–62).
95. Margaret Deanesly, *The Lollard Bible*, Cambridge, 1920, p. 321.
96. See Livario Oliger, *Le Meditationes Vitae Christi del Pseudo-Bonaventura*, Arezzo, 1922, pp. 31–3; Luigi Cellucci, '*Le Meditationes Vitae Christi* e i poemetti che ne furono ispirati', *Archivum Romanicum*, 22 (1938), 30–98 (esp. p. 34).
97. P. C. Fischer 'Die *Meditationes Vitae Christi*', *Archivum Franciscanum Historicum*, 25, pp. 3–35; and see Rosemary Woolf, *The English Religious Lyric in the Middle Ages*, Oxford, 1968, p. 183.
98. See P. C. Fischer, *op. cit.*, pp. 175–209, 449–83.
99. See E. Salter, *op. cit.*, p. 1; *Book*, p. 35.
100. See G. Varanini, *op. cit.*, pp. 489, 543, 550; Almando Balduino, *Cantari*, p. 163; Luigi Cellucci, *op. cit.*, pp. 62, 74–95. The first part of the *Risurrezione* is dedicated to the Harrowing of Hell; its chief source is (predictably) the apocryphal gospel of Nicodemus.
101. *Passione* 10, 1–5.
102. 'Let each man feel what he felt!'
103. See E. Colledge and J. Walsh, *Showings*, *op. cit.*, p. 201–2; H. E. Allen, *English Writings of Richard Rolle*, Oxford, 1931, pp. 23–4.
104. See B. D. Brown, *op. cit.*, pp. lxxviii–xcii.
105. Ed. J. M. Cooper, Early English Text Society, O.S, 60, London, 1875; see also E. Salter, *op. cit.*, pp. 40–1.
106. See E. Salter, *op. cit.*, pp. 102–3.
107. The Latin *Meditationes* appears in *St Bonaventura . . . Opera Omnia*, ed. A. C. Peltier, 15 vols, Paris, 1864–71, XII. See also *Meditaciones de passione Christi olim sancto Bonaventurae attributae*, ed. M. J. Stallings, Washington D.C., 1965, pp. 3–14.
108. See H. E. Allen, *English Writings*, *op. cit.*, p. 18; M. A. Knowlton, *The Influence of Richard Rolle and of Julian of Norwich on the Middle English Lyrics*, The Hague-Paris, 1973, p. 34.
109. See H. E. Allen, *English Writings*, *op. cit.*, p. 18; pp. 25–26, ll. 217–232; p. 27, l. 261.
110. See Harald Lindkvist, Richard Rolle's *Meditatio de Passione Domini. According to MS Uppsala C. 494*, Uppsala, 1917, p. 11; *Some Minor Works of Richard Rolle with The Privity of the Passion by S. Bonaventura*, tr. and ed. G. E. Hodgson, London, 1923, pp. 175–225.
111. See E. Colledge and J. Walsh, *Showings*, *op. cit.*, 1, p. 52.
112. E. Salter, *op. cit.*, p. 53.
113. See R. Woolf, *op. cit.*, pp. 26–7.
114. See Émile Mâle, *L'Art Religieux de la fin du Moyen Age en France. Étude sur*

l'iconographie du moyen âge et sur ses sources d'inspiration, third edn., Paris, 1925, p. 30.

115. *Meditations on the Life of Christ*, tr. I. Ragusa and R. Green, Princeton, 1961, p. 12; *Fanciullezza*, 70, 1. Ragusa and Green provide an English translation of a fourteenth-century Italian version of the *Meditationes*. For information on editions of the Italian text, see O. G. De Luca, *op. cit.*, p. 1003.

116. See I. Ragusa and R. Green, *op. cit.*, p. 15; *Fanciullezza*, 79, 8; 344–352.

117. See, for example, *Fanciullezza* 2, 7; 15, 4–6; 177 (from the *Confessions*: Augustine on sodomy).

118. See *Fanciullezza*, 27–28, 203, 334.

119. I. Ragusa and R. Green, *op. cit.*, p. 17; *Fanciullezza* 86; *Fanciullezza*, 92–95, 174–195.

120. Nicholas Love, *The Mirrour of the Blessed Lyf of Jesu Christ*, ed. L. F. Powell, Oxford, 1908, Prohemium, p. 8.

121. The complete *Myrrour* survives in 47 manuscripts: see E. Salter, *op. cit.*, pp. 1–22.

122. See Elizabeth Salter, 'Continuity and Change in Middle English Versions of the *Meditationes Vitae Christi*', *Medium Aevum*, 26 (1957), 25–31.

123. See *Ludus Coventriae*, ed. K. S. Block, Early English Text Society, E.S, 120, London, 1922, pp. lvii–ix; Cainneach Ó Maonaigh, *op. cit.*, p. 355; E. Salter, *Myrrour*, *op. cit.*, p. 52.

124. See Carleton Brown, *op. cit.*, pp. 169–75, l. 8.

125. *Ibid.*, lines 33–5; compare I. Ragusa and R. Green, *op. cit.*, pp. 68–71.

126. *op. cit.*, p. 197.

127. See D. Wallace, *op. cit.*, pp. 188–253.

128. See I. Ragusa and R. Green, *op. cit.*, pp. 33–4 (and MS illustrations 26–35); R. Greene, *op. cit.*, 45, p. 24; R. Woolf, *op. cit.*, pp. 302–4.

129. I. Ragusa and R. Green, *op. cit.*, p. 15. See also Love's translation: 'Now take hede and ymagyne of goostly thing as it were bodily/and thinke in thyn herte/as thou were present . . .' (*op. cit.*, p. 24).

130. *Book*, p. 46.

131. See I. Ragusa and R. Green, *op. cit.*, p. 56; *Book*, 7, 34–6 (p. 19); Stephen Medcalf, *op. cit.*, p. 118.

132. *Book*, p. 19.

133. See I. Ragusa and R. Green, *op. cit.*, pp. 55–6.

134. See Love, *Mirrour*, *op. cit.*, p. 243; *Book*, pp. 68, 290.

135. See Love, *Mirrour*, *op. cit.*, pp. 78–84 esp. p. 80. See also *Fanciullezza* 362–70, where Jesus is denounced as being 'big and useless', 'a madman', a 'baby' and a 'boy'.

136. See Millard Meiss, *op. cit.*, pp. 3–8 and passim.

137. John Larner, *Culture and Society in Italy 1290–1420*, London, 1971, p. 142.

138. See Millard Meiss, *op. cit.*, pp. 41–2, 132–56; *Fanciullezza*, 167.

139. See W. M. Bowsky, *op. cit.*, pp. 292–3.

140. See E. W. Tristram, *English Wall Painting of the Fourteenth Century*, London, 1955, p. 4.

141. See Joan Evans, *English Art 1307–1461*, Oxford, 1949, p. 87.

142. See E. Salter, *Myrrour*, *op. cit.*, p. 47.

143. See J. Russell-Smith, *op. cit.*, p. 194; *Mirk's Festial*, ed. T. Erbe, Early English Text Society, E.S, 96, London, 1905, p. 171 (lines 25–9); R. Woolf, *op. cit.*, p. 184.

144. See Millard Meiss, *op. cit.*, p. 106.

145. See, for example, 228, 234.

146. *Passione*, 53, 3.

147. *Ibid.*, 111, 4.

148. *Ibid.*, 142, 3.

149. *Ibid.*, 80, 3.

150. *Ibid.*, 80, 4.

151. *Ibid.*, 80, 5.

152. *Ibid.*, 103.

153. See W. M. Bowsky, *op. cit.*, pp. 286–91. San Bernadino's sermons make detailed reference to the famous Lorinzetti frescoes.

154. E. Sandberg-Vavalà, *Sienese Studies*, Florence, 1953, p. 75. See also E. Carli, *Duccio di Buoninsegna*, Milan, 1961, p. 23.

155. See W. M. Bowsky, *op. cit.*, pp. 284–5; John White, *Duccio. Tuscan Art and the Medieval*

Workshop, London, 1979, pp. 95–102; J. H. Stubblebine, *Duccio di Buoninsegna and his School*, 2 vols, Princeton, 1979, 1, pp. 31–62.

156. Compare, for example, *Passione*, 56–64 and J. H. Stubblebine, *op. cit.*, plate 103 ('Betrayal of Christ'); *Passione* 226 and plate 111 ('Deposition'). See also Giorgio Varanini, 'Alcune osservazioni su due recenti scritti dedicati ai *Cantari Religiosi Senesi del Trecento*', *Lettere Italiane*, 19 (1967), 103–20, esp. pp. 119–20.
157. Margaret Rickert, *Painting in Britain: The Middle Ages*, London, 1954, p. 179.
158. Although it is now displayed in the south choir aisle, the Retable was made for the high altar.
159. Such is the testimony of the *Miracoli*: see E. Dupré Theseider, *op. cit.*, p. 262.
160. See Millard Meiss, *op. cit.*, pp. 106–7.
161. See E. Colledge and J. Walsh, *Showings*, *op. cit.*, 1, pp. 52–3.
162. See B. A. Windeatt, 'The Art of Mystical Loving: Julian of Norwich', *The Medieval Mystical Tradition in England*, ed. M. Glasscoe, Exeter, 1980, pp. 55–71.
163. E. Colledge and J. Walsh, *op. cit.*, 1, p. 53; Julian, *Showings*, *op. cit.*, 1, pp. 201–202.
164. See *Book*, p. 324.
165. *Book*, p. 155.
166. *Ibid.*, p. 14.
167. In the sequence of the Passion (as established by the *Meditationes*, developed by Duccio and then taken up by artists across Europe) the loosening of Jesus' arms from the cross causes his body to sway forward; it is then caught by Mary, who has surged up the ladder (see *Passione* 227).
168. *Book.*, p. 94.
169. *Ibid.*, pp. 139–140.
170. *Ibid.*, p. 140.
171. *Idem.*
172. *Ibid.*, p. 148.